To Make a New Race

To Make a New Race

Gurdjieff, Toomer, and the Harlem Renaissance

Jon Woodson

University Press of Mississippi / Jackson

http://www.upress.state.ms.us

02 01 00 99   4 3 2 1

The paper in this book meets the guidelines for permanence and durability of the Committee on Production Guidelines for Book Longevity of the Council on Library Resources.

Library of Congress Cataloging-in-Publication Data

Woodson, Jon.
    To make a new race : Gurdjieff, Toomer, and the Harlem
Renaissance / Jon Woodson.
        p.   cm.
    Includes bibliographical references and index.
    ISBN 1-57806-130-X (cloth : alk. paper)
    ISBN 1-57806-131-8 (paper : alk. paper)
    1. Toomer, Jean, 1894–1967—Criticism and interpretation.   2. American
literature—Afro-American authors—History and criticism.   3. American
literature—20th century—History and criticism.   4. Gurdjieff, Georges Ivanovitch,
1872–1949—Views on race.   5. Gurdjieff, Georges Ivanovitch, 1872–1949—Influence.
6. Harlem (New York, N.Y.)—Intellectual life.   7. Afro-Americans—intellectual
life.   8. Harlem Renaissance.   9. Race in literature.   I. Title.
    PS3539.0478 Z95   1998
    813'.52—dc21   98-42461
                                                                    CIP

British Library Cataloging-in-Publication Data available

To my wife, Lynn Currier Smith Woodson

Contents

Preface - ix
Acknowledgments - xi
Abbreviations - xii

Introduction - 1

1 Jean Toomer: Beside You Will Stand a Strange Man - 29

2 Wallace Thurman: Beyond Race and Color - 47

3 Rudolph Fisher: Minds of Another Order - 75

4 Nella Larsen: The Anatomy of "Sleep" - 97

5 George Schuyler: New Races and New Worlds - 123

6 Zora Neale Hurston: The Self and the Nation - 147

Conclusion - 171

Notes - 179
Bibliography - 183
Index - 191

Preface

This study is the final form of an inquiry that began with my looking in quite another direction. Having discovered a stack of volumes of Melvin B. Tolson's long poem *Harlem Gallery* in 1968, I was delighted to encounter an African-American text as incomprehensible as Pound's *Cantos*, with which I had been long fascinated. While writing a dissertation on Tolson's poetry, I was astounded to realize that he was embodying George Ivanovich Gurdjieff's cosmos in his poems, for I had been coincidentally reading P. D. Ouspensky's *In Search of the Miraculous*. It was many years before I concluded that for Tolson to have written as individualistically and behaved as eccentrically as he did, there must have been a hidden content to the literature of the Harlem Renaissance. Using the coded content of *Harlem Gallery* as a guide, I ascertained which of the Harlem writers had been his teachers, and Jean Toomer did not seem to have been one of them.

While mysterious in other ways, Toomer's role with respect to the writers in Harlem is relatively clear: He brought the Gurdjieff system of self-development to Harlem from France—from Gurdjieff himself—and from Greenwich Village—from A. R. Orage. Toomer documented himself thoroughly in a series of autobiographies. Despite this, there are many gaps in his story, particularly in connection with his Harlem days. The effect of Gurdjieff's teachings on the individuals in Toomer's groups will never be easily known. For example, although the prominent muralist and graphic artist Aaron Douglas was an admitted follower of Gurdjieff, it is difficult to delineate that influence in his art, and, strangely, Douglas claimed there to be none.

This study begins with a chapter on Jean Toomer as background and then concentrates on Wallace Thurman, Rudolph Fisher, Nella Larsen, George Schuyler, and Zora Neale Hurston. Primarily, this is because these writers are better known than others who might have been included, for instance, Eric Walrond, Harold Jackman, and Dorothy Peterson. Generally speaking, Thurman, Fisher, Larsen, Schuyler, and Hurston presented many imponderables to their readers, mainly with regard to their personalities and the details of their lives. The critical consensus is that all of them wrote importantly and significantly, but in certain cases not exceptionally. However, as they are known to literary history, the personalities of the Harlem Gurdjieffians were but masks. They wrote their literary works in ciphers that this study decodes for the first time. Rather than their personalities or lives, this study concentrates on the complexities of their literary works. The writers discussed in this first book-length treatment of "objective" art struggled to find a way to produce "objective" art. The "objective" aesthetic became a form of modernism in the hands of Gurdjieff, however, it was not a new form of art, but perhaps one of the oldest. "Objective" art is conscious art—art that evokes feelings in the reader that the writer consciously transmits with complete awareness of form and content.

Behind all of their writings stands George Ivanovich Gurdjieff (1866–1949), one of the most original, inspiring, and mysterious spiritual teachers of the modern period—a figure known to very few. Gurdjieff was also one of the most innovative of modern writers, although his books have yet to be widely recognized as such. Although often described as a mystic, Gurdjieff cannot be easily categorized. One mark of his importance is the list of those he influenced, for example, A. R. Orage, Frank Lloyd Wright, Katherine Mansfield, and Peter Brook. Gurdjieff introduced a unique and desperately needed spirituality to the modern world, the Fourth Way—the way of the sly man. The spiritual path of the sly man separates its practitioner from other men: He is awake and they are asleep, machines, robots.

I once came across a photograph of the poets who gathered in 1952 for the Festival of Negro Poets in Jackson, Mississippi. Seated in the first row was Zora Neale Hurston; standing behind her was Melvin B. Tolson. They were flanked by such luminaries as Langston Hughes, Sterling Brown, and Margaret Walker. The Harlem Gurdjieffians met under the cover of such race-centered events and turned them to their own private purposes. As Gurdjieffians, they did not believe that they were Negroes or that Negroes existed, and they stated as much metaphorically in their writings. Their public appearances were often theatrical displays of behavior designed to shock audiences into wakefulness and their public speech was often couched in veiled Gurdjieffian terminology. An example of such an event was Tolson's 1966 appearance at the Fisk University Centennial Writer's Conference during which he attacked Robert Hayden (Flasch 42), seemingly for being insufficiently proud of being a Negro. However, when we are aware of the hidden content of the event, Tolson reveals himself as a "sly man." His declaration that "I am no accident—and I don't give a tinker's damn what you think" (Flasch 42) reverberates in resoundingly Gurdjieffian terms.

Acknowledgments

My thanks to John Reilly for reading an early version of this study and contributing brilliant and invaluable suggestions; to Seetha Srinivasan, associate director and editor-in-chief of the University Press of Mississippi, for believing in the potential of this project and patiently nurturing the manuscript through revising and editing; and to Amritjit Singh for his attentive reading of the manuscript, generous guidance, and unstinting forbearance. My thanks and deep appreciation to Dusti Haller, personal librarian and sibyl, and to Jerry Dadds for his Gurdjieff collection and wise conversation. My warm thanks to Carole Doreski for her active and inspirational interest in this project. Finally, I thank Maureen Heher and Lynn Braunsdorf, librarians at the Beinecke Rare Book and Manuscript Library at Yale University, for their kind and efficient assistance.

Abbreviations

BB	*The Blacker the Berry* (Thurman)
BE	*Black Empire* (Schuyler)
BNM	*Black No More* (Schuyler)
BO	*Beyond the Occult* (Wilson)
BT	*Beelzebub's Tales* (Gurdjieff)
CMD	*The Conjure-Man Dies* (Fisher)
DTR	*Dust Tracks on a Road* (Hurston)
HG	*Harlem Gallery* (Tolson)
ID	*Invisible Darkness* (Larson)
ISM	*In Search of the Miraculous* (Ouspensky)
ITD	*An Intimation of Things Distant* (Larson)
KU	*A Kabbalistic Universe* (Halevi)
TO	*Tertium Organum* (Ouspensky)
WS	*The Wayward and the Seeking* (Turner)

To Make a New Race

Introduction

With a once oracular aphorism that has been diminished to a tragic commonplace, W. E. B. Du Bois stated in 1903 that "The problem of the twentieth Century is the problem of the color line" (*The Souls of Black Folk* 239). I have recalled Du Bois's poignant assessment to place in perspective the careers of George Ivanovich Gurdjieff (mystic, psychologist, writer, composer, and teacher of sacred dance) and Jean Toomer (African-American avant-garde writer, social visionary, and disciple of Gurdjieff). A contemporary reading of Du Bois's statement is likely to overlook its implication of the imperiled nature of modern life that was becoming apparent at the turn of the century. Only against the background of widespread belief in imminent social collapse can modernist activities be effectively grasped. The essence of Gurdjieff's message and the agitated reaction of Jean Toomer and Gurdjieff's many other disciples reveal a meaningful pattern in which we see people embracing ideas, methods, and solutions to problems that in retrospect may appear absurd. However, at the time these reactions seemed to be appropriate to people engaged in a desperate search for some means of saving themselves and the world.

Gurdjieff came to America on a mission to save the world. His slow passage began with arduous and mysterious studies in central Asia and moved to the formation of his early esoteric schools in Czarist Russia and Turkey and finally to Europe during the tumultuous years after World War I. Only after harrowing experiences in postwar Germany, a failed attempt to resettle in England, and the establishment of a permanent school in France was Gurdjieff able to launch his American campaign in 1923. He traveled to the industrialized nations of Europe and America to introduce and establish a new teaching, one that would keep the world from destroying itself. He was in search of students to help him achieve this aim. In no way seeking to disguise the desperation that propelled his efforts, Gurdjieff declared: "Unless the 'wisdom' of the East and the 'energy' of the West could be harnessed and used harmoniously, the world would be destroyed" (Patterson xv).

Gurdjieff's assessment of the course of the historical period in which he lived clearly categorizes his response to the cultural matrix as modernist. Peter Fritzsche (10) states that

The epistemological and aesthetic dimensions of modernism signal the discontinuous nature of social experience in the last centuries. Rather than a progressive articulation of power and possibility, civilization records the merely tentative security achieved in the face of inherent dangers. The rise of capitalism, the introduction of industrial technology, the establishment of central state administration, and the proliferation of military power . . . did not automatically advance the security of Europe. The threshold of risk advanced as well. Moreover, an increasingly well-regulated society generated new phobias as the definition and scope of social responsibility expanded. As a result, the practices of discipline . . . coalescing around the regulation of "the social" at the end of the nineteenth century were accompanied by revived premonitions of disaster.

Gurdjieff's belief that the world was about to end coheres with the fundamental characteristic of modernist culture, the presumption that accident pervades all of life and has to be contained and that randomness threatens to overwhelm us and has to be neutralized (Fritzsche 12). Moreover, we should consider that Gurdjieff reached the West only because he and the members of his esoteric theater troupe successfully survived the countless manifest dangers involved in escaping from Russia. During the summer of 1918, they had walked over the northern Caucasus Range to the Black Sea port of Sochi, a journey that caused them to cross the lines between the embattled Red and White Armies five times. Gurdjieff's firsthand experience of the Russian Revolution gave him an exaggerated perception of history. The Revolution of 1917 brought to a close the conventional view that history showed a gradual, progressive course. The revolution sparked other social upheavals, and revolutions broke out in Berlin, Vienna, and Budapest in the two years that followed. Militant strikes threw the shadow of revolution across the remainder of Europe. Between 1914 and 1919, the influenza epidemic killed more people than the ten million slain by the weapons of the first industrialized war, rivaling the horrors of the great plagues of the Middle Ages. The events during these years were so unprecedented that the historical record could shed little light on how life might be restored to normal conditions. The past had in every way become irrelevant and no longer suggested the shape of things to come (Fritzsche 13).

Thus, for those artists, writers, intellectuals, and spiritual seekers who gravitated to Gurdjieff, his arrival in Europe and America had the aura of the coming of a modern messiah. The way of his coming had been prepared by P. D. Ouspensky, the highly acclaimed author of *Tertium Organum*. Ouspensky's blend of mysticism and science had inspired some of the leading American and European intellectuals and artists until his avowal that it was Gurdjieff, not he, that was to be the great spiritual reformer of the modern age. Ouspensky's announcement in 1921 that he had a teacher, one G. I. Gurdjieff, and that this teacher-of-teachers was on his way to England electrified Ouspensky's international following. The culture of the West was already obsessed with the search for "a new totality" (Fritzsche 15), and it was exactly such an "unknown teaching," a systematic approach to all of life, that Ouspensky claimed Gurdjieff would bring from his earlier studies in central Asia. Gurdjieff's system was particularly suited for the educated European audience of the time, because in addition to supplying a new psychology, philosophy, aesthetics, biology, anthropology, cosmology, and philosophy, his system offered an alternative to the catastrophic thinking that characterized modern culture. Prominently positioned within Gurdjieff's system was the Law of the Octave, what his adherents believed to be the key to the eternal laws of history that would allow them to overcome the manifest fragmentation of the world after World War I. Thus, Gurdjieff's system, like other modernist totalities, negotiated the polarities of crisis and renovation that characterize the modern spirit (Fritzsche 11). Like the Marxist and Nazi totalities, it sought to intervene in history and "postulated the commencement of 'new time' " (Fritzsche 16).

Gurdjieff's system was a description of the entire cosmos, but its point of entry was a technique that addressed fundamental human problems. The metaphysics of the system was only really important because it was useful in describing the actual conditions that humans faced. The central insight of the system was that man is not a unified being, but is instead a being in whom the "I" (ego, identity, self) is relative and nonpermanent. The impermanence of the "I" is a result of "consciousness" being the compound result of consciousness, subconsciousness, and instinct (thought, feeling, and organic automism). According to Gurdjieff, all of the catastrophes that take place in life, at whatever scale, arise from the fact that, in his fragmented condition, man does not know himself for what he is and is not. Moreover, the problems of human life cannot be effectively attacked by the systems in place because without recognizing the impermanence of the human personality all of the theories, systems, and therapies that mistakenly assess man's capabilities are invalid. The solution that Gurdjieff hoped to put into effect was understood differently by his many students and interpreters, but it is perhaps best stated by C. Daly King. King saw Gurdjieff's Method, particularly the version taught by A. R. Orage in New York, as a way to escape the life of illusions fostered by a haphazardly modernizing civilization. Convinced that in a few more generations mankind would be reduced to "a welter of blood and misery as the world has never seen" (Webb 354), King advocated "bigger and better men" as the only means by which the degeneration hastened by industrial society could be reversed. For King and the Oragean branch of the Gurdjieff movement, who developed their own ideas in the groups organized in New York, the developmental system introduced by Gurdjieff was not merely a spiritual teaching, a philosophy, or even a physiology, but a new comprehensive science of man.

Given the applicability of Gurdjieff's system to issues that were preeminent within the cultural matrix of the post–World War I era and the professionalism with which his teachings were introduced by British, French, and American teachers, it is not surprising that Gurdjieff attracted many students in Europe and America, particularly artists and intellectuals. Prominent among the many students who were to influence events at large was the African-American writer, Jean Toomer, and this study begins with his affiliation with Gurdjieff's enterprises in America.

Toomer's chief contribution was to formulate and apply an antiracist component to the body of Gurdjieffian doctrine, which did not recognize the concept of race. Gurdjieff's "objective" view of man defined him as "a three-centered organism which experiences two states of consciousness" (Toomer "A New Group, 1926").

Although much has been written about other aspects of Gurdjieff's campaign in America, one chapter has remained locked in a profound secrecy, the activities that comprised the "Gurdjieffian" assault against America's racialist culture. Because of his significant placement in the history of ideas, through the intercession of A. R. Orage and Jean Toomer, Gurdjieff was able to provide an important group of Harlem's writers and artists—referred to in this study as the Harlem group—with powerful new concepts and efficient techniques for the evolution of new states of consciousness.[1] The Harlem group believed these concepts and techniques would allow them to thoroughly transform American culture. This widespread change was possible, the Gurdjieffians believed, because changes arise from the introduction and circulation of ideas.[2] Also, given the primacy of racism in the world's cataclysmic and intractable tendency toward self-destruction, it is no wonder that A. R. Orage and Jean Toomer recognized the need for a rescue mission conducted by the vanguard literary artists of the Harlem Renaissance.

Obsessive concern with race was already an important component of American culture, and in the 1920s it emerged in new forms. The drastic social and cultural transformations that were the results of industrial modernization, the growth of cities, rural-to-urban shifts in population, and unchecked immigration in the years before the 1920s brought about a wide range of violent and ruthless social responses. These reactions took the forms of brutal labor disputes, curtailment of Asian immigration through the Alien Immigration Laws, terror campaigns of the reemerged Ku Klux Klan, and founding of new white supremacist groups such as the Anglo-Saxon Clubs of America. The rate at which people were lynched remained high throughout the 1920s; between 1918 and 1927, 455 persons were lynched in America, 416 of whom were African-Americans. Added to these popular expressions of racism were political, medical, and educational institutions that made racism respectable and spread the gospel of racism throughout American society.

Ironically, racism also became important in attempts to moderate the alarming direction that society was taking. One of the most significant movements to embrace science to address the myriad social dangers was Progressivism, a powerful, mainstream political movement closely allied with the eugenics movement. Influenced by eugenics (the science of race improvement introduced in 1883 by Francis Galton, a nephew of Charles Darwin), racial thought was an increasingly important underpinning to American academia. The importance of scientific ideas about race improvement was not reversed until the end of the 1920s, when the views of racially egalitarian scientists began to make pronounced inroads against the institutionalization of racism in academia. Racism, however, remained a fixture of American society outside of academic debate.

In the 1920s prominent psychologists, sociologists, historians, and creative writers relied upon race theories to explain the characters, intelligence, and human worth of individuals and cultures. Galton's eugenics particularly underscored the negative biological and social effects of race mixing, although racial distinctions were loosely constructed with virtually any observed difference serving as a demarcation. The eugenicist Madison Grant, author of *The Passing of the Great Race* (1916), a milestone in the construction of racial differences in American thought, observed that Europe alone contained three races: Alpine, Mediterranean, and Nordic (Gossett 353–54). As a result of these widely disseminated views, the concept of racial purity became of paramount importance to those who considered themselves members of the superior race.

Jean Toomer was interested in generating from Gurdjieff's teachings a response to the zealous culture of racialism that dominated American life in the 1920s. This flowed naturally from Toomer's enthusiasm for ideas of profound insight and techniques of great effectiveness. However, Gurdjieff himself did not formulate his system, but claimed only to have updated for modern minds a system that had been in existence for all of human civilization. This system was characterized by Ouspensky in the subtitle to his record of Gurdjieff's lectures (*In Search of the Miraculous* 1949) as "fragments of an unknown teaching," the presumption being that the origins of the teaching were lost in the mists of eons. Toomer's attempt to revise Gurdjieff's teachings was a particularly dangerous violation of the system of self-development that Gurdjieff taught.

Gurdjieff claimed that his system and its method of self-development were "objective," that it consisted of "real" ideas in contrast to the illusory material usually encountered in the lives of ordinary men and women. As knowledge of the All or the Absolute, the "objective" was beyond what could be negotiated by the ego and thus was not to be subjected to the dictates of the ego. To Gurdjieff, the common men who applied in great numbers to his Institute for the Harmonious Development of Man, those like Toomer, a "subjective" artist, were in his parlance "lunatics" and "psychopaths." Gurdjieff had rebuked another writer, saying, "You live in dreams and you write about your dreams. Much better for you if you were to scrub one floor consciously than to write a hundred books as you do now" (Nott *Teachings* 37). For a "psychopath" such as the novice Toomer, Gurdjieff's system of self-development was something to do, not to understand. According to the psychological theory on which "the work" (the most common name applied to Gurdjieff's system of self-development exercises) was based, the activities of Toomer's "false personality" retarded the development of his "essence"—the qualities with which he was born. Because human cultures only refine "false personality," normal people have undeveloped "essences" and are psychologically deformed. In

Gurdjieffian terms, one's writing contained one's "essence," and therefore could only express its own lack of development. Although it was possible to create "objective" art, one had to first reach the "objective" level of understanding, the level of mathematics, the level of laws. "Objective" art was the expression of these absolutes, and self-expression was viewed as a vain and destructive activity.

Gurdjieff had first made his mark as a hypnotist, a practice that he abandoned not because he was incompetent but because it did not lead toward his further evolution. In the account of Gurdjieff written by Ouspensky, *In Search of the Miraculous*, Gurdjieff is a teacher of dancing. His ballet "The Struggle of the Magicians" is the first "objective" work of art to come to our attention. It was only about the time that Jean Toomer arrived in France, in 1925, that Gurdjieff began to write in the capacity of an "objective" artist. Gurdjieff's view of this practice must have enraptured Toomer, for he presented "objective" art as the highest of human achievements: "All art encode's one's being, and the highest art can carry that being beyond mortality, but to do so it must be in a form comprehensible only to the initiated" (Taylor letter). The association of art with being was given explicit expression by Gurdjieff: "There is art number one, that is the art of man number one, imitative, copying art, or crudely primitive and sensuous art such as the dances and music of savage peoples. There is art number two, sentimental art; art number three, intellectual, invented art; and there must be art number four, number five, and so on" (ISM 73). There are six qualities of "objective" art: (1) it is conscious; (2) the artist creates knowing what is being done and why; (3) it makes an identical impression on everybody, with variations depending on the level of personal development; (4) it contains exactly what the artist wants; (5) its purpose is the illumination of truth through the recipient's emotional experience; and (6) it originates from objective consciousness (Speeth 140). After meeting Gurdjieff, Toomer quickly came to see that he too wanted to become an "objective" writer.

For his part, Gurdjieff underwent a long recovery from a serious head injury suffered in an automobile accident and remained in France writing his three series of "objective" books. Representing the institute in New York was the teacher that Gurdjieff had trained, the influential British intellectual and past editor of *New Age* magazine, Alfred Richard Orage. Orage was a charismatic individual, and he accumulated about himself a large following of influential New Yorkers who were engaged in the Gurdjieff work. An aspect that has not been subjected to scholarly analysis is the extent to which this group affected changes in the modern culture through the circulation of powerful ideas, but much of what transpired in Orage's circles is unascertainable. However, we are able to track Orage's activities through Jean Toomer's introduction of the Gurdjieff work into Harlem.

Acting as Orage's administrative assistant, Muriel Draper kept lists of the New York membership, organized the meetings, collected dues, and hosted a group that met on Monday nights to hear Orage lecture on the work. One of Draper's lists identifies Carl Van Vechten as a member of the Institute for the Harmonious Development of Man (Draper Collection, Box 20, Folder 635). Muriel Draper was also a close associate of Van Vechten's; she regularly dined with him, coauthored books with him, and, over the course of a lifetime, contributed to a voluminous correspondence between them.

Draper and Van Vechten were both notorious for the bohemian salons that they held independently. However, these salons were similar in bringing together artists, intellectuals, and people of influence of all races during a time when such racial mixing was not a common practice. Draper's salon was frequented by many of the young Harlem artists and writers (Kellner 104). So crucial was Carl Van Vechten to the Harlem Renaissance that Leon Coleman (142) is able to state that "In 1927, when the Negro Renaissance had flowered into a vogue, a copy of *The New Negro* was presented to Carl Van Vechten. It was signed by James Weldon Johnson, Jessie Fauset, Jean Toomer, W. E. B. Du Bois, Zora Neale Hurston, Rudolph Fisher, Walter White, Alain Locke, and many others. There was probably no one who deserved it more."

In specific terms, Van Vechten's satirical novel *Nigger Heaven* had paved the way for African-American writers by stimulating a vogue among whites for literature that concerned the residents of Harlem. Because of the popularity of his novel, Van Vechten was able to secure publishing contracts for Nella Larsen and Rudolph Fisher from Alfred A. Knopf (Watson 100). Van Vechten was also one of the nine patrons of the magazine *Fire!!*, the literary organ of the self-styled younger Negro artists. The single 1926 issue was edited by Wallace Thurman and published many members of the Harlem group. Van Vechten saw to it that Aaron Douglas, who illustrated the advertisements for *Nigger Heaven*, was given commissions for book covers. Van Vechten's closeness to Hurston is documented in her autobiography; she recalls a dinner party that Van Vechten gave so that she could meet Ethel Waters (DTR 243), and she includes Van Vechten in "The Inside Light—Being a Salute to Friendship," a chapter not included in the original edition of *Dust Tracks on a Road:*

With the exception of Godmother, Carl Van Vechten has bawled me out more times than anyone else I know. He has not been one of those white "friends of the Negro" who seeks to earn it cheaply by being eternally complimentary. If he is your friend, he will point out your failings as well as your good points in the most direct manner. Take it or leave it. If you can't stand him that way, you need not bother. If he is not interested in you one way or the other, he will tell you that, too, in the most off-hand manner, but he is as true as the equator if he is for you. I offer him and his wife Fania Marinoff my humble and sincere thanks. (309–10)

Although Amy Spingarn and Eddie Wasserman gave parties attended by black guests, Langston Hughes commented that Van Vechten's parties "were so Negro that they were reported as a matter of course in the colored society columns" (Watson 100). Thus A. R. Orage, Muriel Draper, and Carl Van Vechten, three figures who played major roles in the cultural, intellectual, and artistic life of New York in the 1920s, were Gurdjieffians and antiracialists. Speaking in later years, Fania Marinoff, Van Vechten's wife, described what they had been doing as a crusade to break down the color bar (Coleman 147).

The close relationship between Orage and Toomer suggests that the antiracialism of the New York Gurdjieffians was in part driven by Toomer's ideas and his own personal responses to his racial status. Toomer's metaphysical and mystical ideas about the spiritual evolution of a new American race received practical expression in the racially integrated meetings organized by the Gurdjieffians and in the parties and dinners hosted by Van Vechten, Draper, and others. In addition to the pervasive social influences that resulted from this mixture of ideas and personalities, the antiracial component injected by Toomer into New York in the 1920s had a literary outcome—fiction produced by the Harlem group.

The relationship between Nella Larsen and Carl Van Vechten, well documented by their correspondence, is illustrative and will have to serve in lieu of a more comprehensive record of what transpired between him and the entire Harlem group. Van Vechten and Larsen were the closest of friends: He was her sole defender against the charges of plagiarism that sabotaged her career as a novelist, and he convened parties in honor of her birthday well into the 1930s (Hutchinson 343). Van Vechten took an interest in Larsen's writing and encouraged her to develop her fiction (ID 63). When *Nigger Heaven* was published he sent her a copy, which she immediately read three times (ID 63). Larsen approved very much of what she thought Van Vechten had accomplished, lamenting "it's too close, too true, as if you had undressed the lot of us and turned on a strong light. Too, I feel a kind of despair. Why, oh why, couldn't we have done something as big as this for ourselves?" (ID 64). A further point that emerges from their correspondence is that while Larsen was in Europe writing on a Guggenheim Fellowship in 1931, Van Vechten sent her a copy of George Schuyler's *Black No More* (ID 105)—one of the "objective" texts included in this study. Later that year Larsen was in Paris with her best friend Dorothy Peterson, who, like Larsen, had been a member of Jean Toomer's Gurdjieff group in Harlem. Critics often comment that Peterson's interest in Gurdjieff and Toomer never waned. Writing to Toomer in 1929, Peterson states "It must be a thrill to be back in Fontainebleau again, seeing Gurdjieff and having trips with him. I'd like to be there myself" (Peterson Collection, Box 6, Folder 212). In June 1931 Peterson joined Larsen in Paris, where they remained for the next few months, although what they did there "can only be a matter of speculation" (ID 106).

In addition to his cosmopolitan Jazz Age parties, Van Vechten often gave dinner parties that were characterized by racial mixing. Writing to Dorothy Peterson in July 1927, Nella Larsen recounts a dinner party that she attended at Van Vechten's. Also present were the novelist Isa Glenn and the poet Witter Bynner. Glenn was a member of one of Orage's closest circles, the influential workshop he led for amateur and professional writers. Other attendees were Muriel Draper, Jean Toomer, Melville Cane, Mary Johnston, Hugh Ferris, Samuel Hoffenstein, and John Riordan (Welch 60). Although Bynner cannot definitively be identified as a Gurdjieffian, Toomer had known him since 1919—meeting him for the first time in the company of two other writers who were to become Gurdjieffians (Watson 42). Describing the party to Dorothy Peterson, Larsen wrote, "So we had another G [Gurdjieff] meeting. It was terribly funny, because Isa was quite cool, in spite of the devastating things that all the men plus Fania [Van Vechten's wife] and I said to her" (Peterson Collection, Box 1, Folder 26).

Therefore, it is legitimate to see the Harlem Renaissance suffused with an undercurrent of Gurdjieffian activities and ideas. The lively interracial society sustained by Carl Van Vechten and Muriel Draper provided many occasions for the attendees to pursue the Gurdjieff work without betraying the nature of their activities. A newspaper clipping from a society column describes Dorothy Peterson's tea party to celebrate the publication of *Passing* (1929) by Nella Larsen (Peterson Collection, Box 1, Folder 26). The list of attendees includes nine persons involved in the Gurdjieff work, including Muriel Draper, Carl Van Vechten, Harold Jackman, Aaron Douglas, and the talented, African-American sculptor Richmond Barthe. These associations persisted for many years; five years after Orage's death in 1934, Van Vechten states in a postcard to Dorothy Peterson that he is on his way to see the carving of Orage's head that Barthe had just completed: "I am seeing Orage *questa sera*. I haven't seen the Barthe head" (Peterson Collection, Box 2, Folder 50).

In an important sense, the gap left when Jean Toomer moved away from New York in 1926 was filled by Carl Van Vechten. Van Vechten had already instituted a program of antiracialist social engineering in which he mixed the races at his parties to demonstrate that prejudice against Negroes was the result of ignorance about them—they were just people. Equally important, Van Vechten was a published novelist when he came in contact with the Harlem group, and in 1926 he published "the most controversial 'black' novel to come out of the Harlem Renaissance" (Van Notten 124). As important as Toomer had been to the Harlem group, he wrote nothing about Harlem, whereas Carl Van Vechten produced the explosive novel *Nigger Heaven*. It is well known that Van Vechten advised black writers to portray Negro life objectively, and in his *Oral History* he remarked that "the Negro writing of the Twenties did not achieve complete objectivity" (Coleman 222). However, as Leon Coleman observes, it is difficult to determine what effect Van

Vechten and his novel *Nigger Heaven* may have had because "Van Vechten was not the only advocate of this school of thought; other were Charles S. Johnson, Alain Locke, James Weldon Johnson, Wallace Thurman, George Schuyler, and Langston Hughes" (222). It is thus difficult to assess the similar call for objective writing by Van Vechten, Thurman, and Eric Walrond.

Of particular interest to this study is the idea of objectivity, which has a special significance for literary Gurdjieffians: "objectivity" is the chief attribute of a work of art. In fact, in the Gurdjieffian view, a work of art is either "objective" or it is not a work of art. It was for this reason that one of the subtitles of Gurdjieff's *Beelzebub's Tales* is "An Objectively Impartial Criticism of the Life of Man." What is solely at issue here, though, is what the Harlem group may have meant when they used the word "objective." The Gurdjieffian "objective" bears little resemblance to the "objectivity" invoked by Charles S. Johnson, Alain Locke, and those named above; nor is it the "objectivity" of literary realism. The stylistic attributes of the esoteric "objective" in texts by Gurdjieff and the Harlem group are irony, narrative obscurity, and textual difficulty (intertextuality, intratextuality, numerology, and cryptography), which are much different than the clarity, coherence, sincerity, and objective representation of the discourse of realism. In determining what Van Vechten may have meant by "objective," it is striking to note that it was not to Jean Toomer's post-*Cane* literary productions that members of the Harlem group publicly responded in Gurdjieffian terms, but to Carl Van Vechten's *Nigger Heaven*.

Writing in the *Saturday Review*, Eric Walrond (153) accorded high praise to *Nigger Heaven:* "it abounds in objectivity and truth." The review's conclusion is an emphatic, one- sentence paragraph: "And no colored man, adept as he might be at self-observation and non-identification could have written it." The ten lectures that introduced the Gurdjieff work, which Jean Toomer began teaching in Harlem in 1925 (and Walrond attended in 1926), taught a method of psychological self-development called "self-observation and non-identification." Walrond's use of this specialized terminology in a published review of a novel by another Gurdjieffian is suggestive of a number of interpretations: a rare lack of concern for secrecy, an intentional clue, etcetera. However, it tellingly demonstrates Walrond's application of Gurdjieffian thought to his reading of Van Vechten's novel.

Walrond's general response to *Nigger Heaven* parallels Larsen's reaction on reading Van Vechten's novel—dismay that a black man had not written it and consternation that it was "too true" (quoted in ID 64). These readings are similar to the bitter dissatisfaction that Wallace Thurman later expressed concerning the literary production of the entire Harlem Renaissance, that the African-American writer was too confined by race to achieve real art (Van Notten 303). Moreover, Thurman reiterates this idea in his reviews of *Nigger Heaven* in *Fire!!* and *The Messenger*. However, he further suggests that the Negro author should eschew both propaganda and sensationalism and write objectively about what he knows best, viewing Negroes as merely people who exhibit every facet of life to be found among any people (Coleman 215). Somewhat later, the "Negroes as merely people" formula appeared in *Infants of the Spring* attached to one of the main formulations of Gurdjieff's teachings. Thurman's version was that "Negroes are much like any other human beings. They have the same social, physical, and intellectual divisions" (38–39).

Gurdjieff, Orage, and Toomer stated the principle of man's threefold construction in many different ways, but the most common wording was that there are three centers, the intellectual, the emotional, and the moving (ISM 55). Thus it was the Gurdjieffian meaning of "objective" that the Harlem group understood Van Vechten to have indicated, and his identification as a Gurdjieffian supports such an interpretation. Van Vechten would not have had access to Gurdjieff's *Beelzebub's Tales* while he was writing *Nigger Heaven* because it began to be read aloud to the New York groups too late to have affected his novel. However, by the time *Nigger Heaven* was published, the Harlem group had been introduced to *Beelzebub's Tales* as an example of a thoroughly successful "objective" modern text.

However, the interest of Larsen, Schuyler, Thurman, Fisher, and Hurston in *Nigger Heaven* was not eclipsed by Gurdjieff's text, and they treated Van Vechten's novel as something of a manifesto. What they produced in the first phase of their efforts—from 1928 to 1932—is a unique body of writing that drew various elements from Toomer, Gurdjieff, and Van Vechten. Their antiracial approach to fiction was a wholly original innovation (and it stood in some relationship to Jean Toomer that cannot be described in detail at present). Their writings were "objective" and satirical in the manner of *Beelzebub's Tales*. Also, like *Nigger Heaven*, the works were grounded in the milieu of Harlem's vibrant culture.

In an attempt to advance beyond the "objectivity" accomplished by Van Vechten, the Harlem group innovated "objective" procedures of their own, deriving new approaches to language and structure from the "verbal cabbala" (Waldberg 22) that Gurdjieff employed in *Beelzebub's Tales*. Unfortunately, secrecy prevails exactly at the point where the actualities that brought about this body of writing might have converged: How the form of this literary attack on race was conceived, coordinated, and evaluated can only be determined in so far as the examination of the texts will allow. One relevant clue is contained in Hurston's discussion in *Dust Tracks on a Road* of the difficulties of collecting folk songs. Hurston's discussion also applies to the code used in "objective" texts—the system of "lawful inexactitudes." Orage states that the key to the inexactitudes in *Beelzebub's Tales* may only be discovered by intuition and that "The anomalies that seem to us incongruous and absurd may be a text within a text, which, when rooted out, may comprise an alphabet of the doctrine" (Nott *Teachings* 194). Hurston says very nearly the same thing: "The only way you can know [when the singer was interpolating pieces of other songs], is to know your material so well that you can sense the violation. Even if you do not know the song that is being used for padding, you can tell the change in rhythm and tempo. The words do not count" (DTR 197–98). However, beyond her discussion of "lawful inexactitude," Hurston intimates that it is a peculiarity of African-American language that led the Harlem group to find a unique solution to the problem of writing "objectively." She states that "Negroes can fit in more words and leave out more and still keep the tune better than anyone I can think of" (198).

It was not only Jean Toomer who altered Gurdjieff's system, but also Orage. What Orage taught in New York was shaped by his studies with both Gurdjieff and Ouspensky, which introduced certain emphases not original in Gurdjieff's evocation of his system. Orage's addition to the practice of the work was a renovation that emphasized man's mechanical nature and the need for the technique of self-observation to become less mechanical. These themes are the foundation of the writings of the Harlem group: In the texts written by Toomer's followers, man's mechanicalness became a central theme and self-observation a literary technique.[3]

These departures from Gurdjieff's original ideas, techniques, and methods were brought out in 1930, during his fourth visit to New York. Gurdjieff's examination of the New York groups (with Orage in Europe on a honeymoon) led him to conclude that all of Orage's students were "candidates for the madhouse" (Patterson 134). Gurdjieff's subsequent house cleaning caused a rift in the movement that separated followers into a group that remained loyal to Gurdjieff and a group that pursued Orage's version of the work. There is no clear idea as to what transpired during Gurdjieff's harrowing of Orage's New York groups, for none of the written accounts—those by Gurdjieff *(Life)*, King *(The Oragean Version)*, Nott *(Teachings)*, and Welch—agree on the details concerning dates, conversations, meetings, and personnel. One interpretation of the entire episode is that it was "objective" theater and could not be understood by conventional means (Taylor *Gurdjieff's Deconstruction* 196).

This split had a profound effect on the subsequent shape of the Gurdjieff work in America. Several factions evolved along the lines of what various personalities understood to have happened between Gurdjieff and Orage. It seems that those who were not aware that the rift was a demonstration and a type of initiation separated themselves from Gurdjieff and became followers of Orage. It is useful to note that the subject of Gurdjieff's first lecture delivered to Orage's students in 1930 was initiation. In this lecture, Gurdjieff discussed the differences between exoteric, mesoteric, and esoteric groups. Gurdjieff stated that esoteric groups are to be initiated not only theoretically and practically into all relevant questions, but introduced to all means for a real possibility of self-perfecting (Patterson 134). Although it is not established that any of the Harlem group was in attendance at this lecture, C. Daly King, a loyal Oragean, was present. It is likely that the substance of Gurdjieff's lectures percolated into Harlem through King, whose name appears (in code) in some of the Harlem texts. (There are indications that just as Orage replaced Jean Toomer after he left New York in 1926, King served the Harlem group as a substitute for Orage after his death in 1934.) Gurdjieff's discussion of esoteric groups during his visit to America established the principle that within the work there was a progression from exoteric, public organizing to esoteric, closed groups.

Thus we may suppose that after 1926 Jean Toomer's program in Harlem evolved from the porous public groups of which Langston Hughes and Arna Bontemps were aware into closed mesoteric and esoteric phases, which were conducted in the strictest secrecy. In chapter 9 of *Dust Tracks on a Road*, Hurston emphasizes the importance of secrecy to the Harlem group in this later phase of the work. In a strange, seemingly pointless, three-page episode, Hurston comes into contact with important men while working as a manicurist; however, the point of the passage is manifested in one sentence: "Zora knows how to keep a secret" (159). The unusual concern with secrecy evinced by Hurston is derived from one feature that is particularly pronounced in the Oragean version, a technique called Experiment. The first part of the Oragean Method, Self-observation and Non-identification, was the content of courses taught by Jean Toomer in Harlem beginning in 1925. A second technique, called Participation, would seem to have occupied a mesoteric and private course of study (Webb 308). The third technique, Experiment, was a practice in which the student assumes various roles. The ability to play a role was supposed to enable the student to study the mechanized functioning of human beings and to allow for practice in the changing of habits, thereby establishing more psychic freedom (Webb 308–9). Moreover, the third phase implies a concern with secrecy, a theme that arises pronouncedly in the texts by the Harlem group but which is absent from texts by other Gurdjieffians. Even a cursory study of the various written accounts of the personalities, habits, and interpersonal relationships of the Harlem group suggests that these markedly puzzling individuals were often playing a role and practicing the discipline of Experiment.

A particularly vivid example of a devotion to Experiment, the developmental technique of role-playing, is found in George Schuyler's gyrations between leftist and conservative politics. To account for this aspect of Schuyler's behavior, Henry Louis Gates Jr. diagnoses the writer as a "literary schizophrenic" unable to unite his "fragmented self" (quoted in Gruesser 679) and collapsing under the strain of double-consciousness. This description might accurately apply to an individual lacking Schuyler's philosophical resources. However, for Schuyler and the other members of the Harlem group, the Gurdjieff work posed a solution to the problem of double-consciousness. The work recognized that all humans, not just African-Americans, are bifurcated and require some means of therapy to function more effectively. However, based on what were thought to be "real" ideas, the Gurdjieff work assumed a number of positions that violate conventional standards of decency and honesty. To achieve the "mental freedom" that was the therapeutic goal of the work, the student learned to produce any impression on people that he chose (ISM 267), because "mental freedom" was gained partly by the conscious establishment of a mask or persona. It is often remarked that this role-playing was characteristic of Gurdjieff himself: Kathryn Hulme (52) states that "He could play any role with consummate artistry. Apparently no one who ever met him emerged from the encounter unimpressed one way or another. Nor did any two give similar reports of him beyond . . . the exterior description."

Gurdjieffians took very seriously the realization that normal man is "asleep," and by remaining asleep, normal people constituted little more than a danger to those intent on evolving. Gurdjieff taught that the evolution of large masses of humanity was impossible and opposed to nature's purposes (ISM 57). Because humanity neither progresses nor evolves (ISM 57), it is not in the evolving man's interest to behave as other men do. When we seek to understand George Schuyler's movement from one political position to another, we must consider that as a Gurdjieffian Schuyler was hidden behind his various literary and political disguises, never allowing his true self to be clearly seen.

The literary production of Toomer and his colleagues shows that they were driven by something more than a fad for Negro art: if we only consider their major works we must conclude that the productivity of the Harlem group is nothing less than astonishing. Jean Toomer began holding his meetings in 1925, and his correspondence shows that he was still making visits to Harlem in 1927. Members of the group that had studied Gurdjieff's system with Toomer and Orage published two novels in 1928 *(Quicksand, The Walls of Jericho)*, two novels in 1929 *(Passing, The Blacker the Berry)*, a philosophical work and two novels in 1931 *(Essentials, Black No More, Slaves Today)*, and two novels in 1932 *(Infants of the Spring, The Conjure-Man Dies)*. After this highly productive phase, other factors began to interfere with the literary performance of the Harlem group. After 1929, the Great Depression all but eliminated the interest in African-American writing. Also, Rudolph Fisher, Wallace Thurman, and A. R. Orage died in 1934. Nella Larsen found it impossible to publish her new writings, and she eventually burned the manuscripts of six novels. Nevertheless, the literary phase of the movement continued to operate sporadically. In 1937 and 1939 Zora Neale Hurston produced two important texts, *Their Eyes Were Watching God* and *Moses, Man of the Mountain,* and in 1942 she published a book that purports to be her autobiography. George Schuyler was still publishing in the 1960s.

Melvin B. Tolson is included in this study because though he was not, strictly speaking, a member of the Harlem Renaissance, he was a member of the Harlem group. Tolson came into contact with the Harlem group between 1931 and 1932, during his graduate studies at Columbia University. He wrote a thesis on the Harlem Renaissance, concentrating on those individuals he was able to meet personally. In the introduction he acknowledges the help of Fisher, Thurman, and Zona Gale (Flasch 29; Gale was a prominent Gurdjieffian and a friend of Jean Toomer's). In 1933 he began to publish poems on Marxist themes. Tolson's later, long poems are novelized, high-modernist epics that reiterate everything of an esoteric, Gurdjieffian, Kabbalistic, and alchemical nature that may be found in the texts by Larsen, Thurman, Fisher, Schuyler, and Hurston, although often more heavily coded, more complexly intertextualized, and with more reference to "objective" mathematics. An example of how Tolson's texts are related to the Harlem group's texts is his "Libretto for the Republic of Liberia" (1953), which was generated out of Tolson's close reading of Schuyler's *Slaves Today*, a novel about Liberia. From that beginning, it was extended into a parody of *The Waste Land*, an argument with the major philosophies of history (Hegel and Marx), and an interrogation of historiographers, major and minor (Herodotus, Vico, H. G. Wells, Spengler, and Toynbee). Tolson's *Harlem Gallery* (1965), which approaches the Bible in Kabbalistic polysemy and Joyce's *Finnegans Wake* in unbounded wordplay, is at once encyclopedic and unreadable. Set in Harlem, it alludes to many of the characters and events in the novels by the Harlem group. As a measure of the playful "objective" intricacy with which Tolson compiled *Harlem Gallery*, we can note that the poem's 4201 lines reverse the number 1024—the density of oxygen in the tenth triad of radiations from the Absolute to the moon in Gurdjieff's table of "density of vibrations" (ISM 172).

The prevailing assumption has been that the Harlem group's body of impressive literary productions came after the dissolution of Jean Toomer's efforts to spread Gurdjieff's system in Harlem. Where this study departs from established opinion is in the assessment of the texts that Wallace Thurman, Rudolph Fisher, George Schuyler, Nella Larsen, and Zora Neale Hurston wrote after 1927. The texts produced by these authors have been read in many ways but never as expressions of Gurdjieffian thought—that is, mystical, Kabbalistic, esoteric systemizing—or as texts that consistently valorize Jean Toomer's antiracial ideas.

Moreover, it must be emphasized that Toomer's antiracialism represents a unique cultural component. Although socialism and Marxism proselytized the brotherhood of mankind to varying degrees, this was not done by dispensing with race. For example, Langston Hughes began to move in socialist circles in 1926, and his name appeared on the masthead of *New Masses* in 1930. The joining together of all races was Hughes's great theme, yet at no point did he cease to conceive race or cease to "assert the primacy of [his] experience and the authority of [his] blackness against the supposedly universal values of European culture" (De Jongh 48). Similarly, the antiracism of the NAACP and the Urban League accepted the idea of races and were not antiracialist, affirming that it was as Negroes that the struggle must be carried on for civil and human rights. Zora Neale Hurston, who studied with Franz Boas at Columbia University and served as one of his anthropological field workers, was thoroughly versed in scientific antiracism and could have served as a conduit of Boas's views into the Harlem group. The antiracism of Boas was set on demonstrating the incompetence of the science that propped up the eugenicist movement. Boas performed his crucial defeat of racist science by demanding scientific proof that race determines mentality and temperament. For Boas to counter an unprovable racist thesis with the hypotheses that race, language, and culture varied independently of one another (for which there was partial support from empirical data) was not the same as the unscientific affirmation that "Negroes are just like anybody else" (329), which Hurston maintained in *Dust Tracks on a Road* (1942). Hurston's assertion is a partial presentation of Thurman's original statement in *Infants* that Negroes are like other people because they contain the same social, physical, and intellectual components. In this way, the fundamental proposition of the Gurdjieff work was used to theorize the contemporary, biological conception of race out of existence. Toomer was explicit on this point, stating that "Above race values there are culture values. Above culture there are conscious values. The values of Mankind and Consciousness are identical" ("The Crock of Problems," Jean Toomer Collection, Box 32, Folder 7, 15). Hurston's assessment of race as "so-called" in her satirical discussion of racial purity in *Dust Tracks on a Road*, where she states that "I have been told that God meant for all the so-called races of the world to stay just as they are" (DTR 236), has more of an origin in Toomer's statement "The so-called family tree is largely verbal" ("The Crock of Problems," Jean Toomer Collection, Box 32, Folder 7, 15) than in Boas's anthropology. Toomer's ideas on the irrelevance of contemporary conceptions of race (whether scientific or pseudoscientific), which were interspersed with themes of a future incommensurate with the present order, apocalypse, superconsciousness, and the coming of a new race of mankind, differed qualitatively from other approaches available in 1926. Although Toomer's conception of the future was derived from some of the same occult sources that had given rise to Futurism and Surrealism, his approach represents a new direction. Toomer's linkage of Blavatsky's writings on psychic races to Gurdjieff's metapsychological system of development was a unique fusion of psychological and spiritual materials with which to attack contemporary culture in general—and racism as a specific target.

In 1925 Jean Toomer began to teach Gurdjieff's method of self-development in Harlem. The Gurdjieffian dynamic that Toomer introduced continued to direct the shape and content of the literary works created by some of the important figures who participated in the Harlem Renaissance. In contrast with what was customary for other groups involved in the Gurdjieff work, secrecy and concealment were fundamental practices of the writers of the Harlem group. The Harlem Gurdjieffians not only held secret meetings, they used a variety of cryptographic devices in their literary works, which were at times published under pen names, and conspired to alter the structure of American society. This secrecy seems to have been a reflection of the group's pursuit of an alternative to the dominant position of racism in American culture. Gurdjieff had said that "two hundred conscious people, if they existed and if they found it necessary and legitimate, could change the whole of life on the earth" (ISM 310). The same idea is put into different words and furnished a racial emphasis in Wallace Thurman's novel *Infants*, wherein a character proclaims "if out of a wholesale allegiance to Communism, the Negro could develop just half a dozen men who were really and truly outstanding, the result would be worth the effort" (219).

This idea is also indistinctly presented in one of the coded portions of *Black Empire*, a serialized novel that George Schuyler, as Samuel I. Brooks, published in the *Pittsburgh Courier* from November 1936 to July 1937. In *Black Empire* a list of names is repeated several times: "Dr. [Henry] Belsidus, Sam Hamilton, Rev. Samson Binks, Ransom Just, Bennie Simpson, Patricia Givens, Alex Fletcher, Juan Torlier, Gaston Nucklett, Sanford Mates, . . . [Carl Slater]" (81). Schuyler's wordplay—consisting of anagrams and homophones disguised by superfluous letters and reversed spellings—is not difficult to decipher once the reader becomes aware of the presence of Schuyler's games with language. The obviously ciphered pen name Samuel I. Brooks (see chapter 5) also leads the reader to the hidden level of Schuyler's novel. The message encoded into the list of names reads: be insiders, mass a million, every skin [the] same, some are just, anyone, seven parts, looks left, one railroad, G [will] let you on, time for [the] last call.

The secrecy pursued by the Harlem group was related to their desire to intervene in history through their imaginative writings and to produce "objective" literary works that would raise the level of consciousness of their readers. In addition to Thurman's *Infants*, this intention may be detected in the novels of George Schuyler. In *Black No More* Schuyler presents the idea of world change in a positive light; in that narrative a raceless, utopian world is achieved by men of advanced knowledge by working in secret. In *Black Empire/Black Internationale*— a subtly satirical attack on racialist thought—Schuyler shows a world plunged into a dystopian nightmare of ethnic cleansing, political oppression, and the absolute, authoritarian control by a warped genius driven obsessively by an undeveloped conscience. In this work also the conquest of the world is accomplished by a secret organization.

At this point it is necessary to provide some specifics about the codes with which the Harlem writers constructed their literary works. The chapters that follow are largely concerned with hidden levels of these texts, a feature that has heretofore remained unrecognized. Not only are codes a prominent feature of all of the works by the Harlem group authors, but they exist on a number of semiotic levels. The codes result in such unusual stylistic effects that the consistent wordplay in these texts generally forced the literary works to take on exaggerated and eccentric attributes. Also, it seems, curiously, that the writers of the Harlem group did not take into account that people do not read in the polysemic way that is necessary to extract meanings from their intertextual layerings. Thus, I suspect that the many different styles, contents, and methods of encoding the texts written between 1928 and 1966 represent various experiments of the Harlem group to find a means to signal the esoteric contents of the texts.

It is noteworthy that the most prominent use of codes appears in connection with the names of the various characters. (The chief exception is George Schuyler, whose elaborately contrived pen names are explicit indications of the artificial nature of the surface of his texts; see chapter 5.) Some names do nothing more than announce the existence of the ciphers within the text. In Hurston's *Their Eyes Were Watching God*, the reader encounters the pseudofolkloric sobriquet Coodemay, which can effectively be read as "I am code" by taking the "y" as "i," reading from right to left, reversing direction after "am," and subtracting the extra "o." Although these circuitous methods may seem to produce a foreordained reading, when read against the body of Harlem texts, Coodemay is essentially subjected to a conventional reading. Because Hurston used a system shared by members of the Harlem group, the means used to understand Coodemay may be used to extract a meaning from a name in Thurman's *Infants*. For example, when the name of Thurman's character Dr. A. L. Parkes (the Alain Locke character) is read from right to left it reveals two words, "[c]rap" and "lard." Dr. Parkes is introduced at a donation party where he attempts to recruit the young artists for a "concerted movement which would establish the younger negro [sic] talent once and for all as a vital artistic force" (*Infants* 228). The salon deteriorates into a shouting match in which Dr. Parkes's arguments are dismissed by Thurman's alter ego, Raymond. Raymond's rejection of Parkes's views in the surface text underscores his decoding as "crap" and "lard" in the subtext. Furthermore, we must assume that the wordplay was intended to be transparent. The parallel derogation of Parkes in both the narrative and the subtext was meant to be a sort of Rosetta stone by which the reader is given a key to the hidden level of the text. The "y" used for an "i" is conventional and surfaces again in the name of Thurman's character Eustace Savoy *(Infants)*, which can be read from right to left as "I save you." Similarly, in Hurston's *Eyes* the name Jeff Bruce may be deciphered by reading from right to left to disclose "cur jeff."

Another name that signals the presence of a coded level is N'Gana Frimbo, the African witch doctor and *ubermensch* who is the "murder victim" in Rudolph Fisher's mystery *The Conjure-Man Dies*. If we read N'Gana from right to left and add the missing letters from Frimbo, we solve the puzzle by spelling the word "anagram." With this clue in hand, we may easily solve the long list of anagrams that compose the names of the characters in Fisher's text. A whole class of names found in the texts of Toomer's Harlem group may be read as anagrams, although these anagrams are characterized more by the feature of sound than by orthography; as we shall see, all of the texts emphasize the sonic aspects of communication. Thus George Schuyler's character Patricia Givens *(Black Empire)* hides "seven parts"—a phrase that is shorthand for Gurdjieff's Law of Seven or the Law of the Octave. (An octave may be thought of as either seven or eight notes, because in running from "do" to "do" the eighth note begins a new octave as it completes the last octave. This Law of Seven was said to describe the operation of the universe as a network of vibrations; see ISM 122.)

In most cases the solution of these anagrams demands little more than for the reader to pay close attention to the text. Both Thurman's Paul Arbian *(Infants)* and Larsen's Brian Redfield *(Passing)* conceal the word "brain," which are allusions to Gurdjieff's conception of man as being psychically fragmented into the mutually adversarial functions of instinct, emotion, and intellect. Both Paul Arbian and Brian Redfield represent the intellectual center in their respective texts. Thus Paul Arbian is "all brain," whereas Brian Redfield's dependence on the mental center— the "brain"—causes him to "dread life." By using these simple anagrams and hypograms, the authors attempt to alert the reader by sounding out a quality with which the character has become associated: The irascible character Anne Gray in Nella Larsen's *Quicksand* has a name that declares her "chief feature" to be anger, as does Audrey Denny, whose name proclaims "I deny, I erred." ("Chief feature" refers to the Gurdjieffian idea that every man has a certain fault in his character around which his "false personality" forms; ISM 226.) The pen name Rachel Call ("racial call"), which George Schuyler employed extensively from 1933 to 1938, also constructs a name with double meaning, although here the content has a different emphasis.

A code with a higher order of complexity also pervades the texts created by Toomer's Harlem group, although it is more accurate to say that these texts are synonymous with the code. To demonstrate the nature of this code, it is useful to examine Melvin B. Tolson's employment of this technique. It is no exaggeration to state that his last poem, *Harlem Gallery*, is so saturated with ciphers that every syllable in the text is a component of a sight- and sound-based subtext. Tolson was an inheritor and a survivor: His long poems are informed by the works of all of the Gurdjieffians extending from Gurdjieff himself to Jean Toomer to the members of Toomer's Harlem group. It is for this reason that *Harlem Gallery* contains numerous allusions to all of the texts produced by this diverse assembly. Tolson wanted it clearly understood that rather than having innovated the devices that characterize his complex poetic style, he borrowed them directly from the Harlem Gurdjieffians. Tolson often stated that the "three S's of Parnassus"—sight, sound, and sense—was his formula for writing poetry (Flasch 48). Flasch states: "*Sight* referred to the appearance of the poem on the page; *sound* to the sound of the words (an element which he tested as he wrote by pacing the floor and reciting the lines loudly, regardless of the hour); *sense*, to the image, the appeal of the senses"

(Flasch 48). The sounds form words by a process of accretion, because the sounds are often separated by other syllables and only build up words by repetition; the sounds in *Harlem Gallery* are repeated to the extent that they contribute their "sense" even though they are not presented in the conventional order.

Thus, the concept of the "three S's" that has been attributed to Tolson (Flasch 50) is merely his description of the most common form given to the "attack on reading" in the novels of Rudolph Fisher and Wallace Thurman, where the code was first employed. The code was used subsequently by Larsen, Schuyler, Hurston, and Tolson. Specifically, the concept is introduced in the fight sequence in *The Walls of Jericho* (1928), a passage that Fisher uses to teach the reader to read hermeneutically:

Unintelligible, fragmentary glimpses came through the too narrow doorway—Bubber ducking a cue stick, swung butt-end-to in a villainous arc—somebody reaching for a pool ball in a corner of the one visible table—a figure pitching forward headlong out of *sight*—Jinx with a pianohold, vehemently bending his particular adversary back across the edge of the table—wild swings of bodiless arms, *sense*less twist and tangle of disjoined legs and feet. Accompanying these glimpses, noise, a strident yet muffled tumult: shuffle of feet, grunts, curses, thumps, thwacks, hisses, stifled cries; a deep background of *sound* against which stood out an occasional wooded crash. (272–73; emphases added)

The passage not only sounds out the names of Ouspensky, Orage, Gurdjieff, and Toomer, but it informs the reader of the means to ascertain these names, that is, by the reader's attention to the very same sight, sound, and sense about which Tolson spoke throughout his long career as a poet. In the above passage, Fisher alerts the reader to a "fragmentary glimpse" of the names. Here we may make out Ouspensky in the combination of sounds in "across," "*piano*hold," "du*ck*ing," and "adversary," although the sounds appear in more examples than the one given above. A. R. Orage's initials appear to have been selected for emphasis by the words "narrow," "particular," "arc," and "adversary." Orage may be combined from the sounds in "corner," "doorway," "figure," and "*edge.*" Gurdjieff is presented by "curses," "disjoined," and "muffled." Toomer is heard in "*too,* " "*tum*ult," "pool," "cue," and "Bubber." The names of the teachers of the Gurdjieff work are a consistent feature in the writings by the Harlem group, and the authors used similar means to accomplish these displays.

A typical treatment of these devices is delivered in Hurston's *Dust Tracks on a Road.* The title of Hurston's autobiography is an anagram for "trust code." The events that are depicted in the text are not accurate reflections of Hurston's life, and the text divulges this feature in several ways. One indication of the artificiality of the surface text is that there is an emphasis on the theatrical. The actress for whom Hurston supposedly served as a dresser reacted to her mail irrationally: "She loved her mother excessively, but when she received those long, wordy letters from her, she read them with a still face, and tore them up carefully" (139). In the paragraphs that follow, Hurston includes not only the "torn up" components of the names of G. I. Gurdjieff ("gags"—compare to Grand Exalted Giraw in DTR chapter 5), Toomer ("Baltimore"), P. D. Ouspensky ("tripping," "odd," "ambushed," "paint," "keep"), and A. R. Orage ("particularly," "gloriously," "stage"), but C. Daly King ("she," "playful," "working") and [George] Schuyler ("school," "her"). There are many examples in which Hurston sounds out the names in the paragraphs that describe the young actress. The "torn up" elements resound in complex patterns, and often Hurston includes other indications of the hidden content, such as the use of words that contain significant patterns of doubled letters for emphasis such as "*particularly*," "*tripping*," and "*odd*." (Note Fisher's use of "particular" in the above passage and that the doubled letters that render P. D. Ouspensky's initials occur in a contiguous phrase, "tripping us up at odd moments"; DTR 140.)

It is nearly impossible in a short space to indicate the complex wordplay indulged in by the members of the Harlem group. It must suffice to state that Larsen, Hurston, Thurman, and Schuyler share Fisher's concern with sight, sound, and sense and in various ways sound out the names of the four major esoteric teachers (Gurdjieff, Ouspensky, Toomer, and Orage) with consistent and uniform permeation throughout their literary works.

As a result of Jean Toomer's efforts in organizing a school to teach the ideas of G. I. Gurdjieff and A. R. Orage, many themes that otherwise would not have arisen were introduced into the writings of Toomer's followers in Harlem. Those ideas significantly determined the intellectual and ideological content of an important body of fiction, drama, and poetry. The themes are particularly noteworthy because they are not related to what contemporary readings recognize as concerns of the Harlem writers of the 1920s. These themes include: (1) superman versus normal man; (2) the evolution and involution of races and individuals; (3) "sleep" or mechanical living; (4) "mental freedom" or "mental independence;" (5) the "false personality" and the "mask" (which includes the idea that man has no individuality or unity of personality); (6) man is composed of three centers (physical, mental, emotional); and (7) reciprocal maintenance or man's place in the cosmos (otherwise known as the theme of "cosmic scale"). In the chapters that follow, these seven themes will be examined in the works of Jean Toomer, Wallace Thurman, Rudolph Fisher, Nella Larsen, George Schuyler, and Zora Neale Hurston.

Besides these themes, there are literary elements employed by Gurdjieff that entered Harlem literature, in particular, a predominant tendency to use satire and irony. Among many other things, Gurdjieff was a literary pioneer. Jean Toomer was an ardent admirer of the "objective" literary texts that Gurdjieff wrote, especially the monumental science-fiction satire, *All and Everything: An Objectively Impartial Criticism of the Life of Man,* or *Beelzebub's Tales to His Grandson.*

Gurdjieff began to write the book in 1925 and it became the "Bible" of the groups at that time, when sections of the work-in-progress began to be read aloud at meetings in New York. The first draft was completed in 1927, and plans for its publication arose in 1928. In 1930–1931 the first English-language version of *Beelzebub's Tales* was published in mimeographed form to raise money for Gurdjieff. A. R. Orage was one of the chief translators and editors engaged in the enormous project of accurately rendering Gurdjieff's ideas in the difficult style required by his teacher.

Beelzebub's Tales, Gurdjieff's "prodigious and unclassifiable masterpiece" (Moore 48), is a 1200-page satire on modern science and the scientific mind. The text is presented in the form of a comic ethnology that exoticizes humanity so that everyday activities display their underlying structure. Gurdjieff incites us to ask questions: first to question the authority of science and then the reality of its findings. He substitutes the whole of Western science with an alternative system particularized in a distended, repellent discourse (Waldberg 22–24).

Beelzebub's Tales belongs to a "classic genre" (Waldberg 20) that teaches that "Beneath the humorous surface of the fable we again meet the doctrine of illusion, of *Maya,* of the famous 'sleep' which all the masters speak of, a sleep which must be broken and from which the sleeper must 'awaken' " (Waldberg 21). *Beelzebub's Tales* is comparable to the impenetrable surface of Rabelais and the encyclopedic nature of Joyce's *Finnegans Wake* (Waldberg 22).

In *Beelzebub's Tales* Gurdjieff has set out to destroy existing values. He is so thorough that he undermines the reality of everyday objects: French coffee is described as an oil with no discernible origin; American canned food is deadly; processed meat is filth; the advertising business is insanity; canned soup is made by chasing a chicken through the processing plant; social dancing is "titillation"; American speech consists of five idiotic phrases; and theater (the "manipulation" of actors) destroys the need for the perception of reality. Gurdjieff attacks both religion and rationality, moving from one topic to another and exhausting nearly everything that modern man takes for granted. In short, Gurdjieff's *Beelzebub's Tales* is a demonstration that all of modern life is a manipulative illusion.

Gurdjieff wished to write books that would act on all three centers of his readers. His calculated effect was to destroy the reader's beliefs in all that exists in the world. Although *Beelzebub's Tales* has been called science fiction, that label is a misnomer for a text that is so socially radical, textually innovative, and conceptually encyclopedic. However, *Beelzebub's Tales* had enough in common with science fiction to introduce elements of the genre into some of the attempts at "objective" writing undertaken by Toomer and the Harlem group. As early as the composition of "The Gallonwerps" in 1927, Toomer introduced imaginary technological devices into his writings. In contrast to *Beelzebub's Tales,* the technological devices present in Toomer's fiction are mere signs of the emptiness of modern life and were intended to demonstrate modern man's attempts to compensate for his lack of harmony by populating his world with an increasing array of sophisticated but in-effective prosthetic devices. Toomer's "objective" style was less linguistically grounded than Gurdjieff's, and Toomer tended more to emphasize allegory and character. Because of the extremity of Gurdjieff's language (his dense style, strange neologistic vocabulary, and enigmatic allegories) and the hyperomni-science of his narrative stance, Toomer and his followers did not, or could not, avail themselves of the most pronounced and effective of Gurdjieff's techniques.

Using various components of Gurdjieff's style, Jean Toomer wrote a number of novels that were direct imitations of *Beelzebub's Tales*. Together with Orage, Toomer passed his reverence for the text to his students in Harlem. The Harlem group, in turn, incorporated features of *Beelzebub's Tales* into their own texts, in particular Gurdjieff's tendency to direct his satire downward at his targets from cosmic heights. As we shall see, some of the most compelling writing by members of the Harlem group was in the satirical vein. Other texts by Harlem writers that contain "objective" themes are characterized by the use of heavy irony, and this feature may also be related to texts by Jean Toomer and Carl Van Vechten. There is a close connection between the satirical and the "objective." When the "objec-tive" is destructive, as it often is when aimed at a mass audience in works of popu-lar literature such as *Beelzebub's Tales*, the mode of satire and irony readily suits the purposes at hand. Toomer also passed along from his own appropriations of *Beelzebub's Tales* the use of science fiction as a form of "objective" writing. When coupled with satire, this influence may have produced a powerful effect on the form and content of George Schuyler's futuristic novels.

The seven themes outlined above is one way of categorizing the attempt by the Harlem group to create an "objective" response to racialism. Their antiracial liter-ature represents a reinterpretation of the "objective" literary text, which largely took the form of their responses to *Beelzebub's Tales* in concert with another set of responses to Van Vechten's *Nigger Heaven*. Whereas Jean Toomer's desire to create texts on the level of *Beelzebub's Tales* led to direct appropriation and imitation of Gurdjieff's texts, the Harlem group pursued another direction and produced a new aesthetic. Toomer addressed the social problems that are generated by America's racialist culture in his pre-Gurdjieff novel *Cane* and in such unpublished exposi-tions as "The Crock of Problems" and "On Being an American." However, his at-tempts at "objective" fiction and his plays were not concerned with the subject of race. Thus, it may be said that Toomer's disciples pioneered an "objective" litera-ture that took race as its subject. Toomer's novel *Cane*, with its southern setting, had little influence as a model in this new literary mode; in the writings of the Harlem group, we are able to register their rejection of Toomer's lyrical impres-sionism and racial mysticism.

The Harlem group embraced "objective" satire, as Toomer had done in "The

Gallonwerps" and "Transatlantic," and they began to experiment with an alternative to the modernist aesthetic—an art that had racial subjects without having been derived from the racial ideology of the New Negro movement. In other words, the Harlem group set out to create a new kind of literary art, a "racial" art that was antiracial. Although the Gurdjieffian school of Harlem literature continued to explore ways to apply the "objective" aesthetic, in contrast to Toomer's concern with the transformation of the world through a general change in consciousness, their focus was narrow. The Harlem writers solely directed their efforts at deconstructing the ideology, psychology, and sociology of race.

Toomer was intent upon reproducing the "objective" qualities of *Beelzebub's Tales* in the outer form of his texts so that they would appear like what Gurdjieff called art number four, conscious or "objective" art. Although Toomer's texts were not as difficult to read as *Beelzebub's Tales*, it is readily apparent that they were neither conventional novels nor did they partake of the lyrical-impressionism of *Cane*. If only the surface texts are considered, the texts by Thurman, Fisher, Schuyler, Larsen, and Hurston appear to belong to the categories of popular fiction, art number two, or sentimental art (ISM 298). Thus, the writings of the Harlem group may be described as sentimental-"objective" allegories of spiritual progress. Strictly speaking, it was beyond the capacity of the Harlem group to create "objective" art because they were insufficiently advanced in the Gurdjieff work, and their writings often expressed little more than their rudimentary and rote grasp of esoteric concepts. Although all of their texts expressed how the superman looked at ordinary humans, that aspect of their texts was secondary. Primarily, the texts were designed to put into circulation certain beneficial, antiracialist ideas in the form of parables, myths, and allegories. The Harlem group ascribed to the Gurdjieffian belief that more could be accomplished by circulating beneficial ideas around which people could form a conscience than by institutions that were subject to the degenerative forces of the laws of vibrations, because "the line of evolution is opposed to the line of creation" (ISM 134).

By comparatively examining the thirteen novels, two long poems, and one autobiography that are the focus of this study, it is possible to extrapolate the form of the "textual blueprint" from which their texts may have been generated.[4] This inferential "textual blueprint" specifies that the "objective" text written by a member of the Harlem group should have the following characteristics.

1. The literary text will be divided into twenty-four or twenty-five chapters. The form of the text imitates the form of the cosmos as "three degrees of radiation" or "three octaves." This template assigns each chapter a note in the "do re mi fa sol la ti do" scale. There is room for some interpretative freedom here, as there are twenty-two notes from the first "do" to the last "do" in three octaves, although it seems that there should be twenty-four notes in three octaves. (As we have seen, an octave may be either seven or eight notes.) In the work the two "intervals"—discontinuous vibrations—between "mi" and "fa" and "si" and "do" in each octave are just as important as the notes, for they "cause the line of the development of force to change, to go in a broken line, to turn around, to become its 'own opposite' and so on" (ISM 129). Thus, there are twenty-five points in the Ray of Creation, which may then be represented by the numbers twenty-four, twenty-two, or twenty-five, depending on what is wanted.

In Tolson's poem "Libretto for the Republic of Liberia," this interest in octaves has been exposed: Each of the eight sections bears the name of the note that it sounds—"Do," "Re," "Mi," and so on through the octave. In the novels, the notes are present throughout the chapters as "sound" and usually are sounded in the concluding paragraph of each chapter; in places, the last word in the chapter is the name of the respective note (e.g., in *Jonah's Gourd Vine* at the end of chapter 11, "me" is given for the note "mi"). Truest to the literal interpretation of "three octaves" form are *The Conjure-Man Dies* and *Harlem Gallery*, with twenty-four chapters. *Infants*, *The Walls of Jericho*, and *Quicksand* have twenty-five chapters, although the theory of "intervals" is ignored and the notes proceed without interruption. *Jonah's Gourd Vine* has twenty-six chapters; however, it is clear that the musical scheme is maintained throughout because the final chapter sounds the proper "re" note. Thurman's *The Blacker the Berry* is divided into five titled parts; however, it has twenty-six unlabeled textual divisions that sound the notes with regularity. Much the same can be said for the novels in which there are insufficient chapters to directly allude to the "three octaves": *Passing* (three sections, twelve chapters), *Their Eyes Were Watching God* (twenty chapters), and *Black No More* (thirteen chapters) maintain the musical scheme, ending on the notes "fa," "la," and "sol," respectively. The numbers eight and three are used extensively throughout the eleven chapters of Schuyler's *Slaves Today*, which also end on the associated notes. Here the number eleven is likely to be an instance of the convention of Kabbalistic addition, where $11 = 8 + 3$, which is another way to write the number twenty-four ($24 = 8 \times 3$) because the meaning is "objective" and always refers back to the same cosmic scheme. (Schuyler was married to a student of the occult well versed in Kabbalah.) Hurston may have intended to identify the sixteen chapters of *Dust Tracks on a Road* as two of the three octaves in the ray by repetitions of the phrase "two or three" in the text; the sixteenth chapter uses the convention of doubling to signal the note "do" in the last paragraph of the book, with the words "good" and "do" in the seventh sentence and "do" and "good" in the fourteenth and final sentence. In the anomalously extended texts, Schuyler's *Black Internationale* (thirty-three chapters), *Black Empire* (twenty-nine chapters), and Hurston's *Moses* (forty chapters), the musical scheme is maintained throughout. Hurston's *Moses* may be the only text that alludes to another organizing principle: Although its chapters sound the successive notes, they may also allude to the forty chapters of *Beelzebub's Tales*.

2. Gurdjieff will appear in the text as a character in a disguise. The characteristics by which he is identified are most often his yellow skin and striking eyes. Tolson reduces Gurdjieff to the epithetic compound "jaundice-eyed" in the opening lines of *Harlem Gallery*. In *Quicksand* he is a man who has disguised himself as an African-American woman. In *Infants*, *Passing*, and *Slaves Today* Gurdjieff is an actual woman, in each case with yellow skin and prominent eyes. In *Black Empire* a coded name identifies him as a white woman. Gurdjieff's book, *Beelzebub's Tales*, is alluded to in the projected text as "the book," which was the way it was commonly spoken of by Orage's New York groups. Beelzebub, the protagonist of *Beelzebub's Tales*, is alluded to as the devil, Scratch, Satan, and Beelzebub. In Hurston's *Dust Tracks on a Road* the entire complex is alluded to as "Milton's complete works" (127): "The back was gone and the book was yellowed. But it was all there. So I read *Paradise Lost*" (127). "The book" is *Beelzebub's Tales*, the "yellow" is a conventional allusion to Gurdjieff's complexion, "all there" is a reminder of *All and Everything*, and Satan is the protagonist of both *Paradise Lost* and *Beelzebub's Tales*.

3. The text will be a "legominism"—a text within a text—in which the fundamental concepts in the system are presented. As with all "legominisms," the special nature of the text is indicated through the use of "lawful inexactitudes," or as Margaret Naumburg called them in a letter to Jean Toomer, "conscious discrepancies" (Jean Toomer Collection, Box 7, Folder 18). In Harlem group texts, this feature usually takes the form of misspellings, (e.g., those found in BNM 206–10), inconsistencies in character development, or absurdities in plotting the narrative.

The hidden content in the "legominisms" consists of the body of knowledge taught by Jean Toomer and A. R. Orage known as "the work" or "the Method." The literary text will contain overt allusions to this system by using such words as "work," "working," "worker," "methodically," and "methodicalness." Chapter 8 of Hurston's *Dust Tracks on a Road* uses the word "work" seventeen times in twenty-seven pages; "work" appears ten times in the twenty-nine pages of the chapter that follows. The key to the encoded meaning of "work" is its overuse. The number of occurrences of the word necessarily calls attention to the discourse of the text because the overuse registers on the reader as an anomaly in an otherwise competently written text. Examination of the typescript of *Dust Tracks on a Road* shows that one of the only stylistic changes made in the entire manuscript was crossing out "Their looks drag them one way and their brains another" and inserting the less dexterous sentence "Their looks and charm interfere with their brain-work, that is all" (Hurston Collection, Box 1, Folder 13, 163).

The themes included in the Gurdjieffian Method include: superman, seven types of men, one "I," evolution, involution, sleep, mechanical living, mental freedom, man as a three-story factory, individuality, mask, playing a role, false personality, Ray of Creation, three octaves of radiation, Law of Three, and the Law of the Octave.

4. The text will perform an "attack on reading." The text is its own gloss, explicating the means by which it may be read. Included in the attack are characters who are incompetent readers; references to unreadable writing, ciphers, and wordplay (codes, double talk, puns, clues, syllepses); intertextuality; intratextuality; archaeology of textual figures (textiles, veils, alcoves, houses, rooms, clothes); inscriptions (allegories, chalkboards, calligraphy, signs, manuscripts, paintings); proper names; emblematics; hieroglyphics; represented textuality to orality; represented textuality to corporeality; shifts of consciousness; absurdity; textual artificiality (pseudoresistant texts); textual self-referentiality; textual indeterminacy; and textual obliteration (self-consuming texts, self-destroying texts).

The writers discussed in this study were all invested in an "attack on reading." Larsen's novels approached their "attack" directly through the representation of reading; at the same time, the art of reading depicted in the text (and the subtext) generate much of the novel's meaning. In Larsen's novels texts are always in danger of annihilation, and in places they are obliterated entirely, a feature also shared by Thurman's narratives. Tolson and Thurman create "unreadable" texts, Tolson through allusion and dense syntax and Thurman through narrative disruption. In *Black No More* Schuyler employs a variety of approaches: illiterate readers and signs written by illiterates, intentional misspelling, an incompetent author, and exaggerated names. In Fisher's *The Walls of Jericho* there is an intertextual shift from the biblical story of the battle of Jericho to Tod Bruce's sermon and an intratextual orality by Shine, who repeats the sermon to his two sidekicks in their "rat" discourse, to the narrator's disparaging analysis of Shine's rendering. Hurston's *Moses* is contingent on Moses's search for the "Book of Thot;" not only does Moses locate and read the book, he copies it, washes the ink from the papyrus copy, and drinks it. The episode is an elaborate comment on the insufficiency of normal methods of reading. In *Seraph on the Suwanee* Hurston presents the incompetent reader through Arvay's inability to get a joke, another example of the use of an oral textuality. In *Dust Tracks on a Road* Hurston allows one of her customers to translate a Greek text for her. In Fisher's *The Conjure-Man Dies* the text is the crime that John Archer cannot solve. Readers who think themselves competent are satirized, and reading is transformed into speaking as a clue that sound is the medium of communication.

5. The text will perform an "attack on race." The mimetic level of the text will take the form of a satire in which every form of racialism, color consciousness, and race consciousness is ridiculed. The thesis presented in the text is that racialism can only be combated by fostering in each individual a sense of internal freedom from external influences.

6. Significant names are to be included as ciphers through "sight, sound, and sense." These names include Jean Toomer, A. R. Orage, P. D. Ouspensky, G. I. Gurdjieff, C. Daly King, and the members of the Harlem group. Although the word "king" appears sixteen times in the tenth chapter of *Dust Tracks on a Road*, that this pervasive word is a name is only revealed through deciphering the text. The chapter bears the title "Research," and the first paragraph is instructional: "Research is formalized curiosity. It is poking and prying with a purpose. It is a seeking that he who wishes may know the cosmic secrets of the world and they that dwell therein" (174). The word "king" is a component of both "poking" and "seeking," and "seeking" is a homophone of "C. King." However, Hurston has bidden us to research the "cosmic secrets of the world," and so we are not given Daly until we reach "day" and "delicate" four pages later. The Daly implied by "deli" may be combined with the C. King in the word "sticking" that is given in the previous sentence. The code is used systematically. As noted above, in *Infants* Dr. A. L. Parkes is used to parody Alain Locke's ideas; the name is a cipher for "lard" and "crap." The mysterious magazine cover for a nonexistent Communist magazine that Aaron Douglas designed in 1934 reads "Spark: Organ of the Vanguard" (Kirschke 91). Douglas's "Spark" is consistent with Thurman's "Parkes" in decoding as "crap." "Spark: Organ" accords with other renderings of A. R. Orage, for example, Tolson's "Mr. Morgan's Thirteen

Galleries of Art" (HG 117). The "guard" in "vanguard" conforms with many occurrences of homophones for Gurdjieff in Harlem group texts (see the discussion of Hurston's use of "gourd" and "god" in chapter 6).

7. The text will include a list of names that presents a coded message. The contents of this list seems to have evolved over time, but generally speaking, it is a call to arms and a manifesto.

8. The names of G. I. Gurdjieff, A. R. Orage, P. D. Ouspensky, C. Daly King, and Jean Toomer are the text itself. The surface text is a palimpsest through which the names can be read constantly.

9. The text will include an embedded text. This embedded text is a more specific "legominism" than the subtext in the sense that it contains information of a different nature than is found throughout the subtext. Examples of embedded texts are the Curator's volume of poems, "Harlem Vignettes" in *Harlem Gallery;* Clare Kendry's letters and the Mother Goose rhyme in chapter 3 of the second book in *Passing;* Tod Bruce's sermon on Jericho in *The Walls of Jericho;* and N'Gana Frimbo's description of his kingdom in *The Conjure-Man Dies.* Other texts present similar material through embedded texts that are not clearly demarcated from the main text, such as the "fishing fleet" section of the final chapter of *Seraph on the Suwanee;* the "trial" section of chapter 19, the penultimate chapter of *Their Eyes Were Watching God;* chapter 8 ("Backstage and Railroad") of *Dust Tracks on a Road;* the Happy Hills section of the final chapter of *Black No More;* "Alva," the third part of *The Blacker the Berry;* and in *Moses* the exchange of notes in chapter 15 and the account of the "Book of Thot" in chapter 16.

The chapters that follow are arranged chronologically; the discussion begins with Jean Toomer and his introduction of the Gurdjieff work into Harlem in 1925 and ends with Zora Neale Hurston's last published novel in 1948. During this span of time, the "objective" literary experiments of the Harlem group proceeded without the comprehension of the world. As the Harlem group's texts appeared, beginning in 1928, they met with widely varying receptions depending on the subject, economic and social climate, and quality of the writing. I treat these texts individually as approaches to solving certain formal problems, which is largely the way they have been studied previously (although in this study the formal problems concern the nature of the "objective" aesthetic), and consider the collective thrust of the Harlem group's texts as an attempted intervention into the social (racial) and historical (devolutional) matrices.

Jean Toomer
Beside You Will Stand a Strange Man

Jean Toomer was the subject of numerous literary studies after what amounts to his rediscovery in the late 1960s. Toomer is a controversial writer and is equally celebrated as an African-American literary progenitor of the Harlem Renaissance and defamed as a tragically misguided figure who was unable to come to terms with his racial identity. Fundamentally, Toomer was a violator of taboos, and this contributes to many of the difficulties that arise in trying to understand his complex personality. In particular, Toomer's controversiality stems from his rejection of racialism, a stand that is even today not without many detractors, for "Modernization continues to take the form of ethnicization in many places around the globe" (Sollors 261). In *Beyond Ethnicity* Werner Sollors states that Toomer, "a lightskinned Afro-American whose family had been living on both sides of the color line for generations, viewed racial as well as other 'Linnaean' categories with great detachment and ironical distance. . . . Challenging the 'split spirit' of the past, Toomer expressed a complex vision of the new America of the future. He wanted his readers to understand the essential unity beyond phenomenal diversity, including that created by ethnic categories" (253). The many disturbing and provocative factors, which are expressive of modern crisis, capability, vision, and genius, that must be considered in evaluating Toomer's life and art have surrounded him in mystery, romance, and suspicion. As more was learned about Toomer in the 1960s, among other things, he became notorious for his pursuit of wealthy women. His first alliance was with Margaret Naumburg, the wife of his mentor, Waldo Frank. His pattern of gold-digging seems to have been repeated in his pursuit of the eccentric and generous Mabel Dodge Luhan and in subsequent marriages to two affluent white women. What is perceived as Toomer's conflicted manner in dealing with his African-American identity has also opened him to some unfavorable portraiture. However, it is Gurdjieff's ruin of Toomer's as a first-rank African-American creative writer that is perhaps the most pervasive failure attributed to him, and this idea has become common in discussions of Toomer's career.

If Toomer is placed in the tradition to which he belongs, with the iconoclasts and experimenters of the modern age, we can see that he is a familiar type. Toomer began writing in league with a group of Ouspenskian visionaries who looked to Walt Whitman as a rare modern poet who had achieved cosmic consciousness. In a line of creators that runs from Verlaine, Rimbaud, Corbiere, and Mallarme to

Toomer's colleague Hart Crane and Bob Kaufman (a nearly contemporary manifestation of the type), Jean Toomer may be understood as a classic eruption of the *poete maudit,* the accursed poet. The would-be superman, isolated, tormented by his visions of a new life, more often than not the accursed poet is unable to sufficiently collect his energies, focus his will, transcend his neuroses, and create a new order of language and exertion. The accursed poet stands in marked contrast to such superegoized and successful modernizing writers as Goethe, T. S. Eliot, and Andre Breton. Toomer is, perhaps, difficult to recognize because often the identity of the accursed poet announces itself in madness, suicide, or a similar conflagration of violent symptoms. Toomer's close associate and fellow Ouspenskian, the neosymbolist poet Hart Crane, likewise belonged to this type; after a frustrating career in search of the transcendent form of the American poem, Crane committed suicide in 1932 by jumping from a ship in midocean. In contrast to this more obvious pattern, Toomer's aspirations were couched in a lifetime of obsessive writing that went unpublished, a restless search for spiritual answers, and gradual physical and psychic decline.

Literary critics generally acknowledge Toomer's seminal influence upon the development of African-American literature. He introduced the techniques of literary modernism (modernism in the sense of literary experiment) to some of the most accomplished of the young writers who gathered in Harlem during the 1920s. Toomer was a full-fledged literary modernist who produced experimental fiction and drama that was influenced by Futurism, Imagism, Dadaism, Symbolism, Expressionism, and the lyrical-impressionism of Waldo Frank's Art as Vision group. Two members of the group, Gorham Munson and Hart Crane, were strongly influenced by Futurism in particular (Flint 30–31). This study addresses Toomer's unique brand of modernism formulated from the synthesis of avant-garde literary modernism with Gurdjieff's Fourth Way system of thought (the work) and the radical new forms of literature, theater, and choreography that Gurdjieff pioneered.

The influence of Gurdjieff on Jean Toomer is readily apparent. Before meeting Gurdjieff, Toomer was a member of Waldo Frank's Art as Vision group, which also included Margaret Naumburg, Hart Crane, Gorham Munson, and Kenneth Burke (A. P. Fisher 504). Frank's intimate cadre of disciples pursued mysticism by studying the writings of P. D. Ouspensky, and they produced theoretical statements and creative texts in the style of lyrical-impressionism. The Art as Vision group took its name from Ouspensky's phrase "art is the beginning of vision" that appears in the section of *Tertium Organum* entitled "Art and the Occult." According to Ouspensky, higher consciousness is a matter of "escape from the three-dimensional world" (TO 231). To exercise this escape, it is necessary for the artist to "throw off the chains of our logic" (TO 231). According to Ouspensky, the creative act so affects the emotions that it is possible for the artist to achieve cosmic consciousness. Ouspensky spoke of this higher consciousness as belonging to the higher race of supermen that was then forming within the ranks of normal humanity. The Art as Vision group pursued rapturous states of emotional excess and visionary ecstasy through whatever means were at their disposal, chiefly anesthetic drugs and alcohol. By pursuing this direction, Toomer was able to complete and publish an experimental novel, *Cane*. In 1922 Toomer had traveled to Spartanburg, South Carolina, in the company of Waldo Frank. Both Toomer's *Cane* and Frank's *Holiday* were published in 1923 and were similar in style (ID 27).

The language of the lyrical-impressionist style that Darwin T. Turner (WS 4) saw as characteristic of *Cane* is in most of its modernist practitioners an attempt to render the fragmentary nature of modern consciousness and thus presents the effect of "[a]tomization of the world of the mind and of matter, relativism and subjectivism" (Kronegger 529). In lyrical-impressionism, the writer is ahistorically merged in the present and tries to catch the fleeting sense stimuli as they strike upon the conscious mind. There is no center; thus, in lyrical-impressionism there is an absence of plot, drama, and character. The literary characteristics of the style are sentences without verbs, the use of weak auxiliaries, quality nouns, action nouns, substantivized adjectives, impersonal synthetic pronouns, subjective impressions, a predominance of colors over objects, and the disintegration of the material world (Kronegger 530). All of these qualities are present in *Cane*, which is an assemblage of short prose poems, imagist verses, and a play that all have an indeterminate relationship to one another. Indeed, the experimental form of *Cane* is one of several indications that Jean Toomer was not writing popular literature. Nor was *Cane*, in a conceptual sense, a work of African-American literature. Despite his setting of the narratives in the black South, Toomer was not primarily interested in race as it is ordinarily defined. The author of *Cane* was already a mystic, already engaged in mapping out the limits of humanity, the "new slope of consciousness" of a new type of human being ("The Gurdjieff Experience" WS 128).

Although the outward form of *Cane* can be justifiably described by literary critics as lyrical-impressionism, *Cane* was written to express the superior consciousness of the coming race of supermen, which goes beyond the fragmentary sense impressions embodied in the lyrical-impressionist mode. Jean Toomer intended for *Cane* to be unintelligible to humans of an ordinary range of consciousness, for it purported to embody what Hart Crane called "the metaphorical extra-logical 'truth' of the poet" (Crane 262–63) and what Toomer called the "superior logic of the metaphor" (Bone 81). The visionary aesthetic of the Art as Vision group generated from the idea that the allegorical texts of prehistoric origin (from which Blavatsky supposedly paraphrased the contents of *The Secret Doctrine*) was the language of superconscious men of a former age. The Art as Vision writers sought to recapture this former state of heightened awareness in their own texts. The lyrical, fragmented, surrealistic text of *Cane* was intended by Toomer to project into language all that can be communicated of an inexpressible, transcendental consciousness and was not presented to recapitulate the fragmentary mind of modern man.

Gurdjieff's impact on Toomer's writing was first to invalidate Toomer's practice as a writer of the art-for-art's-sake school. Gurdjieff himself created "objective" literature, and he taught that to do otherwise was to engage in "word prostitution" (Waldberg 27), because the goal of "objective" literature was the destruction of existing values, whereas "subjective" literature merely manifested various pathological states (Nott *Teachings* 127). Toomer arrived at Gurdjieff's Institute for the Harmonious Development of Man as a successful author of "subjective" writing in the mode of Anglo-American modernism, and he met with the standard treatment accorded creative writers and intellectuals who had been accepted for study. He was summarily forbidden to write at all and was assigned chores—hard, physical labor. However, immediately upon his arrival at Gurdjieff's institute, a dilapidated estate called the Prieure located on the outskirts of Paris, he began to subvert Gurdjieff's system of self-development. One aspect of Toomer's personality that comes through clearly in accounts of his early years is his inability to take direction. Forbidden by both Gurdjieff and Orage to use his intellect or his imagination, Toomer instead began to apply them both toward analyzing and reformulating the system itself. In a letter to Margaret Naumburg he states that "At the beginning of the work on the book *[Beelzebub's Tales]*, O[rage] gave me quite a rap for getting involved in the intellectual details" (Jean Toomer Collection, Box 7, Folder 18). Nevertheless, once he reached Harlem Toomer continued in this intellectual direction by elaborating and altering the work with transfusions from other systems of esoteric teachings. The notes that he kept during 1926 show his embroidery of Orage's basic presentation of the Method even as Orage lectured.

The inception of the Harlem group's literary "attack on race" may be traced to Toomer's inability to work on himself and to restrain himself from both altering the Gurdjieff work and assuming the role of teacher. At one of the first meetings that Orage and Toomer held in Harlem in 1926, while lecturing on the work, Orage said, "one should not be dependent upon externality for what happens to one, that this is shameful" ("A New Group, 1926" 2). Toomer added a comment that radically revised the implication of what Orage was saying: "And in this way rubs against the Negro, his possibilities and attitude, in a white world" ("A New Group, 1926" 2). Admittedly, Toomer's phrase "rubs against" is somewhat ambiguous. If the phrase is understood as "touches upon," then Toomer may have seen the solution to the African-American's problem of living in a racist society as a matter of evolving through work on oneself to a higher level of consciousness. Toomer posited creating a mentality in which racial thought no longer affected the psychology of individuals, for no longer would they identify with racial categorization. Toomer's amplification of the importance of race was a major violation of the Gurdjieffian worldview, particularly because the psychological system of the Method is based on "non-identification." In a sense, Toomer's approach to this intricate problem was to paradoxically insist that African-Americans had to disidentify themselves as African-Americans, yet remain conscious that they were African-Americans. The result of this antiracialist therapy is the body of literature discussed by this study—a series of literary works that exploit African-American culture as a means to enforce the view that race is an illusion.

However, it must be pointed out that Toomer's method is in no way derived from or related to W. E. B. Du Bois's "double-consciousness." Du Bois assessed the pathology that came from accepting conflicting views of the self that was racially divided against itself—"two warring ideals in one dark body" (*The Souls of Black Folk* 45). Toomer's application of "self- observation and non-identification" to the psychology of race deconstructed and rejected both the dominant (white) and the minority (black) views of the African-American self. In Toomer's analysis the self is not doubly conscious but unconscious ("asleep"). The self does not suffer from "twoness" (Du Bois 45), but is fragmented into multiple "subpersonalities" unaware of one another's existence.

After a few years of studying the work and creative writing with Orage and a mystical experience in 1926, Toomer began his own attempts to create "objective" literature. He wrote several short stories, a play, and a long poem. His supreme act of subordination was to imitate Gurdjieff's book, *Beelzebub's Tales* in a series of unpublished novels between 1927 and 1933—"The Gallonwerps," "Transatlantic," and "Caromb." Although these texts differ markedly from one another, they reflect Gurdjieff's *Beelzebub's Tales* in many ways. Gurdjieff's "objective" text included the entire corpus of the metaphysical, psychological, and cosmological system. However, the system was rendered in a nearly indecipherable way by the substitution of neologisms for more common terms, such as "Krentonalnian-revolution" for "orbit" and "kldatzacht" for "night"; the style of the text is very dense and circular, making for slow, laborious reading. Another important feature of *Beelzebub's Tales* that is not commonly recognized is that it is completely encoded: "The books of the First and Second Series [are] a coded illusion of a world which hides something real. It is both a repository of ideas and a programme [sic] for disseminating them. Gurdjieff himself indicates the gap between levels of understanding in his recollection of Orage's reaction to his 'shock' treatment.' 'Know the habit of my Teacher,' he recalls Orage saying, 'always to keep deep thoughts under ordinary, so to say meaningless outer expressions' *[Life Is Real]*" (Taylor "Gurdjieff's Deconstruction" 179–80).

Toomer was not alone in this desire to use the literary techniques of "objective" art, for Gurdjieff's monumental literary experiments had a conceptual power similar to the experimental novels of James Joyce. Like Joyce's fiction, they inspired imitation—although, because of limited distribution, only among Gurdjieffians, such as Rene Daumal, Colin Wilson, Zona Gale, and C. Daly King. A comparative study of the writings of Gurdjieff's imitators shows that for each of them the Gurdjieffian influence meant something different. However, in most cases it did not involve writing vast texts in an impenetrable style. One quickly concludes that for most of Gurdjieff's followers, there was little intention to produce "objective" writings, only to encapsulate some of the insights afforded by the system. The science-fiction novels by Colin Wilson, for example, are of medium length and present only one or two Gurdjieffian ideas in each text. Although Daumal's volumes present many more ideas and are allegorical, they are quite short and verbally precise (e.g., *Mount Analogue*). By contrast, Jean Toomer's texts show direct appropriations in style and content from Gurdjieff's texts. They are quite long and encompass much of the entire system on many levels—through allegory and direct presentation of terminology. Toomer attempted to approximate the truly inimitable tone of Gurdjieff's writing—at once ironic, authoritative, ethereal, distant, tragic, and humorous—that was designed to "shock" the reader out of surely distinguishing truth from falsity and reality from illusion.

Detailed discussions of Toomer's activities in Harlem have been consistently overshadowed by his much-publicized rejection of the centrality of racial distinctions, his affairs with Mabel Dodge Luhan and Georgia O'Keefe, his marriages to two white women, the nearly crippling eccentricities of his personality, and the confusion that has resulted because of suspicions about his motives. It is difficult to speak authoritatively about Jean Toomer's movements in Harlem because the firsthand accounts of his activities provided by his contemporaries and biographers are vague. Toomer's own accounts of his activities and associations in Harlem are equally lacking in detail. A further difficulty arises because most secondhand accounts of Jean Toomer's career in Harlem have a pervasively negative character and tend to concentrate on the alleged failure of Toomer's attempts to introduce the Gurdjieff work to the Harlem literary group. Moreover, these discussions usually rely exclusively on the sketch of the Harlem literary scene that Langston Hughes set down in his autobiography, *The Big Sea* (1940).

The dependence of critics on Hughes's account has minimized Jean Toomer's influence on the Harlem writers. Nellie Y. McKay described Toomer's introduction of the Gurdjieff system to the Harlem group:

Late in the fall of 1924, Toomer went to Harlem to try to establish a Gurdjieff group there. Orage, who remained the leading Gurdjieff representative in the United States, is reported to have been pleased by this move on Toomer's part because he thought it was significant that Toomer was in Harlem not as an exponent of black or white culture but of human culture. The group did not last long, as Langston Hughes explains in *The Big Sea*.

Although Gurdjieff claimed that his philosophy required no change in the external patterns of one's life, it did involve an appreciable investment of time for contemplation and study. Such an expenditure of time was impractical for black people—even the intellectuals—because most of them had to work for a living. Thus Toomer's efforts resulted in little success until he went to Chicago's Gold Coast district, where he did well for a number of years in leading groups among people in the area. (*Jean Toomer* 194)

A similar dependence on Hughes's version of Toomer's activities may be seen in Turner's *In a Minor Chord* (1971), Rampersad's *The Life of Langston Hughes*, Vol. I (1986), Kerman and Eldridge's *The Lives of Jean Toomer* (1987), Byrd's *Jean Toomer's Years with Gurdjieff* (1990), Larson's *Invisible Darkness: Jean Toomer and Nella Larsen* (1993), and Davis's *Nella Larsen: Novelist of the Harlem Renaissance* (1994).

From Langston Hughes's autobiography, it is impossible to determine at which point Toomer met with the "failure" that Hughes assigns to his efforts. Also, for most accounts of Toomer's career in Harlem, it is Hughes alone who is summoned to define Toomer's efforts as a failure. Hughes's opinions are also used to characterize the structure and content of Gurdjieff's system of self-development. (Because permanent structures are subject to laws that cause them to run down the scale and pursue a diametrically opposite direction under their former names, it was against Gurdjieffian practice to attempt to be successful in conventional terms; ISM 129.) The dependency on Hughes's autobiography has encouraged critics to indulge in a uniform disregard of Toomer's introduction of Gurdjieff's system to the Harlem writers.

However, the Harlem Gurdjieffians themselves refute Langston Hughes's account of Toomer's efforts to spread the Gurdjieffian system among African-Americans. What they tell us is that once Hughes turned his back on Jean Toomer, Hughes was not aware of the subsequent events—namely, that Toomer's followers continued to pursue the mesoteric and esoteric levels of the Gurdjieff work in secret. Wallace Thurman's novel *The Blacker the Berry* (1929) addresses this issue. The novel is a roman à clef, and Langston Hughes is called Tony Crews. Ray (Wallace Thurman) asks Tony Crews for liquor and we are told that he "held out his empty glass and said quietly, 'We've had about umpteen already, so I doubt if there's any more left'" (143). The Harlem group has been drinking "ice cream and gin" (147), which is an anagram for "I am" and "dancing." The metaphor that Thurman uses is a glass: Crews's glass is empty of two Gurdjieffian techniques, "I am" (a form of meditation called self-remembering; ISM 117) and "the rhythmic gymnastic movements and dances that Gurdjieff adapted from Asiatic sources for use in the work" (Speeth 132). Because no one drinks ice cream and gin, Thurman is presenting a "lawful inexactitude"—a discrepancy used to indicate the presence of a hidden content. Thurman's treatment of this matter is heavily coded, but the unlikelihood of drinking such a concoction gives away his secret. So essential to

Gurdjieff's system of self-development was the "I am" technique that Gurdjieff entitled his third book *Life Is Real Only Then, When "I Am."* Gurdjieff was first known to his American followers as a teacher of sacred dancing; it was the demonstrations of the dances in New York in January 1924 that first attracted such figures as Jean Toomer, Gorham Munson, Mabel Dodge Luhan, Margaret Anderson, and Jane Heap (Moore 200).

Hughes's status as an outsider was also addressed by Zora Neale Hurston twenty years later. In a coded passage in *Seraph on the Suwanee* (1948), she ripostes with a more detailed account of the Harlem group's version, after Langston Hughes had given his own account of this period in his autobiography, *The Big Sea* (1941). In the section of *Seraph* that describes Arvay's visit to the fishing fleet, we are given information about Jean Toomer's Harlem followers. Hughes is commented on in the discussion of a man washed overboard from the *Savannah;* Captain Dutch Smith repeats "over and over" (324) the phrase "I sure hate to lose a man" (324) and we are meant to recognize repetition as a means for reaching the hidden content of the passage. Here we are provided with two clues: a man's name and the name of a book. The repeated phrase approximates the sounds of Hughes in "hate" and "lose." At the same time, the description states that "he had been swept overboard by a big sea" (324), alluding to *The Big Sea,* which contains Hughes's account of Toomer's attempt to spread the Gurdjieff work in Harlem, an account that Hurston sought to refute by this veiled presentation.

Jean Toomer's efforts in presenting the Gurdjieffian system to the writers of the Harlem Renaissance is one component in the only organized attempt to formally shape the ideology of the Harlem avant-garde; its only analog is the achievement of the Garvey movement in providing a pan-African framework for the United Negro Improvement Association (UNIA) writers and artists. Critics often view Harlem Renaissance writers as participants in the insufficiently conceptualized arts movement that the efforts of Alain Locke and Charles S. Johnson could not coalesce (Singh *Novels* 31); the common ground of what did transpire is defined as "the Negro as author and subject of literature" (Singh *Novels* 31). This approach has left many other critical approaches untried. Missing is the recognition of a consistent literary attack on racialist thought and a shared interest in the themes introduced by Jean Toomer through his lectures on self-observation and non-identification. To read texts by the Harlem group as containing, among other things, attacks on race is to be confronted with a need to reevaluate their meaning and, accordingly, to revise the view that Jean Toomer had little effect on his Harlem associates.

As we have seen, the prevailing idea has been that Jean Toomer transmitted Gurdjieffian thought into the Harlem intellectual milieu, and once his efforts ceased, Gurdjieffian activity at the group level came to a halt. Missing from this account is that Toomer had acted on behalf of Orage in conducting the Gurdjieff sessions in Harlem, that is, it was essentially Orage who had organized Gurdjieff groups in Harlem. Toomer's relationship with Orage was similar to that between Orage and C. Daly King. King led a group in Orange, New Jersey, that was regularly visited by Orage, and Orage regularly consulted with King (Welch 48). Although Toomer made important and complex literary, spiritual, and personal contributions to the Harlem group, with regard to the Gurdjieff work, the issue is contact between Orage and the Harlem group. Once Toomer left New York, Gurdjieffian activity within the Harlem group did not cease, it intensified, although it took on a new configuration.

Although it is known that Jean Toomer taught the Gurdjieff work in Harlem, the exact nature of the relationship between Toomer, Gurdjieff, A. R. Orage, C. Daly King, and the Harlem group remains to be determined. Toomer's actual contribution in Harlem was that he inspired and served as a model for an important school of literary experiment, although, again, the details of his relationship to the Harlem group are not generally in evidence.

What Toomer brought to his Harlem colleagues may best be described as the insertion of modernist influences already at work throughout Europe and America, influences that were already directing the course of art, literature, music, and contemporary thought in other parts of New York. As a young man, Toomer had found himself in a state of crisis: His work with the Art as Vision movement had ultimately proven to be insufficient. There is a striking parallel between Toomer's later assessment of his life at this moment and Carl Jung's designation of "the man we call modern" as "the man who stands upon a peak, or at the very edge of the world, the abyss of the future before him, above him the heavens, and below him the whole of mankind with a history that disappears in primeval mists" ("The Spiritual Problem of Modern Man" 457). Toomer states that "The modern world was uprooted, the modern world was breaking down, *but we couldn't go back*. There was nothing to go back to. Besides, in our hasty leaps into the future we had burned our bridges" ("The Gurdjieff Experience" ws 129).

One feature of the revised modernism that Toomer pursued as an "objective" artist that particularly shifted the course of writing in Harlem was "its validation of totality, its veneration of genius and power" (Van Dusen 87). The Harlem Renaissance has commonly been thought of as a movement with little or no ideology. However, Jean Toomer's chief contribution to modernist African-American letters was the transformative power of a totalizing ideology. Toomer's followers and admirers, who had learned from him to see themselves as dwellers in "an empty and aborted interval" (Patterson xix), embraced Gurdjieff's message from above as a means toward the urgent and imperative renovation of the social order (Fritzsche 11). In *The Cosmic Web* N. Katherine Hayles (66) states that "the cultural matrix is capable of guiding individual inquiry in parallel directions, even where there is little or no direct influence between different inquiries." It is revealing to consider that in the first manifesto of a modernist art movement, the Futurist manifesto of

1909, Filippo Tommaso Marinetti indicated that the visionary art movement existed primarily as a means toward the construction of the man of the future: "On the day when man will be able to externalize his will and make it into a huge invisible arm, Dream and Desire, which are empty words today, will master and reign over space and time" (Marinetti 91). Marinetti's followers were so enraptured with the new machine-man synthesis and the idea that the human race could be perfected through "the hygiene of war" that several of the young Futurists enthusiastically embraced World War I and joined machine-gun units. The sculptor Umberto Boccioni and the architect Antonio Sant'Elia died at the front, and Marinetti was wounded. Similarly, Gurdjieff's program was formulated in 1912 in Moscow, where he planned to establish an institute to train students to become helper-instructors so that they could assist in disseminating the teaching. What Gurdjieff sought to create was a place where people would be able to overcome the automatic manifestations of conscience, thereby becoming examples of a new type of man (Patterson 18–19). Another prominent manifestation of totalism in the modern arts, the case of Surrealism, was "the most tightly organized and rigidly controlled movement in all of modern art. [Andre] Breton functioned openly as its 'pope,' who could bless novitiates with inclusion and excommunicate those who fell, in his eyes, out of the stylistic fold" (Plagens 30).

Buffeted as he was by the disruptive forces of history, Gurdjieff was not able to settle and operate his institute until September 1922. His first visit to America was made in January 1924, and it was then that Jean Toomer first encountered him. Toomer's reaction to Gurdjieff and his demonstration of sacred dances was that he was chiefly aware of Gurdjieff's "Power" (Patterson 100). Late in July 1924, Toomer arrived at the Chateau de la Prieure, the large house outside Fontainebleau where Gurdjieff had established his Institute for the Harmonious Development of Man. Gurdjieff was all too aware of Toomer's personal limitations and customarily referred to him as "Mr. Half-Hour-Late," presumably referring to Toomer's habit of speaking slowly (Patterson 118). In the fall of 1924 Toomer returned to New York, where he studied with A. R. Orage, Gurdjieff's deputy in America.

For months after he returned from France, Jean Toomer applied himself to the Gurdjieffian developmental exercises under the tutelage of Orage. He also took detailed notes on Orage's lectures and the psychological exercises used in the sessions that Orage led in Greenwich Village. All of this was preparation for an assignment that Orage was soon to give to Toomer: With Orage's assistance, Toomer was to organize a work group of his own among the artists, writers, and intellectuals of Harlem. In her book *Orage with Gurdjieff in America*, Louise Welch (47) describes Toomer at the start of his new career: "Jean Toomer . . . was encouraged by Orage to undertake groups of his own. A magnetic figure, well over 6 feet tall, Jean with light brown skin, sporting a trim mustache, looking for all the world like an emigre

Brahman, is now best remembered as the author of *Cane* and canonized as a pioneer of the black literary renaissance. Gurdjieff had told Toomer that he ought to work with his own people, and many of them were attracted."

Toomer and Orage held one series of Gurdjieff meetings in the spring of 1925. Although no record of those seminars remains, it is to these first lectures that the published accounts of Toomer's efforts in Harlem refer. For example, Kerman and Eldridge state that "He attracted many to his sessions: Wallace Thurman, the self-styled bohemian of the Harlem movement; Dorothy Peterson, a writer who became fond of Toomer and corresponded with him for about ten years; Aaron Douglas, the most successful of the Harlem painters; Nella Larsen, author of two novels about the color line; and Harold Jackman, a teacher and Harlem activist. Arna Bontemps, a writer and an intense admirer of *Cane*, attended the first session but did not go back" (144). (The above account is particularly skewed in its use of compressed time: when the individuals listed met Toomer in 1925, they had not written their novels or produced their paintings. Thus, Toomer's influence on this group can be made to seem incidental.) According to Kerman and Eldridge, Toomer met with the Harlem group for about a year and then "The group in Harlem eventually faltered" (145). Other published accounts of these events fall into the same pattern. Specific information about who actually attended the first series of lectures and for how long is a matter of speculation. However, it is a matter of record that two members of Toomer's Harlem group, Aaron Douglas and Dorothy Peterson, continued as students in the work for many years. More will be said below on the group's supposed dissolution.

In April 1926 Toomer began to teach another course in the Method that met weekly for ten weeks; the lectures and notes related to that series is called "A New Group, 1926" (Jean Toomer Collection). The meetings cover the entire method for the training in "self-observation without identification." Anyone attending the series of ten meetings would have been introduced to the full complement of the introductory materials included in the Gurdjieff work at that time. This course was exoteric and was open to the public; the attendees were under no onus to pursue their work in secret. Toomer identified the attendees who spoke as "Johnson, Harold, Eric, Dr. Smith, and Dorothy Harris." It is impossible to say whether Toomer was attempting to obscure the identities of those in attendance or whether they were so familiar that he did not need to identify them more fully. Those who can be identified with some certainty are Dorothy Hunt Harris, the wife of the black artist Jimmy Harris, and the Harlem Renaissance writers Harold Jackman and Eric Walrond. Toomer's 1926 notebook shows that the seminars were conducted in an orderly fashion, the students were intensely serious and committed to the Gurdjieff work, and the ideas and values communicated by Toomer and Orage seem to have been received as though they were reasonable, practical, and consistent. The notebook not only records what was said at the meeting by Orage, who often gave the lectures, but also what the Harlemites asked and answered. Toomer also included his own personal thoughts about the meetings. The ten sessions covered: Essential Wishes, Mechanicality of Man, The Method, How We Waste Energy, Observation and The Real "I," Conscious Will, The [Three] Centers, Attitude, Subcenters, and The Octave. The notebook also contained a list of the forty-nine exercises that were given to the students, a glossary of terms that they should be able to define, and a questionnaire used to force the students to examine their assumptions.

During the time that Toomer and Orage led the meetings in Harlem, Toomer continued to attend Orage's groups in Greenwich Village. Perhaps unwisely, Toomer had been engaging in an analysis of the work's ideas, carried on as a replacement for writing fiction, and he began to insert some of his own writings into his lectures. (These writings are preserved in the notebook "A New Group, 1926" along with Orage's lectures.) Because Toomer and his students were supposed to wholeheartedly devote themselves to a nonintellectual and wordless form of self-observation, this attempt to explore writing in a more "objective" consciousness was not developing Toomer toward the necessary integration of his divided self.

Like Sufism and Kabbalah, the Gurdjieff work is a mystical discipline that leads the student to oneness with the Absolute. It is clear that the material in Toomer's notebook, "A New Group, 1926," is designed to take the students to a level of fundamental readiness, where they may begin more demanding exercises that raise the level of consciousness to profoundly different states of experience. In the work, the task of the beginning student is to formulate a vehicle that can integrate the three brains or centers (body, emotions, mind) into a unified organ; one way of expressing this idea is that the astral body is being given control of these lower, material faculties. Many of the exercises that the Gurdjieffians employed were aimed at allowing conscious experiences to be routed through the astral body, so that a separation took place. Thus, there was an experience of being aware of experience as though it was happening to a body in which the awareness or personality was not present. Toomer spoke of the permanent attainment of this type of consciousness as the first awakening, an awakening from the sleeping state to the waking state. The next awakening was from the waking state to the state of self-consciousness: "Self-consciousness is not an increase or an expansion of the waking state" (Welch 63). The personality had to further awaken from the state of self-consciousness to cosmic-consciousness. Gurdjieff's Method—self-observation and non-identification— took the individual only as far as the waking state. From that point, there were two more awakenings necessary before reaching the condition of being fully human in the "objective" sense. Toomer believed that he had attained one of these higher states after he experienced a mystical episode in 1926. Although his "birth above the body" was outside the scope of the work, he indulged in a study of his newly found psychological insights as he began to write a series of spiritual autobiographies called "Exile into Being."

Jean Toomer's synthetic treatment of Gurdjieff's system was hardly unique: Orage, Ouspensky, C. Daly King, and many others added materials from other systems, gave emphasis to certain aspects of Gurdjieff's teachings while ignoring other aspects, and otherwise modified the original presentation. Toomer's particular contribution was that he used Gurdjieff's system to confront the problem of the color line. In this respect, he was a unique link between the disparate elements of modernist aesthetics, esoteric mysticism, and American culture, and Toomer seems to have been acutely aware of his unique placement. It is equally apparent that the talented and highly motivated individuals who made up the Harlem group of Gurdjieffians also regarded Toomer as an extraordinary figure: One of the revelations brought out in the following chapters is the degree to which the writings of the Harlem group repeatedly bear witness to Toomer's centrality.

Jean Toomer's role in the development of the Harlem group was akin to that of a producer and as such his participation was crucial. During his brief presence in Harlem, he infused into its cultural matrix an unprecedented body of systematic, modern, and totalizing ideas that then took on their own dynamic as the Harlem group moved into the larger orbit of New York's Gurdjieffians and subsequently came into contact with important figures from all over the world. (A case in point was that George Schuyler escorted Isak Dinesen to a Carl Van Vechten party; Coleman 148.) After publishing *Cane* in 1923, Toomer appeared in Harlem as the exponent of an avant-garde, experimental school of writing founded on metaphysics. However, influenced as he was by factors of his personal psychology, he was equally committed to becoming a spiritual teacher equivalent to Gurdjieff himself. Toomer had already been attempting to teach the esoteric dances to groups in Greenwich Village, although it was avowed at the time that he did not properly know them. After Gurdjieff reacted to an accident that he suffered in 1924 by superseding the dances with a literary approach, Toomer was enthusiastic about the possibilities of forming a literary avant-garde in Harlem. The techniques of "observation without identification" that Toomer and Orage brought to the Harlem group were designed to transform them into superbeings, possessors of a futuristic, elevated state of conscious awareness. However, the techniques of the work were undertaken in relationship to the texts that Gurdjieff had begun to produce after 1924. Thus, as a relatively successful author of an experimental novel, Toomer might have felt more sure about writing a new form of literature than teaching the movements and dances.

Toomer's version of the Gurdjieff work was an iconoclastic and propulsive creed informed by a messianic component that not only saw the Harlem writers as the authors of a new age of history but as individuals with a limited time in which to effect the salvation of humanity. Through a close study of Thurman's novel

Infants of the Spring ("the only detailed contemporary account of the movement"; Singh *Novels* 32), we see that Jean Toomer arrived in Harlem as a celebrated writer with a determination to change the world. He had come equipped with what he then considered to be some of the most powerful ideas available to modern man. Toomer believed that such ideas in the hands of a few resolute individuals—not politically organized masses—would drive the destiny of the world, thereby deciding whether the human race would develop toward utopian civilization or decline into social chaos, ultimately to unravel through long stages of genetic devolution to a final extinction. This idea propelled all of the groups involved, for Gurdjieff taught that the time allowed for the conscious evolution of humanity was brief: "If humanity does not evolve it means that the evolution of organic life will stop and this in turn will cause the growth of the ray of creation to stop. At the same time if humanity ceases to evolve it becomes useless from the point of view of the aims from which it was created and as such it may be destroyed. In this way the cessation of evolution may mean the destruction of humanity" (ISM 306).

By 1925 Jean Toomer had formulated an extension to Gurdjieff's search for a new type of humanity suited for African-Americans who wished to leave behind the limitations of their cultural moment. However, in contrast to the direction of the Gurdjieff work, Toomer's program was to create a new form of spiritualized American humanity—in effect "a new race of beings that was to be neither white nor black nor in-between" (Rusch 105). It is not clear whether Toomer, who felt that he was himself one of these new beings, conceived the new type as belonging to the human race at all. Apparently, Toomer found a conception of evolution in Blavatsky that he could not abandon, for he commented that "*The Secret Doctrine . . .* is related to a certain method which, I infer, differs from that of Gurdjieff. By implication, therefore, do not mix the two doctrinal structures, but select from *The Secret Doctrine . . .* such material as will elucidate and fill the [Gurdjieff] outlines, as thus far given. (*The Secret Doctrine:* a poor table from which good crumbs fall. Eat these crumbs)" ("A New Group, 1926," "Reading").

In *The Secret Doctrine*, H. P. Blavatsky asserted that the coming "sixth root-race" did not represent a blend of the present biological "races" into a racially fused man, but an altogether new type of humanity that evolves because of an influx of spirit from a supernatural source. Moreover, all of this happens not because of a biologically based evolution but in keeping with "the eternal cycle of Becoming" (191), which marks the waxing and waning of spirit manifested in physical bodies. Thus, Blavatsky's sixth root-race will be a type of man whose spiritual component will be greater than that of present man, the fifth root-race, who must nightly enter the realm of sleep to become aware of his spiritual essence because it is not with him in body. Therefore, Jean Toomer, who saw himself as a member of the sixth root-race, probably felt that he shared very little with men of the fifth root-race. Although he might look like them, race was determined not by the body but by consciousness, and for Toomer it was consciousness alone that separated the man of the future from the man of the present. Moreover, according to Toomer's version of the work, Gurdjieff's Method allowed men of the present to leap into the future by acquiring the future state of consciousness even while inhabiting the bodies of the fifth root-race. In short, Jean Toomer taught Negroes how to be supermen.

In "The Crock of Problems," Toomer gave a definitive appraisal of what he understood to be the position of race in human life: "The so-called family tree is largely verbal. . . . Let there be men and women. . . . I have human values. . . . I am, in a strict racial sense, a member of a new race. . . . Jean Toomer is an American" (Jean Toomer Collection, Box 32, Folder 7, 15). Toomer began to meet with the Harlem writers, artists, and intellectuals to bring a new order of American social reality into being. Like Marinetti's Futurism and like other modernist, avant-garde art movements (Dadaism, Surrealism, Imagism, Expressionism, and Symbolism), which derived their various dynamisms from esotericism, spiritism, and other metaphysical systems (shamanism, Neo-Platonism, Theosophy, and magic), Toomer's Harlem literary enterprise was grounded in mystical teachings. In the final analysis, Toomer's movement maintained goals that were also sociocultural. In drawing on Gurdjieff, Toomer drew on analogous esoteric sources, and his concerns took a form similar to Marinetti's view of the future as a vast site for experimentation (Fritzsche 12). Like Futurism, Toomer's Harlem project was inescapably a modernist thrust into the future. The Harlem writers who joined Toomer did so because he brought into Harlem one redaction of the modernist therapeutic totality, one of the most powerful imperatives within the cultural matrix of the 1920s. As such, Toomer's salvationist program was all but irresistible. Patterson states that "Gurdjieff was quite clear about what he called 'the terror of the situation.' He saw that the lack of conscience and growth of self-will and automism—'Contemporary culture requires automatons,' he said—together with the development of the means of *planetary destruction* would put mankind's very survival in question" (xix). According to Patterson, to accomplish his aim Gurdjieff was forced to abandon the early form of his teaching, esoteric dancing, to "go into the future" (xviii) by authoring a new form of literature that was "A means of transmitting information from initiates to conscious beings over time through the Law of Sevenfoldness" (xviii n. 2).

The characteristically modernist premonitions of disaster and the awareness of the "extraordinary dangers of the present, the fabulous prospects for the future" (Fritzsche 16) in Toomer's exegesis of the Method expressed the Gurdjieffian belief that there existed only a limited time in which to transform the world. This theme may be found throughout the literary texts created by Toomer's followers. In Hurston's *Their Eyes Were Watching God* the character Sop- De-Bottom is a cipher for the phrase "the time's up"; another name, Who Flung, discloses the phrase "how long." In Tolson's *Harlem Gallery* Snakehips Brisky lets slip "risky age," Dipsy Muse provides "used up," and Black Diamond declares that "[I] lack time." Carl Slater, the protagonist of George Schuyler's newspaper serial *Black Empire*, is a cipher that conceals "last call."

Due to secrecy, an incomplete record, and vague or conflicting accounts, it is difficult to establish the relationships between the man Jean Toomer, his novel *Cane*, his introduction of the Gurdjieff work into Harlem, and the writings subsequently produced by the Harlem group. Another component of the confusion is the shifting ground of what constituted the so-called Harlem Renaissance with respect to racial issues. Charles S. Johnson's appreciation of Toomer's breakthrough collection of literary experiments, *Cane* (1923), was based on a recognition that "Toomer still expressed 'triumphantly the Negro artist, detached from propaganda, sensitive only to beauty'" (Lewis 90). Johnson's opinion of *Cane* suggests that, for him, an emphasis on confronting the color line was not the principal criterion for assessing a writer's affiliation with or contribution to the Harlem literary movement. Recent critical readings of Toomer have been more concerned with his ideas on race than any direct influences that Toomer may have had on the writing of the Harlem School, because Toomer's influence is assumed not to have extended beyond his brief course of lectures on Gurdjieff's system. Although *Cane* may have inspired the writers of Harlem to embrace the beauties of "Black life" (Turner "Introduction" x), there is little that came after *Cane* that demonstrates an appropriation of the "poetic realism" ("Reflections of an Earth-Being" ws 20) of Toomer's experimental literary methods.

Toomer's thinking on race was complicated by three factors: his evocation of the idea of a new race of men (Byrd "Jean Toomer" 55, 162; Turner "Introduction" xxiii), the complexity of Toomer's views on race (Byrd "Jean Toomer" 55–56), and the view that Toomer at times attempted to disavow his blackness (ID 148; McKay *Jean Toomer* 180–81; Turner "Introduction" xxiii). Yet the idea of forming a new race in America had not been originated by Toomer, it was one of the chief tenets of the Art as Vision group. Toomer and his Greenwich Village associates of the early 1920s had derived the idea of a new race endowed with expanded consciousness from H. P. Blavatsky's *The Secret Doctrine* and Ouspensky's pre-Gurdjieff book, *Tertium Organum*, which was largely an updated presentation of Blavatsky's occult doctrines.

According to Blavatsky, the new American race was to be spiritually different from existing races. Toomer elaborated this point in his long poem "The Blue Meridian" (1936), which is substantially a Whitmanian paraphrase of the major themes and ideas found in Blavatsky's *The Secret Doctrine*. Toomer meant by "Blue Meridian" (a term that he compounded from Blavatsky's "Meridian of Races" [220] and "azure seats" [240]) that mankind was crossing the balance point between spirit and matter in the direction of spiritual ascent. This meant that the members of the new spiritualized race forming in America (Blavatsky's fifth root-race; 220–21) would have a higher component of spirituality than contemporary men—the men of the fourth root-race—and thus were not in the strictest sense members of the same root-race. The ultimate root-race, the seventh, would be beings of pure spirit. Much of what Toomer said and did in his life and writings may be understood in reference to his view that he was a member of the fifth root-race. In "The Blue Meridian" he speaks of himself as "a strange man" (229). This is an allusion to Blavatsky's description of the forerunners of the sixth root-race, "its pioneers—the peculiar children who will grow into peculiar men and women—will be regarded as abnormal oddities physically and mentally. Then, as they increase, and their numbers become with every age greater, one day they will awake to find themselves in a majority" (249–50).

The spiritual nature of Toomer's "new race" is often obscured in discussions of Toomer's ideas on race. Byrd ("Jean Toomer" 54) states that Toomer held two definitions of race, one biological (organic heredity), the other sociological and psychological (labels and emotion). Byrd concludes that "Rather than accept existing racial classifications, Toomer created one more: American. He labeled himself an American, but an American who was 'neither white nor black'" (55). The Harlem group's concern with the color line, then, is read by critics as yet another break with Toomer. For example, George Hutchinson observes that "Never embracing Jean Toomer's idea of a 'new race,' Larsen rather exposed the violence of racialization as such—the force that had divided her from her mother—in the attempt to make it ethically insupportable, an affront to humanity" (345). Yet we can see in the new society envisioned in the final chapter of *Black No More*, George Schuyler's "chromatic democracy," an equal attention to a rejection of racialization and a depiction of a "new race." Schuyler's text advocates that the existing society be entirely destroyed and reformed along lines that are conceptually beyond what seems possible at the beginning of the text. Here we see Schuyler moving to a phase of constructive social thought that extends beyond the destructive phase of the novel's main narrative. Initially, Schuyler's text closely approximates Gurdjieff's deconstructive satire. The front matter of Gurdjieff's *Beelzebub's Tales* announces the function of the first series "To destroy, mercilessly, without any compromises whatsoever, in the mentation and feelings of the reader, the beliefs and views, by centuries rooted in him, about everything existing in the world." Thus, Schuyler's fictional raceless society is built on the ruins of the world that Gurdjieff wrote his texts to destroy. As we shall see, Larsen also gives indications that her rejection of racialization is an extension of her interest in Toomer's "new race."

The chapters that follow trace Toomer's contribution through the writings of the individuals to whom he passed his theories, visions, and inspirations regarding the future of mankind. Only in rare instances do the texts afford us a sense of the existence of this group—and then it is only through lists of names or in descriptions of social situations that belie the seriousness of the activities, which themselves remain undisclosed. Much more accessible is the sense of how each individual integrated aspects of the Gurdjieff work into her or his life, personality, and art. A sense of the planning behind the individual works—at the group level—may also be attained by treating the individual texts like the pieces of a jigsaw puzzle and combining them to form a larger picture. Therefore, I have attempted to present the outline and substance of the landscape by assembling the individual works into a larger whole.

2 Wallace Thurman
Beyond Race and Color

As the editor of two short-lived but influential Harlem literary magazines, *Fire!!* and *Harlem*, experimental quarterlies devoted to and published by younger Negro artists, Wallace Thurman was an important figure in organizing the avant-garde of the Harlem Renaissance. Thurman followed his Los Angeles associate Arna Bontemps to Harlem in 1924 and found employment as a journalist. In his journalistic work he was a colleague of George Schuyler. Thurman's literary activities were centered on the residence for Negro artists—the "Niggerati Manor" described in his novel *Infants of the Spring*—where he convened the young experimentalists of Harlem, a group including Langston Hughes, Zora Neale Hurston, Aaron Douglas, Richard Bruce Nugent, and Gwendolyn Bennett. Despite his centrality in the Harlem movement, Thurman was an extremely frustrated writer, and he consistently felt that he was unable to achieve great art. Critics generally agree that the two novels that will be discussed in this study are poorly crafted. Nevertheless, his work was avidly read at the time of its first publication, and Thurman is now seen as a writer "who left a genuine imprint on his age" (BB xvii).

Wallace Thurman's novel *The Blacker the Berry* (1929), is an iconoclastic inquiry into the subject of the intraracial color prejudice among African-Americans. Such prejudice was common, however, it was never discussed publicly at the time in which Thurman published his novel. Much of what is avant-garde about *The Blacker the Berry* is Thurman's daring treatment in a published novel—whatever its acknowledged literary worth—of a topic that was an irretrievable transgression of racial etiquette in the view of defenders of the race's reputation. Such race leaders as W. E. B. Du Bois and Benjamin Brawley were extremely offended by Thurman's efforts to address one of the most flagrant, obstinate, and embarrassing practices within African-American society and culture. However, the controversy caused by the novel established Thurman as an important literary figure.

Opinions of *The Blacker the Berry* differ. Amritjit Singh declares it to be "among the better achievements of the Harlem Renaissance" (*Novels* 106). Other readings of the novel have found it to lack "subtlety and complexity" (Walden 206) and to "have many weaknesses in organization and execution" (O'Daniel xviii). Previous readings of the novel have been impervious to the importance of metalanguage in Thurman's style. His novels are particularly dense experiments with syllepsis ("the trope that consists in the simultaneous presence of two meanings for one word"; Riffaterre 77) and subtext ("a text within a text"; Riffaterre 131). Also, previous readings have not particularly valued Thurman's involvement in the literary "attack on racial thought" carried out by the Harlem Gurdjieffians. Singh, for example, plays down the hopeful note on which the novel ends, stating that "in spite of Emma Lou's new self-awareness, the reader is not entirely convinced that her future will be happier or less painful" (*Novels* 111). Because Thurman's fictions are not realistic depictions of how happiness may be attained by his protagonists but texts designed to conceal "subjective" content, the texts can be properly evaluated only after they have been examined with due attention to the rich intertextual and intratextual elements.

On the narrative level Thurman tells the story of Emma Lou Morgan, a self-described "coal scuttle blond" (139) who is too dark complected to be socially acceptable to others of her race and too color struck to rise above the conditions in which she finds herself. Because of the continual rejection that she suffers in her native California, Emma Lou eventually seeks sanctuary in Harlem (which she anticipates to be a Negro utopia), hoping that there she will find acceptance. Instead she is gradually degraded by the lighter-skinned men to whom she is obsessively attracted and with whom she becomes emotionally involved. Finally, she reaches the point where she can accept no further abuse.

Thurman's satire is aimed at highlighting the destructiveness of color-consciousness among blacks. He also emphasizes that Emma Lou's oppression by color-consciousness is caused by the persecution complex that dominates her personality, because she firmly believes that only light-skinned people have value. It takes many years of suffering before Emma Lou reaches a point where the things that she has been told about herself and the nature of the life that she is leading begin to mean something to her. In a moment of psychological insight, Emma Lou realizes that she herself has been to blame for her condition: "What she needed to do now was to accept her black skin as being real and unchangeable, to realize that certain things were, had been, and would be, and with this in mind begin life anew, always fighting, not so much for acceptance by other people, but for acceptance of herself by herself" (226–27).

The Blacker the Berry begins with Emma Lou's thoughts as she faces the ordeal of graduating from high school in Boise, Idaho—from a school at which she was the only black pupil: "Why had she allowed them to place her in the center of the first row, and why had they insisted upon her dressing in white so that surrounded as she was by similarly attired pale-faced fellow graduates she resembled, not at all remotely, that comic picture her Uncle Joe had hung in his bedroom? The picture wherein the black, kinky head of a little red-lipped pickaninny lay like a fly in a pan of milk amid a white expanse of bedclothes" (4). Handicapped as she is by her color-consciousness, Emma Lou is only able to formulate absurd solutions to her perceived difficulties: "High school diploma indeed! What she needed was an efficient bleaching agent, a magic cream that would remove this unwelcome black mask from her face and make her more like her fellow men" (5).

Seeking respite from racial isolation among the black students in a Los Angeles university, Emma Lou encounters a group of five students on her second day of classes. She is unable to manage an introduction; all she can do is smile as she passes by them. The omniscient narrator relays the group's reaction to the dark girl's overture, which is that she is a "hottentot" (33) and unfit to join their group. This assessment is delivered just as Emma Lou approaches: "One of the group of five had sighted Emma Lou as soon as she had sighted them" (33). The responses to Emma Lou that we are given proceed from this simultaneous sighting. This passage is little more than a pretext to introduce the names of the five students, Helen Wheaton, Bob Armstrong, Amos Blaine, Tommy Brown, and Verne Davis, for the names of these empty-headed purveyors of intraracial prejudice present word games lacking in "objective" consequence. The names may be deciphered, respectively, as "what in hell," "barnstorm," "blame us," "row my boat," and "never advise." This passage presents intratextual coherence between the trivial actions of the students on the narrative level and the vapid messages derived from their names by means of a hermeneutic reading. The seemingly insignificant contents of the names underscore the purposelessness of the college social group. Although Emma Lou is desperate to find acceptance by the five students, they can offer her nothing worthwhile, for they are as inconsequential as their names. At the same time, their names represent an important feature of the novel's structure and provide a key to the subtext. Should the reader employ the method of close reading described by Thurman as Emma Lou reads her mother's letter "over and over," the exaggerated presentation of the students and their names should allow the reader to recognize that in addition to the surface text there is a subtext that contains word games. Once a reader deciphers the names of the five students, the other names in the narrative become relatively transparent.

The structure of *The Blacker the Berry* is entirely shaped by the methodology of "the attack on reading" that is a fundamental characteristic of the texts written by the Harlem group. Generally speaking, Thurman's narrative is a self-destroying text designed to collapse in such a way that reading it exposes the underlying "objective" structure of the subtext. Even in its failure, Thurman's method produces a much different effect than Larsen's more supportive narratives *Quicksand* and *Passing*. In a provocative assessment of *Infants* John Williams states that "more wants to happen than the repeated topics on race relations, but it does not" (quoted in Singh "Foreword" xxiii). The insufficiency noted by Williams is a feature of the intentional "artificiality" of Thurman's narrative, for the novel's design does not allow the reader a comfortable reading.

Thurman differs from the other members of the Harlem group in the degree to which his text is invested in *intratextuality*. Instances of intertextuality used in concert with a self-referential "attack on reading" are rare in *The Blacker the Berry*, a narrative in which the characters do little reading. One occasion when reading does take place occurs when Emma Lou receives a letter from home:

Emma Lou finished rinsing out some silk stockings and sat down in a chair to reread a letter she had received from home that morning. It was about the third time she had gone over it. Her mother wanted her to come home. Evidently the hometown gossips were busy. No doubt they were saying, "Strange mother to let that gal stay in New York alone. She ain't goin' to school either. Wonder what she's doin'?" Emma Lou read all this between the lines of what her mother had written. Jane Morgan was being tearful as usual. She loved to suffer, and being tearful seemed the easiest way to let the world know that one was suffering. Sob stuff, thought Emma Lou, and, tearing the letter up, threw it into the waste paper basket. (98)

Thurman mounts his "attack on reading" primarily by showing that in his text words do not reveal their meanings unless one is willing to read "between the lines." Because she is able to access the subtext of the letter, Emma Lou is able to transcend the emotional manipulation inherent in the surface text and to discount its value as truth. She ends her reading by shredding the letter, because in the terms of her limited understanding of the text, it is worthless. Thurman's idea is that the alert (or alerted) reader will treat his novel in a similar way, discounting the allure of verisimilitude to read the novel on the level of its subtext; it is the subtext alone that contains real meaning. The above passage also shows that Emma Lou was able to read in this way only by means of applying a particular technique. What we are allowed to witness is not her reading of the text but her "rereading" of the text; only through extreme concentration can the subtext be detected and deciphered.

Because she is a "normal woman" and "asleep" in Gurdjieffian terms, Emma Lou Morgan's "reading" of the text as an act of "reading between the lines" is a parody of hermeneutic reading. Her subtext is lodged in the sociolect and is an illusory or suppositional reading compared to the "objective" reading that the hermeneutic subtext necessitates.[1] Her technique is the correct one, but her preparation is inadequate: Because "objective" writing requires that the reader be familiar with the semiosis of an entire esoteric *system*, Emma Lou is not equipped to penetrate into the real or esoteric subtext. In fact, the subtext of the letter under discussion, a letter that is meaningless to Emma Lou, contains two Gurdjieffian connotations. By stating that Emma Lou had read her mother's letter about three times, Thurman alludes to Gurdjieff's "Friendly Advice" in the front of *Beelzebub's Tales*, where he declares that the reader is to "Read each of my written expositions thrice." Also, Emma Lou's thoughts about her mother's commitment to suffering alludes to one of the central ideas that Gurdjieff taught, the counterintuitive proposition that people enjoy suffering. Gurdjieff stated that "A man will announce any pleasure you like but he will not give up his suffering. . . . No one who is not free from suffering, who has not sacrificed his suffering, can work" (ISM 274). The two presentations of the devil in the text, when Emma Lou resolves to "Go to the devil" (44) and a conversation that tells of someone who has gone to see "Flesh and the Devil" (76), belong to this same intertextual treatment of *Beelzebub's Tales*. Here the devil stands for an intertext (Riffaterre 128–29). However, it rather fails to indicate a relationship to Gurdjieff's text, for to project beyond the text the word "devil" must also indicate its presence as a sign of the intratext, and these two occurrences of the devil are too insubstantial to summon forth *Beelzebub's Tales*. As shown below, some Harlem group texts do contain a sufficient number of devils to compose a subtextual "critical mass" that is capable of exposing the artificiality of the surface text.

Although Thurman provides a route into the hermeneutic level of his novel, he does not do so by directly undermining the process of reading as reading through a directly self-referential assault on the act of reading, as we will see in the texts of Hurston, Schuyler, and Larsen. In those texts, themes of illegibility, illiteracy, Biblical hermeneutics, interpretation, comprehension of jokes, and the act of reading itself were incorporated into the narratives. In contrast, Thurman's text largely forgoes intertextuality, and, with few exceptions, does not thematically incorporate reading. Thurman has replaced the activity of reading with that of joining. Much of the activity revolves around Emma Lou's examination of groups of people as she considers the possibility of enlisting in their ranks. This theme is particularly determining, because the purpose of Thurman's text is to invite the readers of its subtext to adopt antiracialist behavior.

Above all, Thurman's narrative is artificial. He strives to evidence this through the use of emblematic names for characters; an asymmetrical system of naming characters, whereby some characters have full names and others do not; the motif of sound; the use of settings with confined or hidden spaces; and a vocabulary that is meant to underscore the artificiality of what is being narrated. Perhaps the perception of the "failure" of *The Blacker the Berry* by critics indicates their partial discernment of the artificiality of the narrative. Thurman's effective method for demonstrating the artificiality of his text is to undermine the narrative with "incompetent" writing to such a degree that the resulting prose is perceived as weak and lacking finish. His device of writing "poorly" only becomes problematic when the artifice fails to announce itself, and, as a consequence, the priority of the surface narrative is never questioned by the reader.

Given the importance of role-playing in Orage's version of the work, it is not surprising that Thurman's texts show an interest in reticence, as do other texts by the Harlem group. Like Nella Larsen's *Passing*, *The Blacker the Berry* is overdetermined by "silence, secrecy, and concealment" (Davis 324). Emma Lou is devoted to cosmetics that will cover her too dark complexion. Her first job is working as a maid for the actress, Mazelle Lindsay. Subsequently, she can only find employment as the maid of another actress, Arline Strange, a white woman who plays the part of a mulatto. (A considerable portion of Hurston's *Dust Tracks on a Road* narrates her work as a maid in the employ of an actress. False identities, secret organizations, and subterfuge are also important features of all of Schuyler's fiction. We may also note the importance of concealment in Fisher's *The Conjure-Man Dies*.)

As a further indication of the artificiality of the proceedings, Alva, Emma Lou's paramour, is employed as a presser in a costume shop. When he speaks he uses "phrases with a double meaning" (BB 130). Alva lives by extracting money from women who he *pretends* to care for, such as Emma Lou, and he teaches his friend Braxton to do the same. His sole reason for including Emma Lou in the outing in the "Rent Party" chapter is to maintain the ruse that he cares for her. Throughout the text, Thurman points out instances of duplicity. For example, when Emma Lou is taken to a cabaret the guise of authenticity is insufficient to fool even her: "Everything seemed unrestrained, abandoned. Yet, Emma Lou was conscious of a note of *artificiality,* the same as she felt when she watched Arline and her fellow performers cavorting on the stage in "Cabaret Girl." This entire scene seemed staged, they were in a theater, only the proscenium arch had been obliterated. *At last the audience and the actors were as one*" (105; emphases added). Throughout Thurman's text there is the atmosphere of a mystery that waits to be disclosed: The audience in the Lafayette theater consists of "people [who] were always looking for someone or something, always peering into the darkness, emitting *code* whistles" (176; emphasis added). In a cabaret, Emma Lou cannot account for the odor of liquor because none is in view: "Then she noticed a heavy-jowled white man with a flashlight walking among the empty tables and looking beneath them. He didn't seem to be finding anything" (102).

Thurman's text is a tapestry of wordplay, and he continually employs ciphers. Some of Thurman's codes are constructed by use of the expected order of letters, with intervening letters provided to disguise his words. Of course, the transparency of Thurman's corruptions is intended to reveal the artificiality of his narrative, so that when we realize what he is doing, we can no longer read the names of his characters at face value.

The most artificial name in *The Blacker the Berry* is that of the actress Clere Sloane (191). The name can be read as "clear one," which is unavoidable because Clere is not a conventional name. Although it suggests the name Clare, it strongly invites a reading as an homophone of "clear." Sloane seems more problematic, however, it reveals its intended meaning readily once Clere has been recognized, because the implication is that something is clear. Another name that is little more than a hint is Emma Lou Morgan's lackluster acquaintance, Anise Hamilton (169). Again, the text indicates that the name is emblematic: The name is attached to "a simple-minded oversexed little thing" (169), whose name declares her personality as "a nice mild one." This reading is given away by Thurman's distortion of the spelling of Anice. Because the correct spelling of the name is the one that the reader must restore to Anise, Thurman forces the reader to interpret Anise as "a nice." Again, having come this far, the reader soon realizes that the name Hamilton hides the rest of a phrase, for "mild one" coheres with the facts provided by the narrative about Anise Hamilton.

Many of the names in *The Blacker the Berry* belong to a second category, names that direct the reader to the specific contents of the subtext. The protagonist's name is transitional because it contains an emblematic or disruptive name and a name that must be read hermeneutically. Emma Lou may be read as "I am low" or "aim low"; aiming low is Emma Lou Morgan's strategy in selecting men. Her choices are inferior specimens from the classes of men who will not reject her. A typical example of Emma Lou's tendency to "aim low" is Benson Brown, who is described as a "negative personality" (210): "He was as ugly as he was stupid, and he had been as glad to have Emma Lou interested in him as she had been glad to attract him. She actually seemed to take him seriously, while everyone else more or less laughed at him" (210). Given the context, Benson Brown may be read as "no one." This is accomplished by deriving "one" from Benson and "no" from Brown: This reading is consistent with "clear one" and "a nice mild one," but its indirection resembles more the designs of Larsen and Hurston. However, this interpretation is faithfully supported by the narrative.

Emma Lou Morgan's name presents an uncharacteristic difficulty, for her surname remains unincorporated into the phrase "aim low"; it must be combined with another name for its meaning to be made plain. During her early college days in California, Emma Lou cannot meet the more refined type of students with whom she wishes to associate. Instead of making friends with the popular black students, she is forced into an unwilling alliance with the clownish Hazel Mason: "She didn't want to be associated with any such vulgar person" (30). When Morgan is combined with Hazel Mason, the conjoined names sound the word "organization." The combination of the two names reinforces the unlikely social alliance of Emma Lou and Hazel.

It is Thurman's use of intratextuality—the parallel between wordplay and narrative action—that allows his subtext to be located and read. One of the most interesting features of Thurman's style is the consistency with which the events in the narrative are reflected in the subtext by some type of wordplay. In this case, the hermeneutic meaning of the names is achieved by combining "organ" with "az" and "ason." Following this lead, we read Campbell Kitchen (191) as "come be in it," Gwendolyn Johnson (203) as "we do join," Alma Martin (37) as "all are in," and the given name of Emma Lou's boyfriend, John, conveys an imperative "Join!"

Other names indicate the nature of the esoteric organization that occupies

Thurman's attention. It is a secret organization, for Weldon Taylor's name (50) cautions that "we don't tell." The name of a California college student Grace Giles (42) yields specific information about the organization: Her name is a composite of "raceless" and George Ivanovich Gurdjieff's initials, G. I. G. We should also consider that Grace Giles comes from Georgia, which intratextually affirms the association of Grace Giles and Gurdjieff. Other facts also tie Grace Giles to Gurdjieff. We are told that she was registered in the School of Music (42), which "was located some distance away, and Grace did not get over to the main campus grounds very often, but when she did, she always looked for Emma Lou and made welcome overtures of friendship" (42). Gurdjieff's school was called the Institute for the Harmonious Development of Man and was located in France, and he made trips to visit his American followers from time to time. Also, music is suggested by the word harmonious in the name of Gurdjieff's institute.

The Blacker the Berry is composed of five sections. The first is named after the protagonist, "Emma Lou"; the second after a place, "Harlem"; the third after a character, "Alva"; the fourth after an event, "Rent Party"; and the final section delivers an opinion about the outcome of the narrative, "Phyrrhic Victory." This is a decidedly mysterious plan and requires some comment. Only two of the sections are named after characters. After we learn about Emma Lou's history in "Emma Lou," we follow her to Harlem, where nothing of consequence happens to her until she encounters Alva. He dominates the narrative after his appearance in the third section; Alva takes Emma Lou and a group of Harlem writers and artists to a house-rent party (to be read as "Ouspensky"). The Phyrrhic victory of the final section mostly represents Emma Lou's emotional separation from Alva. Alva comes to dominate the narrative; he is Thurman's fictional Gurdjieff, and as such, his subtext is the "objective" reality over which Emma Lou's subordinate narrative is laid as a textual veneer.

The Blacker the Berry, then, is a text that appears on its surface to be a narrative about intraracial color prejudice, while in reality it is a Gurdjieffian initiatory text given the form of a satirical novel. As such, its chief concern is ultimately with Gurdjieff and his system and not with the inadequately contrived Emma Lou Morgan and her derisory racial travail. Even Thurman's grudging solution to the racial dilemma is framed in explicitly Gurdjieffian terms—"salvation within one's self" (225) and "mental independence" (227)—by Campbell Kitchen, Emma Lou's levelheaded benefactor. A discussion of Campbell Kitchen is presented below.

The name Alva is itself a considerable departure from Gurdjieff and requires explanation. We must read the name as an anagram of "love" with the proviso that the vowels have been substituted. Thurman establishes the equivalence of "love" and "Alva" because he places these words adjacent to one another. "Alva loved" appears twice in one paragraph and "loved" twice in the same sentence: "*Alva loved* her for herself alone, and *loved* her so much that he didn't mind her being a coal scuttle blond" (139; emphases added). On the previous page we are told that "Geraldine, who of all the people he pretended to *love*, really inspired him emotionally as well as physically" (138; emphasis added). Also, Geraldine suggests the first syllable in Gurdjieff's name (although the name is to be read as "danger"), and there is a suggestion of the Gurdjieffian "three centers" in the reference to inspiration that is emotional and physical (although the mental center is not named). Alva appears to Emma Lou in a cabaret, where he takes pity on her and asks her to dance. It is with dancing that Alva is thereafter associated, and it is in a dance hall that Emma Lou locates Alva after their initial contact. To cement the association of Alva and Gurdjieff, Thurman makes Alva a theorist of dance: "Dancing, said he, was a matter of calisthenics, and calisthenics were *work*. Therefore it, like any sort of physical exercise, was taboo during hot weather" (138; emphasis added). Here, not only do we have an association of Alva with dancing, but a double-entendre that informs us that dance is "work" and the Gurdjieff work was dance of a sacred variety.

Characteristic of Gurdjieff were his yellow coloring ("ecru" according to Solita Solano; Moore 221), "unusual bearing and gaze" (Moore 161); affectation of Asian disguises—"The Tiger of Turkestan," "A certain Hindu," and "A Teacher of Dancing" (Moore 409); and dual reputation as either a charlatan or a great spiritual teacher (Moore xiii). The Gurdjieff of the period during which *The Blacker the Berry* was written is a somewhat remote figure, because the Harlem group had no direct contact with him. This is reflected in Thurman's novel in the way that he portrays Alva. When we examine what we are told about Alva, we see that Thurman first emphasizes his "smiling oriental-like face, neither brown nor yellow in color, but warm and pleasing" (107). Later, we are told that "His skin was such a warm and different color, and she had been tantalized by the mysterious slant and deepness of his oriental-like eyes" (121). Emma Lou also appreciates "the pleasing lines of his body" (127): "She watched the rhythmic swing of his legs, like symmetrical pendulums, perfectly shaped; and she admired once more the intriguing lines of his body and pleasing foreignness of his face" (128). This description is reminiscent of Jean Toomer's initial reaction to Gurdjieff: "I saw this man in motion, a unit in motion. He was completely one piece. From the crown of his head down the back of his head, down the neck, down the back and down the legs there was a remarkable line. Shall I call it a gathered line? It suggested co-ordination, integration, knitness, power" (Moore 201).

Also suggestive of Gurdjieff is the description of the child that Alva fathers with Geraldine: "There was only one feature which remained unchanged; his abnormally large eyes still retained their insane stare. They appeared frozen and terrified as if their owner was gazing upon some horrible, yet fascinating object or occurrence" (217). The description of the child is another example of a "lawful inexactitude," here designed to attract the reader's attention to the discrepancy between what a baby should be aware of and Alva's offspring. Because the baby is Gurd-jieff, and therefore aware of man's dangerous position in the universe, his eyes are fixed on what Gurdjieff called the "terror of the situation"—the realization that men are irresponsible machines (Waldberg 5).

Employing a technique that was used by all of the Harlem group, Thurman attempts to direct the reader's attention to the level of the sounds in the text. Gurdjieff's name—along with those of other important figures—has been syllabically encoded into the text so that the syllabic elements sound throughout the narrative. The pioneering Thurman, however, seems more experimental than those who followed him. Lacking the complexity of their intertextual and self-referential "attack on reading," Thurman was not satisfied merely to elicit the names of Gurdjieff, Ouspensky, Orage, Toomer, and (C. Daly) King through sound. In addition to evoking names through syllabic patterns, Thurman has linked action and setting to sound, so that certain activities take on a reflected signification in the subtext. The reader is informed of this relationship between text and subtext throughout the narrative by the trope of entering a closed space.

A particularly unambiguous sequence begins in the concluding pages of "Harlem" with Emma Lou noticing "Men standing in groups or alone" (91); as she passes them, "There were a few remarks passed. She thought she got their import even though she could not hear what they were saying" (91). By narrating this perceptual event, Thurman directs the reader to what can be found in the text by paying attention to what cannot be clearly heard. The narrative returns to the subject of men in groups a few pages later as "Alva" opens. We are informed that Alva belongs to the Elks and that "Fraternal brothers must stick together" (96). Having broached the topic of exclusive, ritualistic groups, we are introduced to a feature of Alva's living quarters:

Alva put on his dressing gown, and his house shoes, then went into the little alcove which was curtained off in the rear from the rest of the room. Jumbled together on the marble topped stationary washstand were a half dozen empty gin bottles bearing a pre-prohibition Gordon label, a similar number of empty gingerale bottles, a cocktail shaker, and a medley of assorted cocktail, water, jelly and whiskey glasses, filled and surrounded by squeezed orange and lemon rinds. The little two-burner gas plate atop a wooden dry goods box was covered with dirty dishes, frying pan, and egg shells, bacon rinds, and a dominating though lopsided tea kettle. Even Alva's trunk, which occupied half the entrance space between the alcove and the room, littered as it was with paper bags, cracker boxes and greasy paper plates, bore evidence of the orgy which the occupants of the room staged over every weekend. (96–97)

In being led into Alva's alcove, the reader is also entering the subtext, or more exactly is imitating the act of entering the subtext. Should it escape the reader that by going beyond into the curtained off space the world of the narrative has been left behind, then the reader will remain in the "sleeping" world. The space beyond the curtain constitutes a reification of the subtext, and the reader will realize the significance of the space by reading its contents. Gurdjieff's system is strewn around the reader in apparent disarray, yet to the discerning eye, the detritus within the adytum is the cosmos, and Alva, dressed in his robe, is a high priest possessed of magic words of power: "Alva surveyed this rather intimate and familiar disorder, faltered a moment, started to call Braxton, then remembering previous Monday mornings set about his task alone" (97).

Alva's role as a magician becomes apparent by reading the name of his roommate, Braxton, as Abraxas: Alva is about to call upon Abraxas. Idries Shah states that "All true magicians were expected to know Words of Power to call the spirits—(abracadabras like *Sabaoth*, from the Hebrew, or *Abraxas*, from the Gnostics" (*Oriental Magic* 94). Abraxas was both a mystical word used as a charm and carved on jewels and a god worshiped by the Gnostics and Gnostic-Christians. The Egyptian Basilides regarded him as the Supreme Deity, the source of Mind *(Nous)*, the Word *(Logos)*, and other emanations, including the 365 heavens of his system. Abraxas was usually represented with the head of a cock or a lion, a human body, and serpents as legs, and he bore a whip and shield *(Webster's New International Dictionary)*. Given the ritualistic import of the contents of Alva's alcove, we are to understand that the marble washstand is an altar, and that the "little two-burner gas plate" (96) suffices for "the burning brazier for fumigation" (Shah *Oriental* 94) that the magician requires for the summoning of the spirit Abraxas. Thurman has provided two additional clues to the magical context of the subtext. The god Abraxas is figured forth in the word "cocktail," an allusion to the cock's head and serpent's tails. The statement that "It was Braxton's custom never to rise before noon" (94) is an allusion to the "rulership of the hours by angels" (Shah *Oriental* 99). The close connection between the Gurdjieff work and Gnostic doctrines is detailed by Nott (*Further Teachings* 227–37) and Ouspensky (ISM 339).

In addition to ritual magic, the passage describing Alva's endeavors in his alcove contains several references to alchemy. The equipment required for alchemical experiments are but "a crucible, an egg philosophical, and a retort with its receiver" (Barrett 69; a retort is a vessel used for distillation, and is characterized by a long, bent-back neck). Alva's alcove contains "a dominating though lopsided tea kettle," in which we can recognize the alchemist's retort. This kettle sits atop the "little two-burner gas plate" (96), which serves as the alchemist's crucible, or stove. Verisimilitude does not allow Thurman to place the "egg philosophical" upon the stove, because, unlike the lopsided tea kettle, it has no place in Alva's makeshift kitchen. Thurman handles this piece of equipment simply by referring to its characteristics: the egg is a glass vessel, and we see that the kitchen is replete with bottles, glasses, and a cocktail shaker. There is also a mention of "egg shells," which suggests the philosopher's egg. Additionally, Thurman has supplied the name of Roger Bacon, a famous alchemist, in mentioning "bacon rinds." We may also interpret the cocktail shaker as a reference to the dragon-serpent Ouroboros, symbol of The Great Work (Sadoul 117), a beast that appears in a famous alchemical text as a serpent with the head and body of a cock with its tail inserted into its mouth.

The conduct of alchemy—the bringing forth of the stone—was commonly called The Great Work or simply The Work, which we can read as a pun on the Gurdjieff "work." Thus, Thurman's elaborate presentation of alchemical lore may have been intended to alert the reader to his interest in the Gurdjieff work and not to alchemy itself. Moreover, the alcove passage uses the word "presser" twice and "pressing" once to inform the reader that Alva was employed as a presser—a role that has no inherent relevance in the narrative. "Presser" is a curious word, and it would seem that Thurman wants attention paid to it. When we must consider not only Thurman's interest in alchemy but his concentration on particular words, it is helpful to reflect upon the secretive nature of alchemy. Alchemists are as famous for their use of ciphers, abstruse symbolism, confusing terminology, and unintelligible processes as they are for their ability to transmute base materials into gold. Through coding their texts they protected the occult powers over which they held mastery. Fulcanelli, the most famous contemporary alchemist, quotes the statement that "Our art is entirely cabalistic" (131) to indicate the importance of ciphers to the conduct of alchemy. Cabala, alchemical wordplay, uses simple devices: When the syllables in "presser" are reversed, we get "serpres," in which we can recognize "surprise," which is comparable to other examples of wordplay in the text. For example, we can compare "presser/surprise" to "Geraldine/danger." Thurman does not like to leave the reader hanging, and we can find the solution to this puzzle in the text, "Alva seemed surprised" (148). Lest this reading appear forced, it must be urged that Thurman has assembled *The Blacker the Berry* with attention to every detail. When Alva takes Emma Lou to the rent party instead of Geraldine, whom "he always took" (138), "There was no *danger*" (140; emphasis added). In other words, if Alva did not take Geraldine to the party, because she is "danger" on the hermeneutic level, there will be no "danger" if Emma Lou attends in her place. Thurman has provided a trivial, although nonetheless effective, wordplay intended to alert the reader to the text's philosophically substantial perplexities.

Thurman's inclusions of magic, Gnosticism, and allusions to occult practices and paraphernalia did not come about through any overt interest in such pursuits, because Gurdjieffians were opposed to them. It seems that Thurman placed these elements in *The Blacker the Berry* to indicate the secretive nature of the esoteric school to which he belonged and interjected magical imagery into the metaphor of groups and the act of joining. Because it served as a Gnostic crypt, the disorder of Alva's alcove contains the cacophonous fragments of the names of the principle

Gurdjieffians: Gurdjieff ("curtained off," "Gordon," "ginger," "jelly"); A. R. Orage ("rear," "marble," "stationary," "bearing," "similar," "assorted," "orange," "bore," "orgy," "staged"); and Ouspensky ("dressing," "house," "then went into," "empty," "medley," "jelly," "whiskey glasses," "squeezed," "gas," "wooden," "pan," "space between," "greasy," "evidence," "occupants," "weekend"). A distinct feature of Thurman's novel is that he rarely gives more than the first syllable of Gurdjieff's name; also, Gurdjieff's name is represented rarely in comparison with Orage's name, which occurs on nearly every page. This practice perhaps can be explained by Thurman's lack of personal acquaintance with Gurdjieff and his intimate knowledge of Orage.

In addition to sounding out names, Thurman introduces a key Gurdjieffian word, "work." James Moore explains that the term, "'The Work'. . . emerged modestly in Petrograd in 1916 simply as Gurdjieff's convenient contraction of 'the group's work'" (3). Gradually, however, it became a portmanteau expression, pressed into service as a noun and an adjective to denote virtually anything specifically "Gurdjieffian" (3). To clarify that he speaks of "the work" and not mere labor, Thurman associates this word with the fact that Alva "was forced to get up at seven o'clock" (97), thereby connecting his work with the Law of Seven, a fundamental esoteric idea. The same conjunction of Gurdjieff's name and the number seven occurs toward the end of the novel: "*Seventh* Avenue was the *gorge* into which Harlem *cliff* dwellers crowded to promenade" (223; emphases added). By creating patterns that open into the hermeneutic level, Thurman enforces the illusory and insubstantial nature of his narrative. Thus, we read Emma Lou's perception that the nightclub acts that she watches are mere parodies: "Yet Emma Lou was conscious of a note of artificiality, the same as she felt when she watched Arline and her fellow performers cavorting on the stage in 'Cabaret Gal'" (105). In particular, we are constantly presented with evidence that Thurman's narrative is inherently "artificial" (to use his word), for the text is saturated with repetitions of the word "work." Once recognized, this device necessarily undermines the verisimilitude of the text's mimesis and forces a hermeneutic reading. There is an exaggerated concern with employment throughout the narrative: the word "work" occurs twenty-seven times in the text. Emma Lou's concern that she have "congenial work" [69, 98] keeps the topic alive; note the "gee" sound in "congenial," which suggests Gurdjieff's cognomens G. and Mr. G.

Thurman also focuses much attention on Braxton, considering that his chief attribute is that "No matter what his condition, Braxton would not work" (164). The following paragraph repeats this assertion and expands Braxton's refusal into a formulaic presentation of Gnostic doctrine: "It is a platitude among sundry sects and individuals that as a person thinketh, so he is, but it was not within the power of Braxton's mortal body to become the being his imagination sought to create" (164). This is comparable to Colin Wilson's description of Gnosticism: "Man's true home is the Divine Light. By the use of his will and intellect, he will eventually achieve freedom" (202). We have seen that in a sense Braxton, as Abraxas— the manifestation of *Logos*, the Alien, the Abyss, the Non-Existent (BO 201)—materializes the immateriality of the esoteric level of the text. This is nothing less than an act of literary magic. Braxton's refusal to work, which on the mimetic level casts him as a figure of even less social worth than the dissolute and parasitic Alva, reverberates with a hidden, counter meaning that represents a transvaluation, for "The chief characteristic of the Gnostic doctrine is its tendency to make heroes of the villains of the Old Testament—Cain, Esau and so on" (BO 201–2). On the hermeneutic level, Braxton's refusal to work is a sign of his divinity; he is beyond a need to "work" on himself, and as such is the agent who makes it possible for all beings to evolve to the level of divine light. On the narrative level, Braxton serves no purpose, and the reader may well question his existence in the text; Braxton belongs within the text because he does not and will not "work," which has only subtextual significance.

Given that the subject of this study is the Harlem Gurdjieffians, we must pay close attention when they appear in the texts. In other texts by the Harlem group they have been confined to the subtexts, present only as figures cloaked in ciphers and intimations; as such, they are discernible in Thurman's *Infants*, Hurston's *Seraph*, and Schuyler's *Black No More*. However, in the fourth section of *The Blacker the Berry*, Thurman presents his associates veiled by nearly transparent pseudonyms. When Emma Lou arrives at Alva's room, some of the celebrities have arrived. She is introduced to Tony Crews (Langston Hughes), Cora Thurston (Zora Neale Hurston), Paul (probably Bruce Nugent), and Truman Walter (Wallace Thurman). Aaron Douglas and his wife Alta arrive somewhat later. (The principal reason for the appearance of these figures in *The Blacker the Berry* may be to indicate that Langston Hughes was not a member of the group, as has been discussed in chapter 1.) We may well wonder at the composition of this group of partygoers. Bud (Rudolph) Fisher is mentioned in passing in the course of the conversation, but significant figures are missing. Thurman's feeling may have been that, by including everyone, he would have transgressed the rules of secrecy.

Thurman made no attempt to render the gathering realistically. Emma Lou's entrance thrusts her into an ongoing conversation about intraracial color prejudice. For the Harlem celebrities to be conversing about intraracial color prejudice is too much of a coincidence, and thereby begins the erosion of the mimetic quality of the narrative. "They're just damning our 'pink niggers'" is how Paul describes the discussion. We do not get Emma Lou's initial reaction to the topic or the manner of its handling; before long there is another interruption as a white youth, Ray Jorgenson, arrives. Emma Lou is then turned loose by the narrator: "Emma Lou was aghast. Such extraordinary people—saying 'nigger' in front of a white man! Didn't they have any race pride or proper bringing up? Didn't they have any common sense?'" (144). Even Alva enters into the fray, when he sees an opportunity to move Emma Lou toward an enlightened view of color. Truman delivers a long, reasonable dissertation on the social causes of intraracial and interracial color prejudices and their interrelationships; Alva directs his comment toward Emma Lou: "'But all light-skinned Negroes aren't color struck or color prejudiced,' interjected Alva, who, up to this time, like Emma Lou, had remained silent. This was, he thought, a strategic moment for him to say something. He hoped Emma Lou would get the full significance of this statement" (147).

All of this passes by Emma Lou without any useful effect: "She couldn't comprehend how these people could sit down and so dispassionately discuss something that seemed particularly tragic to her. This fellow Truman, whom she was certain she knew, with all his hi-faluting talk, disgusted her immeasurably. She wasn't sure that they weren't all poking fun at her" (148). Even when Truman remembers her from college, and Emma Lou realizes where she had seen him before, she is ashamed of herself and nearly sobs. Despite Truman's advocacy of freedom from color prejudice, Emma Lou is dismayed at encountering someone from a time that she experienced as entirely humiliating, although it should be obvious that Truman never would have rejected her during their college days. Emma Lou cannot recognize that it is up to her to change her perception of the world. In another sense, Emma Lou's inability to transcend racialist thought is a comment on the reader's inability to see into the subtext and to read the text hermeneutically. Thus we can also read "She couldn't comprehend all this talk" (148) as a comment on the reader's inability to read the text adequately. Appropriately reading the text exposes the insubstantiality of the narrative, or rather, indicates that whatever literary frailties exist are the intentional requirements of the "attack on reading."

Emma Lou has been profoundly altered by her exposure to Alva's bohemian friends. The next morning her landlady ejects her from her room; even this event reveals that something has happened to Emma Lou. She begins to formulate some notion that she has all along been "asleep": "it seemed as if she had slept for hours. She felt like someone who had been under the influence of some sinister potion for a long period of time. Had she been drugged?" (157). Having reached this point, Emma Lou begins a long reflection in the course of which she begins to evaluate her relationship with Alva and the nature of his influence on her. She realizes that Alva is beyond her control, for her efforts to stop him from drinking gin had a bad outcome. However, she also now admits that he is "master of all situations" (159) and "he used more subtle methods" (159) in conducting their relationship than she had realized, one result of which was that she gave him money without being conscious of how she had begun doing so. Energized by being able to think of nothing but Alva, she leaps from her bed to make new arrangements.

The nature of Emma Lou's new arrangements are filled with hermeneutic significance. Alva refuses to move in with Emma Lou, but he does take control of her move: "Then the finding of a room had been irritating to contemplate. She couldn't have called it irritating of accomplishment because Alva had done that for her. She had to admit that he had found an exceptionally nice place too. It was just two blocks from him, on 138th Street between Eighth Avenue and Edgecombe. It was near the elevated Station, near the park, and cost only ten dollars and fifty cents per week for the room, kitchenette and private bath" (181–82). We recognize in its location, "on 138th Street near Eighth Avenue," allusions to the Law of Three and the Law of Eight. The mention of an elevated station connotes "ascending octaves." "Edgecombe" is an anagram adjacent to "Eighth Avenue," and was intended to mean "become eight," an allusion to the superman, or man number eight.

Despite Emma Lou's change in direction, she has not accomplished enough. Nothing short of penetrating into the Harlem Gurdjieffians would adequately serve her need for "mental independence," and this she cannot manage. The narrative details her growing separation from Alva as he becomes ever more deeply involved with Geraldine. Once Alva finds that Geraldine is pregnant, the "Rent Party" chapter ends, and there is a gap of two years between the "Rent Party" and the final chapter "Pyrrhic Victory." The chapter offers a few pages of catching up with the events of Emma Lou's life before we are again returned to the subject of "organizations." Emma Lou has taken up with a new friend, Gwendolyn Johnson ("we do join"), and together they engage in Emma Lou's habit of "aiming low" by enlisting in inferior organizations. In the concluding pages of the novel, Emma Lou reestablishes contact with an abandoned, alcoholic, destitute Alva, who has custody of his deformed, mentally deficient son. Moving into the vacuum left behind by Geraldine, Emma Lou labors heroically to put things right. The concluding episodes are replete with Gurdjieffian allusions: Gurdjieff's name is sounded out at various places in the text ("garbed," "curtly" [212]; "chafed" [213]; "gorge," "cliff" [223]), as are the names of Ouspensky and Orage.

In the narrative's denouement, Emma Lou comes under the influence of Campbell Kitchen, "possibly Thurman's version of Carl Van Vechten" (Singh *Novels* 111). Kitchen's philosophy is stated vaguely regarding "salvation within one's self" (225), but in "mental independence" (227) we can recognize his advocacy of a Gurdjieffian principle. Jean Toomer directed his Harlem sessions toward solving the problems caused by America's racialist culture primarily through the cultivation of "mental independence" (Jean Toomer Collection, Box 66, Folder 2). Because of Kitchen's influence, Emma Lou resolves to achieve "economic and mental independence" (227). The idea that directs Emma Lou toward new possibility is Kitchen's belief that "What she needed to do now was to accept her black skin as being real and unchangeable, to realize that certain things were, had been, and would be, and with this in mind begin life anew, always fighting, not so much for acceptance by other people, but for acceptance of herself by herself" (226–27).

Infants of the Spring (1932) is a roman à clef that traces the fortunes of the residents of Niggerati Manor. Thurman's plot is thin: a wealthy patron furnishes a rent-free building for Harlem's young writers and artists to live in. Their antics become more and more extreme, until a scandal and a trial cause the patron to revoke her largess. The events are loosely based on the infamous "267 House" on 136th Street provided by the owner of a Harlem employment agency, Iolanthe Sydney (Lewis 193).

In Thurman's *The Blacker the Berry*, the word "artificiality" (105) appears in the text and may be understood to apply to the text itself. In *Infants* the artificiality of the text has been increased considerably, depriving the narrative of nearly all verisimilitude. Moreover, there are instances in *Infants* where the this quality is so manifest that the reader cannot help but to realize that the text consists exclusively of text-destroying words. Nowhere in *Infants* is the narrative's intratextual attack on reading more in evidence than in chapter 15, for little happens in that chapter. Pelham has been arrested and is to be arraigned: the chapter details what happens when Raymond, Paul, Stephen, Eustace, and Euphoria attend the proceedings in the Washington Heights court. In the chapter's four pages Pelham's friends learn nothing, for "No one could distinguish what was being said" (154). The text provides every extraneous noise that Pelham's friends hear, every "droning interchange" (154), "grumbling monologue" (155), and "great hubbub" (155). As a result of their inability to hear anything meaningful, his friends leave the court "knowing no more than they had on the night before" (157). To take Thurman at face value, one would have to think him a very poor writer indeed. Yet when we look at what Thurman says, it is clear that the text gives as much as it needs to, indicating that the reader is in danger of coming away without knowing anyhing unless attention is directed toward the sounds that relate what is "below the surface" (156).

The protagonist of *Infants of the Spring* is a character called Raymond, whose name becomes Ray after fifteen pages. Of the twenty-five chapters, all but seven (chapters 2, 3, 4, 7, 8, 11, and 21) feature Raymond's name in the opening paragraph, often in the opening sentence, and several times as the first word. The text also exploits the tropes of antanaclasis (repetition of a word with a different meaning each time) and syllepsis (one word with two mutually incompatible meanings) with the words "ray" and "light," respectively. Thus the first act of the novel is Raymond's Promethean lightbearing, as he "pushed the electric switch and preceded his two guests into the dimly lighted room" (11). Subsequently, we find "trying to make him see the light" (12), "spotlight" (22), "Can't you see the light of creation in his eyes?' " (26), "rays of light gleaming though the cracks in the studio door" (63), and at the narrative's conclusion, "blindingly white beams of light" (284) and "dominating white lights in full possession of the sky" (284).

The theme of light receives more specific development as the ray. Stephen is ready to "bolt" (15), perhaps an allusion to the Kabbalistic lightning bolt. Besides the words "ray" and "light" coupled together (63), there are "the sun's unretarded rays" (208) and "blindingly white beams" (284), which appears in the concluding paragraph. The light, beam, bolt, and ray represent the Gurdjieffian concept of "the ray of creation" and may be associated with the Gnostic idea of effecting spiritual salvation by ascending the ray. Thurman also used the name Ray in *The Blacker the Berry*, in which he was the white, European member of the group of Harlem bohemians for whom Alva played cicerone at the rent party. The same European visitor turns up as a character in *Infants* with the name Stephen Jorgenson, a cipher for "even organization." We can presume that Thurman preserves this particular character, because, to point out the irrelevance of race, he requires a white character to be in the midst of the younger group of Harlem writers.

Raymond Taylor, the Wallace Thurman character in *Infants*, "realizes that his 'modicum of talent' was not enough to create great literature" (Singh *Novels* 34). The problem of creative energy (another word that resounds throughout the text) with which Ray struggles is analogous to the "ray of creativity"; although he represents the "ray of creation" on the hermeneutic level, he also manifests the "objectively" creative potentialities locked up in humanity. Ray is the "ray of creation" in Thurman's novel because in Gnostic thought man is a portion of the ray (Nott *Further Teachings* 231).

The problem with Ray's self-development is that although he desires to become a superman, he is not sure that he has the capacity. Strangely, Ray has decided that the sign of superiority is the ability to accomplish great writing, which perhaps reflects the effect on Thurman of Gurdjieff's "objective" *Beelzebub's Tales*. For most Gurdjieffians, *Beelzebub's Tales* was a bible for the scientific, modern world. To more clearly formulate his answer, Ray attempts to imagine what it is that he is trying to become. In essence, this is what Raymond seeks to name in depressed ruminations that arise after the Nietzschean intoxication that he experienced on the previous evening: "Always he had protested that the average Negro intellectual and artist had no goal, no standards, no elasticity, no pregnant germ plasm. And now he was beginning to doubt even himself" (145).

Ray realizes that his aesthetic failures result from the disharmony within him: "The struggle to free himself from race consciousness had been hailed before actually accomplished" (147). Early in *Infants* we learn that Ray "pronounced [himself] a Nietzschean" (59). Ray tries to decide whether he is a Nietzschean, a question raised by Stephen, but he cannot answer this to his own satisfaction (59). On the narrative level, Thurman uses Ray to satirize the idea that anything can be achieved through art or that an individual can evolve by working alone.

However, we are not meant to read the episode as nothing more than Ray's tormented insights. Thurman speaks in parables, and he tells us that he does so: Ray declares that he is "a disperser of pearls to swine" (147). On one level, the purple passages through which we witness Ray's soul-searching can be dissolved into a

Gurdjieffian vocabulary lesson. By using the words "shock," "essence" (in "essentially"), "intellectual metabolism," "light," and "attitude" (in "new attitude toward life"), Thurman employs some of the one hundred terms that Gurdjieff's students were supposed to recognize. On another level, the passage is suffused with wordplay, which further establishes that the passage is not to be taken at face value. We can make out A. R. Orage's name in "pa*r*aded," "cath*a*rsis," "pe*a*rls," "ca*r*efully," "pe*a*rls," "superi*o*rity," "eff*o*rt," and "cour*age*." Orage is particularly important to our ability to assign a motive for Thurman's derisory treatment of the Nietzschean "Superman." Prior to his association with Gurdjieff, Orage had disseminated a creed of his own origination that was a fusion of Theosophical and Nietzschean ideas. Orage's creed went out through his influential journal *New Age* and his book *Consciousness, Animal, Human, and Superhuman* (1907).

Although we may not at first realize it, the superman theme is most effectively dealt with in *Infants* in the description of Raymond's mental breakdown. Raymond collapses because he realizes "objectively" the unfavorable position in which man, in his unevolved state, is placed, the so-called "terror of the situation." While visiting the imprisoned poet Pelham, Raymond begins to notice the unreal quality of reality. Although his experience takes up a number of pages, the crux of Raymond's insight is contained in one sentence: "The people flabby puppets jingling at the end of strings over which a master hand has lost control" (204). This reflects the fundamental Gurdjieffian proposition that man is "asleep" and all of man's actions are mechanical or automatic. Thurman's "master hand" is the "one 'I'" possessed by "real man." The concept of man's mechanical behavior also enters the text through the "objective" description of characters. In love with two women, Stephen "had precipitated confusion by vacillating from one to the other like a self-controlled automaton" (167). Also, when Raymond runs from the jail "Automatically, he plunged into the first subway kiosk he saw, then as abruptly plunged upward into the open air" (206). Although the actions that engage Thurman's characters are informed by Gurdjieff's psychology, Thurman does not pursue this theme or treat it consistently where he has begun to develop it: When Raymond recovers from his collapse on the street, we are told simply that: "Consciousness returned" (208).

In this important episode, for a brief time Raymond was "conscious" and was able to see the world as it is. Oddly, Thurman obscures this vital point by calling the state of "sleep" (waking consciousness) to which Raymond returned at the end of his ordeal "consciousness." Raymond had not, in fact, returned to consciousness, he has again fallen into "sleep." Thurman's point is more or less lost on the reader through maintaining this conventional usage. However, a satirical treatment of the paucity of normal consciousness may be intended because the first thing that Raymond hears upon waking up is "How's the coon?" It is very likely these "objective" lapses and inconsistencies that Thurman had in mind when he pronounced his novel a failure: "I have tried to make the novel elastic without having first learned the boundary lines so that I could steer a clear course. The results you know. Sheer chaos" (Van Notten 249).

Throughout modern thought, the nature of the superman has always been problematic. For many thinkers it has been enough to wish to be the superman to attain that status. However, in the Gurdjieffian system, simply to desire higher consciousness is not enough: Gurdjieff's system of self-development was often called "the work," because it required a heroic effort to raise one's consciousness. Raymond implies that he ascribes to the Gurdjieffian view when he states that "The pygmies have taken us over now, and I doubt if any of us has the strength to use them for a stepladder to a higher plane" (221). The concept of the evolutionary ladder (another form of the "ray of creation") that Raymond expresses is derived from a fundamental Gurdjieffian concept. Orage noted that "All beings can be classified according to their reason. Every one of them is on a step of a ladder, evolving or involving—*Jacob's ladder*" (Nott *Teachings* 196; emphasis added). Here Thurman has altered Gurdjieff's explanation of evolution, for *normal* man is the superman and the work is a means, not an end. Thurman implies that the end is accomplished by using the "masses," whereas in truth the esoteric school asked only that a person work on himself. In contrast, Thurman's superman is above all the independent man—amoral and irreligious. Thurman has omitted the religious, moral, and humane aspects of the superman concept, reducing him to an egotistical interpretation.

In his attempt to be systematic, Thurman is very close to Toomer, perhaps because he felt that he needed to reflect the complexity of the entire system. In contrast, the other Harlem Gurdjieffians were content to craft more aesthetically conventional texts that were each limited to the development of only one aspect of the system. Rudolph Byrd observes of Prince Klondike in Toomer's "The Gallonwerps" that his "remarks and observations are nothing more than restatements of fundamental beliefs within the Gurdjieff system" (104), a description that also applies to Raymond's utterances in *Infants*. Thurman includes the themes of the superman, race and evolution, "sleep," mental freedom, and the three centers, although he does not develop any of the themes to any great extent. Most of the "objective" themes in *Infants* are barely more than aphoristic presentations of Raymond's rootless "convictions."

For all Gurdjieffians, it was Gurdjieff himself who represented developed man, man with a "real 'I.'" As we shall see, Gurdjieff appears as a masked character in most of the texts by his Harlem followers. In *Infants* Thurman's Gurdjieff is an objectionable—and therefore highly noticeable—character, the Pig Woman:

There also lived on the third floor a mysterious witch-like person, labeled the Pig Woman by Raymond, because of her resemblance to an outstanding character in a contemporary *cause celebre*. She was aged, wrinkled and black. Her torso was the shape of an arc, and she limped as she walked along mumbling to herself. It was not known how long she had been living in the house. Euphoria had found her there. She still remained. Three times per week she left home at six in the morning and she always returned exactly twelve hours later. The other days she remained at home, unheard, unseen—a silent mysterious person who held converse with no one in the house except herself. Nor was she ever known to have visitors. (115–16)

Thurman's description of the Pig Woman is remarkable for saying nothing of consequence on the narrative level. However, the passage is hermeneutically replete with significance. The number three is given twice; this may be taken as a reference either to the Law of Three or the idea that man has three centers. The pattern of the Pig Woman's life—"three times," "six in the morning," "twelve hours"—reproduces one of the alternative enumerations of the "ray of creation," which, in addition to taking forms that run from the Absolute to the Moon or that resemble the musical octave, spans the numbers between three and ninety-six: Absolute, one, do; All Worlds, three, si; All Suns, six, la; Sun, twelve, sol; All Planets, twenty-four, fa; Earth, forty-eight, mi; Moon, ninety-six, re; Absolute, zero, do (ISM 137).

The Pig Woman is a marker for several vacancies. We are told that the Pig Woman resembles someone, but not who; the famous *cause celebre* is likewise unidentified. More to the point, however, is that Thurman's anagram, Pig Woman, reads "I am G." The paragraph that follows the one quoted above presents the Pig Woman uttering "a series of hoarse guttural shrieks" and "wildly gesticulating" (116). Although the need for communication is urgent, the other characters are not given the cause of the disturbance by the Pig Woman; they must figure it out for themselves. Raymond tries to silence the Pig woman, whereas Paul's reaction is to laugh.

The absurd antics that the passage narrates—for no discernible purpose within the narrative—are but a pretext for the wordplay that Thurman develops through the significant *sounds* that he inserts. Moreover, Thurman has thoroughly alerted the reader to the sounds in the passage, which presents a list of familiar names. First tumbles out A. R. Orage: "arranging," "ravaged," "hoarse," "guttural," "parrot," "eager." The association of the Pig Woman with Gurdjieff is more subtle; it is made by a series of the letter g in the phrase "The Pig woman leanin*g* over the banisters wildly *g*esticulatin*g*." This is presented with a rough approximation of Gurdjieff's name sounded phonetically by "scurry succeeded" (116), which is emphasized by the next sentence, which contains the phrase "burned in the furnace." Ouspensky's name also appears in the passage, for we note that the words "r*u*shed," "ca*us*e," "*poin*ted," "bea*ting*," "ceili*ng*," "gr*een*," "dre*ss*ing," "sil*ence*," and "lad*y*" phonetically reproduce the components of Ouspensky's name, although with little respect to syllabic order.

Surprisingly, Jean Toomer's name makes an appearance in the sentence that narrates the Pig Woman's exit: "And she s*tum*bled into h*er room eeri*ly sobbing to herself" (117; emphases added). This is particularly interesting because Thurman names Jean Toomer in the narrative; Raymond asserts that Jean Toomer is the only Negro who exhibited elements of greatness (221). Thurman's handling of Toomer's name is entirely unique among the techniques employed by the Harlem group. The passage that names Jean Toomer in the surface text also sounds out his name in "regime" and "humor, your flight too" (200). We hear Toomer's name on the following page in "two sets of people, your own and mine." Below Jean Toomer's name, the text repeats his name: "symptomatic of my generation. We're a curiosity . . . even to ourselves. It will be some years before the more forward" (221). Toomer's name in the subtext possibly serves both as a pointer to the subtext's existence and to the Gurdjieffian nature of Thurman's novel. Because there are, in a sense, two Jean Toomers (the Ouspenskian and the Gurdjieffian phases), we can see this passage as Thurman's indication that Toomer the writer means much less to Thurman than Toomer the teacher.

Thurman's text is saturated with odd verbal effects intended to prepare the reader for his wordplay, however, it is not a very effective alarm. Eustace Savoy is given to such utterances as "But you musn't dride the hinks" (21) and "Then I'll shise and rine" (21). This device is meant to point to the overabundant use of the letter g in adjacent passages. Another example of the same device is even more expository: " 'No ganymede? Guess I'll have to drix the minks.' He plunged into the alcove and began his task, humming, *All God's Children Got Wings* the while" (159). Seven occurrences of the letter g appear not only around but in the sentence containing the wordplay. We should also note that the Niggerati drink gin and ginger ale throughout the narrative; for example, "Paul returned with three quarts of gin and an equal amount of pale dry gingerale" (159). The word "gingerale" contains the first syllable, sounded phonetically, of Gurdjieff's surname; "three quarts" further points to Gurdjieff's system, which contains important concepts manifested as the number three.

As befitting a text written to dispense Gurdjieff's system, the novel gives the master the last word. The novel that Raymond Taylor and Artie Fletcher "salvage" after Paul's bathtub suicide is reduced to its title, "Wu Sing: The Geisha Man," for "only the title sheet and the dedication page were completely legible" (283). Paul's illegible novel presents Thurman's final "attack on reading." While the passage announces the illegibility of the surface text of *Infants of the Spring*, it also points to the illegibility of the title of Paul's novel, which "Ironically enough" is "completely legible" (283). Paradoxically, Thurman confronts the reader with a subtext that has dissolved. All that remains of Paul's novel is the title, which, although legible, is coded. Deciphered, "Wu Sing: The Geisha Man" reads "G in us: G is the man."

Wallace Thurman's second novel, *Infants of the Spring* is useful in delineating the relationship of Jean Toomer and the Gurdjieff work to the Harlem group. Although critical appraisals of *Infants* have been generally low, because it is a roman à clef, this satirical portrait of the younger, bohemian Harlem writers has been recognized and valued as a unique look at the Harlem Renaissance by one of its most dynamic members. In his foreword to the 1992 edition of the novel, Amritjit Singh observes that "*Infants* has been read often as a satiric account of the Harlem Renaissance—as a measure of Thurman's final loss of faith in its possibilities and his despair at its failures" (xiv). Similarly, Daniel Walden states that "Thurman, brooding and magnetic, to a significant degree ridiculed the Renaissance of which he was a part. While he was at the center of this movement, he denounced the quality of the literature because it laid at best a shaky foundation for the future. . . . In Thurman's vision the Renaissance was doomed to fail" (206). As with other texts examined in this study, we find that *Infants* does not address the themes expected in a novel of the Harlem Renaissance, nor does it address them in expected ways, particularly if we take the Harlem Renaissance to be "a new awakening of black culture in the United States" (Wintz 2). Instead, we are given a concerted attack on black culture in general terms, an attack that ranges far beyond the limited theme of intraracial color prejudice that occupied Thurman in *The Blacker the Berry*. Moreover, Thurman offers the skeptical view that neither white nor black cultures are sufficiently endowed with the means to encourage the advancement of individuals toward a truly conscious state of awareness.

Infants shows Thurman and his racially and sexually mixed associates coexisting in a rooming house—Niggerati Manor—as they engage in a constant round of parties and casual erotic adventures. The protagonist, Raymond, is Thurman's mouthpiece. Thurman's satire is reserved for Raymond's associates, yet Raymond is equally unable to complete the novel that he had started three years previously. Raymond finds that his creativity is blocked because he does not believe himself capable of producing a literary work of genius. Nor is Raymond pleased with the way the Harlem Renaissance has been progressing: "He was disgusted with the way everyone sought to romanticize Harlem and Harlem Negroes" (36). In one of the most animated episodes in this nearly static narrative, Raymond's mentor, Dr. A. L. Parkes ("crap" and "lard")—the Alain Locke figure—asks Raymond to host a regular salon at Niggerati Manor. Raymond concurs, but only because he expects to enjoy the ridiculous spectacle of combining so many buffoons. The first to arrive at the initial salon is Sweetie May Carr ("what race I am"), a thinly disguised Zora Neale Hurston. Thurman then gives the same satiric leveling to Tony Crews ("not work"), who represents Langston Hughes. DeWitt Clinton ("not in it"), the Countee Cullen character, receives less attention than Crews. Raymond is almost approving of Cedric Williams ("small circle"), the Eric Walrond stand-in, "one of the three Negroes writing who actually had something to say, and also some concrete idea of style" (233). Raymond also looks approvingly on Dr. Manfred Trout ("our man"), a depiction of Rudolph Fisher.

Having convened the salon, Raymond is content to witness as Dr. Parkes tries to persuade the gathered writers that Negro writing is a matter of "going back to your racial roots, and cultivating a healthy paganism based on African traditions" (235). Thurman's satirical treatment of Dr. Parkes's ideas exaggerates the actual views held by Alain Locke. In his comments on this passage, Amritjit Singh helpfully restores the context of history: "Thurman distorted Locke's philosophy in attributing to him a return to African roots and atavism" (*Novels* 144 n. 118), and Singh directs the reader to Locke's essay "The Legacy of the Ancestral Arts" as a further corrective. In that essay, Locke does advocate "the resources of a racial art" (267), but he does so without urging the essentialist stance. Locke asserts that racial art "represent[s] essentially the working of environmental forces rather than the outcropping of race psychology" (255), and he sees the "American Negro" as subject to alienation and misunderstanding as the "average European Westerner," when faced with works of African art (255). In fact, Locke is rather remote from a position that could be construed as racialist: He advocates African art because of the "growing influence of African art upon European art in general" (255–56). Thurman is not interested in a fair representation of Alain Locke's thought as much as he is trying to make the explicit *language* of racialism appear unconscionable and insupportable aside from any consideration of what the language is being used to advocate. For Locke to broach the moderate view that Negro art will be improved by "a cultural pride and interest" (256) in African art, he, in Thurman's view, betrays an unacceptable indulgence in racialist categorization. Thus, Thurman's satirical reply to Locke, his "attack on race," is conducted in hyperbolically absolutist terms. His handling of Parkes indicates that Thurman viewed racialist thought of any calibration as extremism, and, consequently, gave no quarter in the struggle to expose racialism as entirely untenable.

Thurman's satire is also directed toward the younger generation, the "fledgling writers of the Renaissance" (Walden 206). The Niggerati make no coherent response to Dr. Parkes' invocation, because, Raymond discloses, "most of them had not the slightest understanding of what had been said, nor any ideas on the subject, whatsoever" (235). In the discussion that does ensue, Paul, the most decadent of the assembled artists, questions the validity of Dr. Parkes's assumptions about the centrality of race and ethnicity: "How can I go back to African ancestors when their blood is so diluted and their country and times so far away? I have no conscious affinity for them at all" (237). Raymond agrees with Paul: "Is there really any reason why *all* Negro artists should consciously and deliberately dig into African soil for inspiration and material unless they actually wish to do so?" (237). Paul asserts that "I'm not an African . . . I'm an American and a perfect product of the melting pot" (238). Here, Paul echoes the position taken by Schuyler in his satirical essay "The Negro-Art Hokum" (1926), in which Schuyler states that "Aside from his color, which ranges from very dark brown to pink, your American Negro is just plain American. Negroes and whites from the same localities in this country talk, think and act about the same" (310). Schuyler's closeness to Thurman's position better defines how Alain Locke's ideas are distorted into those of Dr. Parkes; like Schuyler, Thurman wishes to illustrate the danger of any and all racializing activities, no matter how reasonable and moderate. In "The Negro-Art Hokum" Schuyler formulated his view that any concept of racial difference will be used by the Negrophobes and racists to prove the Negro's inferiority (Singh *Novels* 37). In discussions of Thurman's views, it is generally observed that he "opted for individuality" (Walden 206). Likewise, in the discussion of racial art led by Dr. Parkes, Cedric Williams (Eric Walrond) and Raymond Taylor (Wallace Thurman) "stress individuality" (Singh *Novels* 35). In Thurman's advocacy of "individuality" we can recognize Toomer's unique adaption of the Gurdjieffian doctrine of "non-identification," the idea that "one should not be dependent upon externality for what happens to one" ("A New Group, 1926").

After Paul and Cedric's attempt to refute Dr. Parkes's argument, the discussion descends into anarchy, with Communist slogans vying with calls for common sense. In the midst of this argument, Raymond offers his opinion: "One cannot make movements nor can one plot their course. When the work of a given number of individuals during a given period is looked at in retrospect, then one can identify a movement and evaluate its distinguishing characteristics. Individuality is what we should strive for. Let each seek his own salvation. To me a wholesale flight back to Africa or a wholesale allegiance to Communism or a wholesale adherence to an antiquated and for the most part ridiculous program are all equally futile and unintelligent" (240).

Having said his piece, Raymond is followed by a few others' exchanges, and then "Pandemonium reigned" (242). Thurman has provided Raymond's rather long speech because *Infants* is little more than a vehicle for these convictions. Although Thurman may have had some interest in satirizing the various types of Harlem artists and intellectuals, his satire is thin; Thurman's technique is directed much more toward weaving Raymond's convictions into his narrative.

What, then, are Raymond's convictions? They are diffuse and decontextualized versions of the concepts taught by Orage and Toomer. In some instances they have been intentionally misidentified; in other places they are nearly unrecognizable. However, the question we must ask is what is the source of Raymond's odd antiracial convictions, the ideas that Dr. Parkes finds so shocking. In the passage quoted above, Raymond combines two striking ideas, that movements cannot be made and that we should strive for individuality. These ideas challenge the basic assumptions of nearly every ancient and modern system of belief, however, they can be easily located as "real" ideas derived from the Gurdjieff work.

A corollary to the Law of the Octave is that "straight lines never occur in our activities" (ISM 128). In notes that Toomer took at a meeting, Orage discussed this idea and gave the Christian religion as an example of a movement that had turned into its opposite: "The Grand Inquisitor doubtless sincere in the belief that he was doing right strictly in line with the original doctrine" (Jean Toomer Collection, Box 68). Orage further observed that only by understanding the Law of the Octave could one move in a straight line: "Be conscious of the octave as it operates in one's own impulsive life." By having Raymond state that the course of a movement cannot be plotted, Thurman is referring to a fundamental "cosmic law." Thus—leaving aside the specific issue of race—Raymond's thought is opposed to Dr. Parkes' because Parkes has not based his academically derived concepts and actions on principles that are "objective" and "real."

Raymond's access to "real" ideas accounts for the pervasive aura of superiority through which he conducts his various undertakings. Similarly, Raymond's adherence to a raceless individuality is based in Gurdjieff's system, although he presents a somewhat confused version of things. From the discussion above we can see that individuality is not really the answer, for Ouspensky and Orage note that even individual activities will not move in straight lines unless properly attuned to the movement of vibrations in the octave. Raymond seems to be using "individuality" to mean "mental independence," which was a major theme in Thurman's first novel, *The Blacker the Berry*. In *Infants*, Raymond's insistence on the relevance and appropriateness of "individuality" is consistent with the meaning of "mental independence."

In keeping with the esoteric nature of the Gurdjieff work, *Infants* relays no declaration of Thurman's connection to the Gurdjieff movement. Thus, we can see *Infants* as an experiment in moving several of Toomer's important ideas into a mass audience, the most significant of which was the need for a raceless society. Thurman's strategy with *Infants* is particularly interesting, for in Raymond he has created a character with powerful convictions about art and society and turned him loose on the most important members of the Harlem literary avant-garde (such as Langston Hughes) and more influential circles (such as Alain Locke). Raymond is brilliantly set up to ridicule and demolish the most cherished ideas about Negro art, culture, and society that were in circulation at that time.

Moreover, Raymond Taylor is also equipped with an unidentified countertext, Gurdjieff's *Beelzebub's Tales*, which he decries to those whom he seeks to strike down with his convictions. It is likely that Thurman treats the Harlem writers scornfully because he is only too aware of their failure to carry out an ambitious program for producing and disseminating "objective" literature in the form of an "attack on race." Certainly, Thurman demonstrates the vapidity, laziness, and degeneracy of his Harlem associates and the artistic impoverishment of their writing. Although competent in most cases, the novels that the Harlem writers had published by 1932 were not, in Thurman's public view, the works of literary genius that students of Gurdjieff's methods might have been expected to produce. Given the hermeneutic nature of the texts of Thurman and his colleagues, we can only speculate as to whether Thurman had his tongue in his cheek when he delivered his opinion about Harlem writing. However, at this point it would appear highly likely that Thurman's derogatory treatment of his peers was just another pose.

In effect, *Infants* is the only published account of the Harlem group's plan to create a body of "objective" literature. Admittedly, the indication that this plan existed is sketchy; however, there is enough implied in *Infants* to indicate that either Jean Toomer, Wallace Thurman, or the entire group working in concert designed a program that would allow them to produce "objective" literature with which to influence the course of events in American society. The following quotes from *Infants* represents a portion of the esoteric ideology of the Harlem group, which was grounded in Toomer's use of the Gurdjieff work as the sociological, philosophical, and psychological basis for a literary "attack on race": "It is mass movements which bring forth individuals. I don't give a good god damn what becomes of any mass" (218); "And if out of a wholesale allegiance to Communism the Negro could develop just a half dozen men who were really and truly outstanding, the result would be worth the effort" (219); "No intelligent person subscribes to the doctrine of Nordic superiority but everyone can realize that now the white man has both the power and the money. His star is almost at the zenith of its ascendancy. There are signs of impending eclipse but meanwhile he holds the whip" (142); "The pygmies have taken us over now, and I doubt if any of us has the strength to use them for a stepladder to a higher plane" (221); "Negroes are much like any other human beings. They have the same social, physical, and intellectual divisions" (39–40).

3 Rudolph Fisher
Minds of Another Order

In his introduction to *The City of Refuge: The Collected Stories of Rudolph Fisher,* John McKluskey describes Dr. Rudolph Fisher as

> one of the Harlem Renaissance writers who attempted to affirm the complexity of black urban culture while steering clear of exotica and oversentimentality, two dangers of his moment. . . . In just less than ten years, fifteen of his short stories were published. Of these, "The City of Refuge," his first, and "Miss Cynthie" are the best known today. Both were included in *The Best American Short Stories* collections for their respective years of publication. Fisher was also the author of two novels, *The Walls of Jericho* and *The Conjure-Man Dies.* The first novel has been touted as one of the more successful Harlem novels of the period; the second is a successful detective novel and the earliest black detective novel published in book form. (xii)

Fisher's short stories are allegorical treatments analogous to the "teaching stories" often used by Gurdjieff to demonstrate the "objective" view of the human condition. Fisher translated Gurdjieff's allegory of the cart, horse, and driver into his short story "Dust" so faithfully that Margaret Perry complains of "the insistent personification" in the story in which the roadster is compared to "a cruelly spurred horse" (8). Perry states that "The reader nearly forgets this is a car" (8). The same analogy was also used by Orage and Toomer and appeared early in the lectures on "self-observation without identification," such as the series that Fisher attended in 1926. The most detailed written version of the parable is recorded in Ouspensky's *In Search of the Miraculous:* "The driver is the mind. In order to be able to hear the master's voice, the driver, first of all, must *not be asleep*, that is, he must wake up. . . . The horse is our emotions. The carriage is our body. The mind must learn to control the emotions. The emotions always pull the body after them" (ISM 92).

Fundamentally, *The Walls of Jericho* (1928) is an expansion of the earlier short story "Dust." In "Dust," as Pard discovers that the "lyncher . . . red-necked hillbilly . . . cracker" (151) who he has run off the road is in reality a black man, we witness the epiphany in which the self is revealed as nothing more than a delusion: "Man is divided into a multiplicity of small I's" (ISM 60). In *The Walls of Jericho* Fisher depicts the developing self beyond the single moment of revelation. In both texts the agent of revelation is a woman, although the doctrine of tolerance—only suggested by Billie's comments in "Dust"—is fully spelled out in *The Walls of Jericho* by the words of Reverend Tod Bruce's sermon and figured forth, as well, by the action of the novel. *The Walls of Jericho* functions as an allegorical treatment of Fisher's ideas about the illusory nature of the categories of race, color, and class.

John McKluskey describes the novel as

a Harlem panorama. We are introduced to nearly every layer of social class as Fisher knew them during the late 1920s. The passing theme and class conflict are introduced in ways often comic. Still further, it is a novel that attempts to hold together its many disparate parts through the exploration of the notion of self-delusion. However, the work centers on an evolving relationship between "Shine," a piano-mover, and Linda, an ambitious maid. Shine deludes himself about the possibilities for vengeance from a fellow black. All this is fueled by a metaphor crystallized late in the book. With Linda, Shine listens to a minister shape the story of Joshua and the walls of Jericho. . . .

Prepared for this wisdom by his involvement with Linda, who challenges him to accept his vulnerability, Shine takes the Jericho metaphor to heart in the last third of the book. He struggles to maintain his tough facade for his friends and at the same time come to terms with his underlying tenderness. This is shown not only in the love relationship but also in his inability to injure two rivals—one apparent (Merrit), the other real (Patmore)—in later action. . . . Near the novel's end he can state: "The guy that's really hard is the guy that's hard enough to be soft." (xxviii–xxix)

By naming his protagonist Joshua Jones and having him go by the humiliating nickname of "Shine," Fisher indicates the two levels on which his novel operates. As Shine, his protagonist represents the entire black race, and the novel represents Fisher's prescription for the social advancement of the masses—what is now called the underclass. Through the Shine character, Fisher confronts the interracial and intraracial complexities of America's schizoid culture. By calling his protagonist Joshua Jones, Fisher alludes to the "Book of Exodus," providing an intertextuality that forces comparisons to the story of Moses in his conquest of Canaan and the establishment of the promised land. The intertextuality is emphasized by a twofold subtextual narration of Tod Bruce's parable, first incompetently, with the meaning of the sermon censored (by Joshua Jones), and a second time with the full meaning restored by the omniscient and "objectively conscious" narrator. Moreover, the narrator points out that the reverend's use of the fall of Jericho to represent his doctrine of the development of the self is less apt than it might seem: "Bruce spoke quietly, without show but with impassioned conviction; and though many of his hearers no more grasped his message than did Shine, there was none who felt the same when Bruce ended as when he began. His honesty and sincerity were contagious and the very defects in his imperfect analogy revealed a convincing absence of artifice, a contempt for trifling disparities, and impressive disregard for minor obstacles in conveying a major idea" (183).

Tod Bruce's "major idea" that "No man knows himself till he comes to an impasse; to some strange set of conditions that reveal to him his ignorance of the workings of his spirit; to some disrupting impact that shatters the wall of self illusion" (185–86) appropriately applies to the racial situation, for as Bruce says, "A man may think he is black when he is white" (185). In Tod Bruce's view everything is an illusion, even race: Without mental freedom there is no possibility of perceiving reality. Fisher's doctrine, inserted into *The Walls of Jericho* by Tod Bruce, is derived from Gurdjieff's comment about the condition of the common man: "He does not see the real world. The real world is hidden from him by the wall of imagination. He lives in sleep" (ISM 143). The metaphor of the walls of Jericho alludes to Gurdjieff's more general metaphor that equates the defensive wall of the ancient city with sleep.[1]

Thus on the "objective" level Fisher's novel is about "sleep." However, he has compressed and distorted a complex array of ideas into a relatively simple and compact idea that does not reflect Gurdjieff's system exactly. According to Gurdjieff

If a man throughout the whole of his life were to feel all the contradictions that are within him he could not live and act as calmly as he lives and acts now. . . . He must either destroy contradictions or cease to see and to feel them. A man cannot destroy contradictions. But if "buffers" are created in him he can cease to feel them and he will not feel the impact from the clash of contradictory views, contradictory emotions, contradictory words. . . . Awakening is possible only for those who seek it and want it, for those who are ready to struggle with themselves and work on themselves for a very long time and very persistently in order to attain it. For this it is necessary to destroy "buffers," that is, to go out to meet all those inner sufferings which are connected with the sensation of contradictions. (ISM 155–56)

Thus, what Tod Bruce calls the "wall of self illusion" is Gurdjieff's concept of "buffers." The idea of "buffers" was important in the version of the work presented in Harlem by Toomer and Orage, and the Harlem group incorporated it into their coded texts. It follows, then, that in *The Walls of Jericho* the central metaphor, what the narrator calls the "imperfect analogy," originates from one of the fundamental concepts in Gurdjieff's system. So important is this concept to Fisher that he completely halts the narrative progression to address the reader directly through the embedded text of Tod Bruce's sermon. The sermon concludes by foreshadowing the denouement: "I urge you therefore to besiege yourselves; to take honest counsel with the little fraction of God, of Truth, that dwells in us all. To follow the counsel of that Truth and beset the wall of self deception. So will the towering illusion tumble. So will you straightaway enter triumphant into the promised land" (187).

By generating a significant portion of his narrative from an episode centered on the General Improvement Association's (GIA) costume ball, Fisher demonstrates the illusory nature of the world as perceived by normal human consciousness and pursues the themes of artificiality and theatricality, which were so effectively explored by Wallace Thurman. In the "Uplift" section of the narrative, Fisher's satire takes aim at a broad range of targets including the personality of W. E. B. Du Bois, miscegenation, Negro characteristics, and integration, although the narrator is careful to indicate the actual nature of the proceedings. Fisher's GIA alludes to both the United Negro Improvement Association (UNIA) and the National Association for the Advancement of Colored People (NAACP). Although the GIA approximates the form of UNIA's name, as a white woman, Agatha Cramp would not have been allowed to join the ranks of Garvey's back-to-Africa movement. Fisher's GIA is patterned on the integrationism of Du Bois's NAACP. However, by fusing these organizations as he does, Fisher parodies them both. In Fisher's view, neither organization was capable of usefully bettering the structure of American society. There is also a pronounced irony in having the occasion be a costume ball; with their illusions or "buffers" in place, the characters are already wearing the costumes of their "false personalities." The Gurdjieffian view is that "Man consists of two parts: *essence* and *personality*. . . . Essence is the truth in man; personality is the false. Culture creates personality" (ISM 161–62). In contrast to the "buffering" effect of socialization, it is the intent of the Gurdjieff system to "take off all masks" (ISM 157). However, at the ball the characters are devoted to maintaining their illusions or "masks."

The most important illusion at the costume ball is that "The bars are down. This is for the Race. One great common fellowship in one great common cause" (71). However, the narrator reveals that even at the one dance where there is supposed to be intraracial unity, there are divisions of caste and class: "Out on the dance floor, everyone, dickty and rat, rubbed joyous elbows, laughing, mingling, forgetting differences. But whenever the music stopped everyone immediately sought his own level" (74). The narrator's insight into the psychosocial realities of life in Harlem is so distant from a normal view that he seems to become wholly an other, a voice belonging to another order of being. The narrator emphasizes the mechanical, unconscious, externally determined nature of the dancers: "So dense was the crowd of dancers, so close each couple to the next, that an observer from above might easily have lost the sense that these were actually people. They seemed rather some turbulent congress of bright colored, inanimate things, propelled by a force over which they had no control" (102). This passage may be compared to Thurman's description of Raymond's breakdown (actually a breakthrough) in *Infants*, when he grasps the mechanical nature of human life: "The people flabby puppets jingling at the end of strings over which a master hand has lost control" (204). Both of these passages are grounded in the conceptual origin of Gurdjieff's system, that man can do nothing, that things simply happen: "Man is a machine. All his deeds, actions, words, thoughts, feelings, convictions, opinions, and habits are the results of external influences, external impressions. Out of himself a man cannot produce a single thought, a single action. Everything he says, does, thinks, feels—all this happens. Man cannot discover anything, invent anything. It all happens" (ISM 21).

Fisher's passage is also a presentation of esoteric physics; he describes the dance as a play of forces of which "an observer from above" (102) is aware, for we are shown the dance while looking down from the terraces of the Manhattan Casino. The narrator indicates this force four times in the passage (102), labeling it variously as "stream," "undertrend," and "current." Here Fisher alludes to Gurdjieff's complicated discussion of cosmic physics: "The influence of the moon upon everything living manifests itself in all that happens on the earth. . . . All his [man's] movements and consequently all his activities are controlled by the moon" (ISM 85). The consequences of man's cosmic situation are spelled out by Gurdjieff in explicit terms: "'Progress' and 'civilization,' in the real meanings of these words, can appear only as the result of *conscious* efforts. . . . And what conscious efforts can there be in machines? . . . It is precisely in unconscious involuntary manifestations that all evil lies" (ISM 52).

The thrust of the Shine-Linda subplot is that Linda—an embodiment of the Moses archetype—is moving toward a higher level of consciousness and hoping to move Shine, the embodiment of black mass-man, along with her. This reading results from the fundamentally allegorical nature of Fisher's text. In Fisher's short story "Dust," the woman, Billie, functions as Pard's conscience. Conscience or consciousness (for Gurdjieff these are the same thing) is defined as an "objective" or permanent idea of good (ISM 158) and is a faculty developed after removing the "buffers" that prevent one from seeing the truth of the human situation, or in Fisher's terms, after realizing that one is surrounded by a wall of illusion. Allegorically, Linda is Shine's conscience, for she leads him to a more conscious view of himself. By contrast, Fred Merrit has no conscience—all that he has is a portrait of his dead mother. The portrait is what is left of Merrit's conscience, now a mere projection, a symbol entirely external to his being. When he loses the portrait in the fire set by Patmore, the loss nearly destroys him. Although Merrit seems able to continue, his psyche is open to involuntary and unconscious evil impulses, and he is last seen awash in a sea of mental confusion.

Merrit plays out his most revealing attributes in an encounter with the hypocritical Agatha Cramp, his white neighbor. Agatha Cramp has joined the GIA to give herself something to do. At the costume ball she converses with Merrit, whom she believes to be white. To amuse himself and to discomfit Agatha Cramp (for he will see to it that she eventually learns that he is black), Merrit pretends to be white and drops provocative, doubly meant comments into their conversation. The description of Merrit emphasizes the contrast between his outer self (his "mask" or "costume") and his inner self: "And so beneath his pleasant manner, there was a disordered spirit which at this moment almost gleefully accepted the chance to vent itself on Miss Agatha Cramp's ignorance" (107). As we might expect, all of the characters in the novel lack an integrated self—a union of mind, body, and emotions. However, it is Merrit who demonstrates this Gurdjieffian concept in action.

In Gurdjieffian terms "Man has no individuality. He has no single, big I. Man is divided into a multiplicity of small I's" (ISM 60). In the scene where Merrit plays racial cat-and-mouse with Agatha Cramp, one of his "small I's" comes out for a while. Merrit's race-bating subpersonality is not interested in the consequences of such a devious course of action; it simply wants the fun it can have at that moment. Moreover, Merrit strikes out at Agatha Cramp because he is upset about the flirtation between a white man and a married African-American woman (Tony Nayle and Nora Byle): "That he should allow it to disturb him so profoundly meant that it went profoundly back into his own life, as it did into the lives of most people of heredity so diverse as his" (107). Merrit, himself a light-skinned mulatto, is divided against himself and cannot accept either half of his diverse heredity. Merrit represents the self divided against itself of Du Bois's double-consciousness.[2] However, more to the point, Merrit is the victim of his own fragmentation, is immune to salvation, and is resistant to the formation of a universal, unitary man that is the blending of all races into a new American race. Here we see Merrit swayed by external events and stimuli, entirely mechanical, and lacking anything that can be termed "mental freedom." His own pain causes him to lash out at Agatha Cramp, who, although a member of the dominant race, is a woman faced with her own self-administered psychic tortures.

In his attempts to shock Agatha Cramp, Fred Merrit confronts her with opinions on the color question that are extremely threatening to her assumptions of racial superiority. Merrit predicts the inevitable conversion of America into a black nation: "Wouldn't it be amusing if the Negro let others worry their brains out devising and developing the civilized luxuries of life—while he spent his time simply living, developing nothing but his capacity for enjoyment; and then when the job was finished, stepped in and took complete possession? Suppose—just suppose, for one can never know—that this irrepressible laughter, this resiliency, is caused by the confidence that he will reap what his oppressors have sown" (123). What Merrit depicts for Agatha Cramp's contemplation is a veritable racial apocalypse, the coming to pass of every social horror that she can conceive (a theme expanded upon by Schuyler in *Black Empire;* see chapter 5). The all-black world, which Merrit conceives as his utopia, is for Fisher a racialist dystopia, because the novel discredits racialist thought whether it is harbored by blacks or whites.

However, the depiction of utopias is a matter of subtleties, and even when the results of certain processes give identical results, the meanings may not be the same. Fisher places the black monoracial utopia (really a dystopia) in the context of Merrit's nasty, ironic, verbal assault on Agatha Cramp to suggest that he does not condone Merrit's views. Fred Merrit and Agatha Cramp represent the tragic side of racialism in *The Walls of Jericho:* Although the novel limits their conflict to verbal aggression, the potential (and the means) for greater violence surrounds them both. The novel also maintains a suspenseful suggestion that Agatha Cramp plans to burn down Merrit's home. In the wider scheme of things, the threat of a race riot motivated by Merrit's move into a white neighborhood hangs over the novel from its opening pages: "In Patmore's the discussion concerned a possible riot in Harlem, a popular topic among those men who loved battle" (5). At the conclusion of the novel, Merrit dimly realizes that Shine and Linda are leaving him behind in the old world. However, he is unable to move beyond his racial preoccupations:

He had preposterous feelings, far too absurd to admit: an impulse to run after the departing Bess, crying, "Wait—for God's sake—" as if she were carrying off some chance of his own; a terrifying sense of some slow crushing futility, allowing them to escape, but holding him captive, surrounding, insulating, oppressing him, like the haze of this morning's mist, beyond which he could perceive but out of which he could not emerge; as if he moved and must always move in a dismal, broad, gray cloud, outside of which were clear blue skies that he could know of but never reach. (292)

What has Fisher intended by making us think of Moses in this scene? Moses is the religious leader who cannot enter the promised land, and similarly, Merrit remains behind in the divided world. However, Merrit is no prophet. He remains behind because he is a "mechanical" man and his mental formulations are depraved. In Gurdjieff's terminology, Merrit is "already dead." The root assumption of Gurdjieff's system is that normal man is "asleep." Eventually even the possibility of awakening can expire: "It happens fairly often that essence dies in a man while his personality and his body are still alive. A considerable percentage of the people we meet in the streets of a great town are people who are empty inside, that is they are actually *already dead*" (ISM 164).

To emphasize Merrit's unfortunate condition, we are given a last look at his mind as he briefly recapitulates the psychic mileposts in his life. These instances pass before him without his being able to attach any meaning to them. As Merrit's life unrolls, ironically, the walls of Jericho, which served to awaken Shine, is reviewed uncomprehendingly by Merrit as "Tod Bruce in his pulpit drawing some remote and ridiculous analogy" (293). Merrit, confined in his race-obsessed inferno, is alone, continuing to propound race-obsessed insights—"jigs were inherently smart" (293), while Joshua Jones and Linda—awake to the possibilities that exist in their ever-expanding mental freedom—"drop abruptly out of vision, into another land" (293).

Thus far the discussion of *The Walls of Jericho* has been largely concerned with the narrative level of the text; however, Fisher's text contains a hermeneutic level as well. The following is a brief examination of Fisher's performance as an "objective" novelist in *The Walls of Jericho*. Fisher's novel is distinguished from the other texts by the Harlem group by his minimal use of devices that open his text to hermeneutic interpretation. Fisher's "attack on race" is pursued on the mimetic level of the novel, and his investment in an "attack on reading" is negligible. Although the title of Fisher's novel conducts us into the subtext, it is only by recognizing the pattern common to texts by Hurston, Thurman, Larsen, and Tolson that we are able to recognize the existence of wordplay in Fisher's title.

Given the preponderance of words that approximate "gurd" in Thurman's texts ("gingerale," "vulgar," and "Niggerati"); the occurrence of similar homophones in Larsen's *Passing*, such as "Gertrude," (196) "georgette" (196), and "manicured" (196); "gourd" in the title of Hurston's first novel, *Jonah's Gourd Vine*, and "G" near "eir" and "ere" in *Their Eyes Were Watching God*, we recognize the significance of the homophone "jer" in "Jericho." (We can add to this list the "jure" homophone in the title of Fisher's second novel, *The Conjure-Man Dies*.) In each of these texts, the inclusions of approximations of the "gurd" homophone is intended to establish a "lexical overdetermination" (Ulmer 23), which will allow the reader to decipher the provider word as a rendition of Gurdjieff's name. Fisher's text provides this overdetermination by setting much of the activity on "Court Avenue," which approximates the sound of Gurdjieff's name more closely than does "jer." It also provides numerous repetitions of the homophone, which eventually accumulate into a recognition of "Gurdjieff." This recognition can only be made after the discovery that reading the text is contingent upon "first voiding, displacing, or repressing any established meaning" (Riffaterre 83)—in other words, by apprehending that the text is a code and setting about to decipher it. Fisher piles up homophones for "Gurd" in "giraffe" (15), "Great Gordon Gin" (89), and "regard" (15). He approximates the sound of the complete name by combining "*gar*ment" (11) and "*ges*tures" (11) in one case and "Acco*rd*ingly" (11) and "*aff*ection" (11) in another. Read hermeneutically, the passage states quite emphatically that something is hidden within it:

Accordingly their own expression of this affection had to take an ironic turn. They themselves must deride it first, must *hide* their mutual inclination in a *garment* of constant ridicule and contention, the irritation of which rose into their consciousness as hostility. Words and *gestures* which in a different order of life would have required no suppression became with them necessarily inverted, *found issue only by assuming a precisely opposite aspect, concealed a profound attachment* by exposing an extravagant enmity. And this was a distortion of behavior so completely imposed upon them by their traditions and society that even they themselves did not know they were *masquerading*. (11; emphases added)

Instances where Fisher approximates the sound of "Gurdjieff" may be discovered throughout the text, yet compared to his colleagues, Fisher's accessible clues are rarities. Fisher generally renders names through the repetition of their component sounds, not as words. Although he continually sounds the names of Gurdjieff ("currents . . . jests" [139]), Orage ("Courage" [5], "disparage" [9]), and Ouspensky ("is . . . spinster . . . skirts" [44]), the names do not sufficiently announce their presence.

From the "objective" perspective, the entire text is a fuguelike intercourse of the importance of these significant homophones ("gurd," "chief"; "or," "age"; "us," "pen," "ski"; "too," "mer"), which cumulatively present these sounds so constantly, consistently, and emphatically that ultimately the names themselves break through and the subtext is perceptible to the reader. The collapse of the walls of Jericho after repeated blows of the ram's horn is at issue in Fisher's text: The collapse of the mimetic text that makes audible the subtext is the activity that generates the text itself. Only once does Fisher arrange a passage so that it has sound as its subject. However, what is important here is not only sound but the interpretation of sound:

A familiar sound came from outside. Bess had been parked in the street below. Jinx and Bubber had grown impatient and were "laying" on the horn, by way of suggesting that the driver hurry and return. The sound came faint but clear through the open windows.
"Know what that is?" Shine asked her.
She smiled and answered, "I guess that must be the ram's horn." (261)

Fisher imagines that the walls of Jericho fall when the reader becomes aware of the subtext, and the sounds of the esoteric level are at last accessible: Jericho can then be entered by the wandering pilgrims. "Jericho" is revealed to be "Gurdjieff." The passage quoted above—which is a key to the subtext—contains the phonetic components of "Gurdjieff": "grown," "suggesting," "guess"; "hurry," "return"; "driver," "sound," "parked"; "suggesting," "guess," "Bess"; "familiar," "faint." The passage quoted above renders the sounds of Gurdjieff's name, although not in the proper sequence, and it concludes a chapter that has many, more complete homophones of "Gurdjieff." The passage thus summarizes and calls attention to the activity of sounding out Gurdjieff's name, which has been continuous throughout the chapter.

The contents of the subtext of *The Walls of Jericho* do not differ from what his associates have concealed in their novels. However, Fisher is more laconic and more ambiguous in his constructions. In many examples, even when it is clear that a passage contains a cipher, it is difficult to be sure of Fisher's intention because his devices are obscure. For example, Gurdjieff's *Beelzebub's Tales* was commonly referred to as "the book"; therefore, we know that when Linda says "I'll bring the book, Miss Cramp" (69) we are to take "the book" as a reference to *Beelzebub's Tales*, but this was very much the jargon of insiders. Similarly, the passing references to the "devil" (41, 51, 65) and "devil" followed by the reinforcing word "scratch" (51) in the subsequent paragraph are also allusions to *Beelzebub's Tales*. Likewise, there can be little doubt that Fisher is referring to the Gurdjieff work in his description of piano moving: "Every man who enters this work thereby invites this pursuit" (223).

Other requisite Gurdjieffian matters appear in Fisher's text with little concealment. The concept of the "mask" is present in the costume ball (71) given by the GIA. There are several mentions of the numbers three (4, 24, 61, 167), seven or eight (144, 150, 253), and allusions to the Laws of Three and Eight.

Fisher strikes a distinctive chord only at a few places in his novel. Foremost is his rendering of an idea that does not appear in other texts by members of the Harlem group, namely, the description of esoterism. Fisher depicts the esoteric project as a building in imitation of Gurdjieff's parable of the orderly house as a stage in the development of the harmonious self. *The Walls of Jericho* is a text in which buildings figure prominently. Fisher's description of esoterism in the figure of Patmore's Pool Parlor also originates in that parable, although with a different emphasis. In Fisher's treatment, the building is not the harmonious self but the esoteric school, specifically, Gurdjieff's institute. He states that

Pat*more*'s *P*ool *P*arlor occupied the remodeled ground floor of a once elegant apartment-house: *two* long low adjacent rooms, with a smaller one in the rear. You could enter either of the larger *two* from the street, and a doorway *join*ed them within. There were no pretenses about these *two* rooms: one was a pool room, its stolid, green colored tables extending from front to back in a long squat row; the other was a sal*oo*n, with a mahogany bar counter, great wall mirror, a shining foot rail and brass spitt*oo*ns. In the sal*oo*n you could get any drink you had c*our*age and cash enough to *or*der; in the pool room you could play for any stake and *use* any langu*age* you had the in*genu*ity *to* devise. The third room was off the pool room and behind the sal*oo*n; this gave itself over to that triad of swift exchange, poker, black-jack, and dice. (4–5)

The italicized syllables in the above passage indicate components of the names of Jean Toomer, P. D. Ouspensky, A. R. Orage, and G. I. Gurdjieff (more commonly known as G. or Mr. G.). This passage has been superabundantly endowed with fourteen occurrences of the phoneme "oo," which is a device meant to attract the reader to the sound of Jean Toomer's name ("joined . . . two . . . more") as it echoes throughout the paragraph. Having attained that stage of recognition, the reader will be able to progress onward to the other names concealed in the paragraph. Moreover, with "use any language you had the ingenuity to devise" the paragraph alludes to Gurdjieff's interpretation of the biblical story of the confusion of tongues: "The *Esoteric* or innermost circle of all consisted of people who had attained the maximum development possible to man, full consciousness, unity and will. . . . The next circle to this was the *Mesoteric* or middle circle. . . . The third circle was the *Exoteric* circle. . . . Beyond these concentric circles there lay the outer region of the Confusion of Tongues, the great area in which dwelt the whole of the rest of humanity" (Walker 188–90). This reading usefully locates the esoteric project in its derivation from language and further illuminates the "objective" method through which Fisher and the other Gurdjieffians have created their texts.

The cardinal feature of esoterism in Ouspensky's interpretation of the story of the Tower of Babel was that between the members of all of the circles "what one understood, all of the others understood in the same way" (Walker 190). The Confusion of Tongues is most clearly represented in *The Walls of Jericho* by Agatha Cramp: "Miss Cramp sat staring about with eyes that comprehended nothing, the turbulence in her own mind confusing every perception" (139).

According to Gurdjieff, his institute was an esoteric school. However, his schools in New York were exoteric, having only beginners as members. Orage commented in the early 1920s that the school he convened was "Not esoteric, nor even mesoteric. These are very far from us. If we can start an exoteric group, we shall do well" (Nott *Teachings* 29). Thus, the description of Patmore's Pool Parlor may specifically apply to the structure of Gurdjieff's New York schools: Admission was available to the public, and the groups were openly conducted. It was only the Harlem group that set up secret meetings: Henry Patmore is an anagram for "inner room." Thus within the third room of Patmore's Pool Parlor, the "triad of swift exchange" (5) that transpired was the "line of work" that constituted Toomer's "attack on race" in addition to the two esoteric lines of evolutional work, work on oneself and work on other people (Walker 193).

Fisher has endowed his text with another clue to the nature of the Harlem group's enterprise in a passage that signals its hermeneutic content: "Joshua Jones, be it confessed, was himself no cipher among the ladies. There had been girls aplenty: Sarah Mosely, Babe Merrimac, Lottie Buttsby, Becky Katz, Maggie Mulligan, and others. An acknowledged master of men is usually attractive to women, and in his world of sinew and steel, Shine had the necessary reputation; there was no end of stories about what he could do with his hands" (80). Read hermeneutically, the passage offers itself as a "cipher" and refers to the "master of men," whom we know to be Gurdjieff ("*girl*" "con*fess*ed"). The motivation for these contrivances is that Fisher must draw attention to the list of Shine's former girlfriends, which when decoded declares: "some harass," "be merry," "lots [of] us," "takes a million." The hidden message informed the readers that they were wanted as recruits in a struggle against the forces of racialism. Although it is clear that the narrative level of *The Walls of Jericho* presented a case against race and color discrimination, without Fisher's ciphered message, the reader would remain unaware of the African-American Gurdjieffians who were organizing to change the structure of American culture. Given such ambitious plans, we realize that the reader should take literally the utopian conclusion of *The Walls of Jericho*, which frames the truck with Linda and Shine beneath a "sunrise like a promise" (293) as it begins its voyage "into another land" (293), the promised land that waits beyond the racially divisive ethos of Miss Cramp, Fred Merrit, Patmore, and the other proponents of racialist thought.

Rudolph Fisher's *The Conjure-Man Dies* (1932) is a detective novel set in Harlem. The novel resurrects John Archer, the Harlem doctor who appeared in a short story in which Fisher struck a blow against the dependence of African-Americans on folk superstitions in medicine. The novel pairs Archer with Detective Perry Dart, a black, New York City police officer, and involves them in a case with a number of unusual aspects. The African conjure-man and Harlem fortune teller N'Gana Frimbo is found murdered. While assisting in solving the crime, John Archer discovers that Frimbo has only faked his death, and a strange relationship grows between them. They engage in a number of intellectual discussions in which Frimbo imparts some exotic views of African rituals and alludes to the possession of profound powers. In one of these conversations Frimbo reveals that he is a superman. Frimbo maintains that he is free and undetermined by the laws of cause and effect and the laws of accident that operate on the Earth: "Imagine, for instance, an order in which a cause followed its effect instead of preceding it—someone has already brought forward evidence of such a possibility. A creature of such an order could act upon our order in ways that would be utterly inconceivable to us" (227).

Frimbo refuses to reveal the method that he uses to exercise his free will or the source of his knowledge; however, he does give an abstraction of the principles involved: "I simply change the velocity of what is going on. I am a catalyst. I accelerate or retard a reaction without entering into it. This changes the cross currents, so that the coincidences are different from what they would otherwise be" (228).

The Conjure-Man Dies is particularly useful in demarcating the advances made in "objective" writing by the Harlem group. Although it may have been a good career move for Fisher to extend the geography of African-American literature into the realm of the detective story, that genre also proves a good vehicle for a writer who wishes his reader to look upon the text as a hermeneutic problem. By turning to the genre of the detective story, Fisher selected a form better suited to his semiotic and "objective" needs than what the satirical novel of manners could provide. This genre was not pursued by Fisher; however, Schuyler capitalized upon it and turned out a number of popular newspaper serials based on intrigue, mystery, and conspiracy.

In *The Conjure-Man Dies* the plot hinges on an act of deception. The reader's attention is drawn to this central act (in which a man dies and rises from the dead) and to other, lesser acts of deception: Ultimately, Fisher designed the narrative to break down and thereby reveal itself as a deception, a text concealing a subtext.

Parallel and complementary to the deceptive acts that drive the narrative is the theme of sight, which is brought to the reader's attention through every conceivable means. Characters are described according to defects of their vision (e.g., "unseeing eyes" [31], "cross-eyed" [50], "the cast in one eye" [66], "protruding eyes" [107], and "cock-eye" [133]) and are hyperbolically threatened with having their eyes poked out or are blinded by glaring lights. Characters are plunged into darkness, and they hold conversations in darkened rooms. Dr. John Archer joins the case because "This promises to be worth seeing" (22), and Frimbo's crisis is initiated by the words "Frimbo! Frimbo! Why do you not see?" (70). The culmination of the sight motif comes during Bubber Brown's narration of his case (in a self-referentially parodying subplot in which he assumes the role of a clownish private detective): "I couldn't use nothin' but my ears—couldn't see a thing" (52). Fisher thus informs the reader that "reading" by eye will not reveal the subtext—this is accomplished by using nothing but the ears.

Another route into the subtext is through the novel's intertextual relationship to the detective stories of the Sherlock Holmes corpus. This intertextuality is signaled by the stilted literary diction that John Archer adopts soon after Detective Perry Dart asks him to consult on the case. Although Archer and Dart apply professional techniques (the meticulous interrogation of witnesses and suspects, an examination of the "corpse," the comparison of fingerprints, an analysis of the evidence, and a logical examination of the facts), their efforts lead them to accuse an innocent man, Jinx Jenkins. Archer speaks ironically when he says that he has plans to write a murder mystery (155), as though he is the equal of Arthur Conan Doyle and can rival the famous Sherlock Holmes, who is, in the words of Dr. Watson, "the most perfect reasoning and observing machine the world has ever seen" (quoted in Rosenberg 110). However, when Archer is shown to be mistaken in his accusation of Jinx, the irony reflects back on him. The attentive reader cannot escape the implication that Archer is, despite his overweening certainty, altogether unequipped to solve the case by the means at his disposal.

The undermining of his detective, John Archer, is only the beginning of Fisher's "attack on reading." In contrast to the doctor and the detective, Bubber Brown is an untrained pseudodetective. Nevertheless, he cleverly subverts the investigation by planning his attack on the case several moves ahead of the detectives and throws suspicion away from himself so that he will be free to assist his accused friend, Jinx Jenkins. As Brown sets off on his own to solve the case, Jinx urges him on from his jail cell: "All I got to say is, Sherlock, do your stuff" (196). By setting up Bubber Brown to solve a case that Archer and Dart cannot solve, Fisher signals that he has not actually written a detective mystery. Not only has he descended into parody and comedy, robbing his text of every possibility of establishing a credible atmosphere of suspense, danger, and intrigue, but he has caused the reader to doubt the efficacy of the conventional tools by which Archer and Dart attempt to read the text of their mystery. The device that most seriously damages the text as a detective novel is that Fisher plays off a pair of clowns against Archer and Dart. Where clowns conventionally serve to elevate the hero, Bubber and Jinx are allowed to demote Archer and Dart. The text forces readers to question their own ability to competently penetrate into the real text, thereby bringing an awareness of the esoteric subtext.

Fisher's "attack on reading" is complex; it relentlessly assaults the reader with impasses, paradoxes, and riddles. This concerted "attack on reading" is not solely confined to the intertextual arena, for the attack at the intratextual level is equally destructive of the reader's complacency. Within the novel there are difficulties with text even beyond the convolutions presented by the murder case. The foremost example of an intratextual dilemma is Perry Dart's inability to negotiate John Archer's pseudo-Holmesian discourse. In fact, rather than imitating Holmes, Archer violates Holmes's prime directive, namely that "Whenever you have eliminated the impossible, whatever remains, however improbable, must be the truth" (quoted in Rosenberg 3). For his part, Archer's version of Holmes's modus operandi is delivered as an absurdity: "And I too am of the common persuasion which Mr. Frimbo so logically exposed, that one who comes to life was never dead. Logic to the contrary notwithstanding, I still believe the dead stay dead. And, while the corpse may be hard to produce, I still believe you have a murder on your hands" (182). As the investigation proceeds, the exchanges between Archer and Dart are increasingly marked by Dart's discomfort with Archer's language. Archer, nevertheless, behaves as though the successful solution of the case depends upon his use of a discourse of detection. Finally, Dart can bear no more. Archer issues a long speech that concludes: "But now, if these two blood specimens reposing in my bag present certain differences which I anticipate, I shall advise you to proceed with the total demolition of yonder dwelling—a vandalism which you have already contemplated, I believe?" (184). Dart's reply is telling: "Gosh, doc, it would be so much easier in French. Say it in French" (184).

The same speeches that Dart cannot comprehend repeatedly sound Gurdjieffian names syllabically. Jean Toomer's name, for example, sounds throughout the two quotes from *The Conjure-Man Dies* presented immediately above and is heard in "And I *too* am of the common persuasion" (182). The reader is meant to realize that Fisher's text, like Archer's speech, is not decipherable by the normal methods: Like French, it is another language altogether, and unless one approaches it with the correct tools, the text remains indecipherable. Archer's reply to Dart's plea for a translation into French is an ironic depiction of an improbable action. If the reader takes Archer's witticism literally, it is a reification of the "attack on race": "And if you shouldn't find the elusive corpse there—a possibility with which I have already annoyed you tonight—you may proceed to demolish the house next to the right, then, the next to the left, and so on until all Harlem lies in ruins" (184). However, this passage also provides an "attack on reading." If we read the text hermeneutically, we indeed reduce the narrative to ruins and the "mystery" dissolves into the sham that it is. Moreover, if we read Archer's speech literally, we realize that it is a clear statement of the aims of the Harlem group, to so devastate racialism that nothing like Harlem could ever again exist.

Despite the overdetermined meanings contained in the passage, it is also possible to read it as mere banter, an implication that is to a degree supported by the text. In a similar exchange, Archer and Dart are examining blood cells with a microscope:

"What are they doing?"
"Nothing," Dart grinned. "Must be Negro blood."
"Jest not, my friend. It is Sunday. All blood reposes. But keep looking." (203)

We can interpret these racialized high jinks literally, but they are equally loaded with ciphers. Closest to the surface we encounter the ever-present clue of the word "grinned" placed adjacent to the word "Negro" (one of the text's running gags). By itself, this signifies nothing; however, like other inclusions, this juxtaposition arises so often in *The Conjure-Man Dies* that the cumulative effect alerts the reader's suspicion that an anagram is intended—"grinned" is to be read as "nigger." The word "jest" may be combined with a previous occurrence of "god" to render "Gurdjieff." On another level, the dialogue reiterates the Gurdjieffian precept that "In order *to do* it is necessary *to be*" (ISM 22). As a spur to cast the attention in the direction of visual phenomena, the surface text provides a microscope through which the reader is urged to "keep looking" (203).

The contents of the hermeneutic level of *The Conjure-Man Dies* differ very little from what was created by others in the Harlem group. The twenty-four chapters that comprise the novel allude to the cosmic scheme known as the "ray of creation" or "three octaves of radiations." This subject is elaborated by a beam of light produced by an extension lamp used in the room where the mind-reader, Frimbo, held his interviews. By having Frimbo read minds, Fisher indicates yet another occurrence of subtextual reading. We first encounter this light when Jinx's consultation with the psychic is recounted by the narrator: "He sidled between the chair and table and sat down facing the figure beneath the hanging light. He was unable, because of the blinding glare, to descry any characteristic feature of the man he had come to see" (66–67). The police use the room to interrogate the assembled witnesses and suspects, thus justifying further descriptions of the powerful light. For instance, during the interrogation of Spider Webb, we read, "In the bright illumination of the horizontal beam of light, Spider's face twitched and changed just enough to convince Dart that he was on the right track" (135–36).

The subtext is replete with such familiar inclusions as the number three (36, 44, 74, 137), "mask" (37, 57), the three divisions of man (171), the devil (81, 170), and the ciphered and phoneticized names of Gurdjieff, Ouspensky, Orage, and Toomer.

However, two inclusions are particularly unique to *The Conjure-Man Dies* and require some exposition. Fisher is meticulous in arranging his subject matter to complement the hidden level of his texts. Joshua Jones, the protagonist of *The Walls of Jericho*, was a piano mover; this warranted discussions of pianos, which could then be used to symbolize the Gurdjieffian cosmic scheme—three octaves of radiation. Likewise, Fisher's selection of a murder mystery allows for the presentation of a wide range of esoteric materials. Decisive among the inventions present in *The Conjure-Man Dies* is the murder weapon itself. While investigating the corpse of the murdered conjure-man, Dr. Archer draws from the dead man's throat "a large, blue bordered, white handkerchief" (21). Because the murder weapon is a handkerchief, the word "handkerchief" subsequently occurs in the text many times. Following its initial appearance by only a few pages, Archer makes a pun on the murder weapon: "He wouldn't do the expected thing—not if he was bright enough to think up a gag like this" (23). The word "hand*kerchief*" offers the ear "Gurdjieff," and Fisher underscores this reading by presenting the word near "gag," for Gurdjieff's initials are G. I. G. However, Fisher is not finished; he couples the handkerchief with a "club": "I'll bet the chap handled the club with the handkerchief" (91). Here Fisher's text points to the existence of a secret organization dedicated to the elimination of race.

In the novels by Wallace Thurman and in Fisher's *The Walls of Jericho* we encounter list of names that can be read as a coded message. Fisher not only includes such a list of names in *The Conjure-Man Dies*, he repeats it with small variations (80, 135, 298). The most concise rendition is: "Mrs. Arimintha Snead, Mrs. Martha Crouch, Easley Jones, Doty Hicks, Spider Webb, and Jinx Jenkins" (298). If the names are treated as anagrams, it reads: "Need men," "Tomorrow," "Sly ones," "Do it," "We spy," "Join in," confirming the message that Fisher included in *The Walls of Jericho*. Through the coded lists of names in *The Conjure-Man Dies* Fisher intended his readers to recognize that his novel announced an antiracial project that would fundamentally alter the structure of American life.

Before concluding this discussion of *The Conjure-Man Dies*, the appearance of Gurdjieff in the text requires some elaboration. Other members of the Harlem group have introduced Gurdjieff into their texts in unexpected disguises; yet Fisher seems not to have done so in his first novel, *The Walls of Jericho*. Instead Fisher gives his reader pieces of Gurdjieff distributed among the characters in the form of striking eyes and yellow skin. But with *The Conjure-Man Dies*, the case is quite different: It is evident that the "psychist" N'Gana Frimbo, an African chieftain, is meant to represent Gurdjieff. James Moore delineates the controversy about Gurdjieff's significance as a matter of whether "he was a charlatan" or, as Peter Brook stated, "'the most immediate, the most valid and the most totally representative figure of our times'" (1). After hearing Frimbo speak for a while, John Archer wonders, "What is he—charlatan or prophet?" (223). When Frimbo first appears, he is disguised in the headdress of his tribe. Later, on the night that John Archer visits Frimbo, we are told that his appearance is "Matter-of-fact"; in other words, Gurdjieff's disguise has been taken away and his identity revealed.

Gurdjieff's unusual eyes were one of his most distinctive features, and his eyes were mentioned by everyone who wrote about him. Fisher begins his description of Frimbo by mentioning his eyes: "But the deep-set eyes still held their peculiar glow, and the low resonant voice was the same" (213).[3] There is, too, the matter of the name that has been given the character, N'Gana Frimbo. If N'Gana is reversed, the resulting "anagn" suggests the word "anagram." If we follow that clue and read "Frimbo" as an anagram, the letters can be rearranged into "form b i," which can be recognized as a Gurdjieffian exhortation to "form [the] Big 'I.'" Were it necessary to sum up Gurdjieffian self-development in a single phrase, we could do no better: Gurdjieff himself stated that the goal of the work is "Individuality, a single and permanent I, consciousness, will, the ability to do, a state of inner freedom" (ISM 159).

It is also noteworthy that Frimbo takes Archer "to that rear third-floor chamber," a location that indicates the esoteric nature of the subtext. The third room on the third floor alludes to both the concept of man as a "three-storied factory" and to the role of Gurdjieff as a teacher of hidden wisdom. Once they have situated themselves in the inner sanctum, Frimbo commences a series of revelations that strike at the foundations of John Archer's scientific beliefs. It is particularly interesting that Fisher has chosen to make his detective a medical doctor with an expressly scientific bent, for Gurdjieff's *Beelzebub's Tales* is, among other things, an attack on modern science. *The Conjure-Man Dies* makes a similar attack on science. Using the conventions of the detective story, Fisher exposes the shallowness of modern science by providing an alternative conception of the universe. Archer is amazed at the rightness of what he hears, for Frimbo's (Gurdjieff's) teachings do not contradict the evidence of science, they instead extend this evidence to unsuspected consequences. Archer is forced to reveal his enthusiasm for what he hears: "'You astonish me,' said the doctor. 'I thought you were a mystic, not a mechanist'" (214). Frimbo's reply is classic Gurdjieffian icon-breaking: "'This,' returned Frimbo, '*is* mysticism—an undemonstrable belief. Pure faith in anything is mysticism. Our very faith in reason is a kind of mysticism'" (214).

The concepts described by Frimbo are taken from some of the more abstruse parts of Gurdjieff's system. Frimbo's claim to have freedom of will is drawn directly from the Gurdjieff-Ouspensky literature; according to Gurdjieff "the possibility for man thus gradually to free himself from mechanical laws exists"

(ISM 84). The vocabulary that Frimbo uses is virtually the same as that used by Gurdjieff, and the idea being expressed is the same: "The fewer laws there are in a given world, the nearer it is to the will of the Absolute; the more laws there are in a given world, the greater the mechanicalness, the further it is from the will of the Absolute. We live in a world subject to forty-eight orders of laws, that is to say, very far from the will of the Absolute and in a very remote and dark corner of the universe" (ISM 81).

Frimbo's claim that he is able to change the order of events is an allusion to one of Gurdjieff's ideas that was of extreme importance to Toomer and the Harlem group. Gurdjieff's system was based on the idea that by understanding the nature of universal laws, it is possible to gain control over historical events. Indeed, the Harlem group crafted their literature to be placed in the world in specific ways designed to alter the order of historical events. The group intended that their literary works act on their cultural moment as "additional shocks" that would correct the movement of certain events and influence outcomes in desired ways.

Given this context, it is not surprising to see Fisher create Frimbo, who speaks so authoritatively of such matters as controlling the very fabric of coincidence— of the coordination of time and space. Frimbo speaks of the "change in velocity" (CMD 228) with the power to reconfigure coincidences; this is an allusion to Gurdjieff's Law of the Octave, which describes "the discontinuity of vibration and . . . the deviation of forces" (ISM 130) in the universe. The technique that Frimbo alludes to is based on the assumption that events will not turn out as they have been planned unless certain forces are set in motion to correct the course of events; according to Gurdjieff, all events give opposite results from what was originally intended without mankind noticing what has happened. The language that Gurdjieff used to discuss this topic is ridden with jargon. However, the paragraph below comes closest to describing Frimbo's version of the means for changing the course of events:

The right development of these octaves is based on what looks an *accident*. It sometimes happens that octaves going parallel to the given octave, intersecting it or meeting it, in some way or another *fill up its "intervals"* and make it possible for the vibrations of the given octave to develop in freedom and without checks. Observations of such rightly developing octaves establishes the fact that if at the necessary moment, that is, at the moment when the given octave passes through an "interval," there enters into it a "additional shock" which corresponds in force and character, it will develop further without hindrance along the original direction, neither losing anything nor changing its nature. (ISM 131)

The Gurdjieffian Harlem group had formulated a plan to alter the course of history, and this plan was based on their analysis of history as subject to the Law of the Octave. Thus, as a work of "objective" literature, Fisher's text exists more as a "legominism" than anything else, and his subject is the historical plan itself.

Fisher's "legominism" is presented in the form of an inserted text—Frimbo's description of his life in Africa, "twenty years past and five thousand miles away" (216). Frimbo's narration begins by establishing the proper mood: The initial paragraph contains such words as "unaware," "out of sight," "mysterious," "it must reveal itself," "invisibility," and "indeterminate." This vocabulary alerts us of hidden content; we are also told that the ritual is "completely symbolic" (218). The passage describes a ritual that takes place in a square. Looked at hermeneutically, the episode is a series of numbers, anagrams, and geometric figures: one hundred fighting men; twelve years old; a town of a thousand people; the village of Kimalu; Malindo, the feast of procreation; forty-eight tribes; a circle one hundred fifty feet in diameter; forty-eight torches; a chest; dancers; a baby; and a python.

Fisher uses the Buwongo ritual to symbolize the Gurdjieffian concept of "man as a three-storied factory." This concept is connected to a complicated system of diagrams that explain how man can better use the energy available to him, a problem that Gurdjieff poses as a question: "What then is a man to do when he begins to realize that he has not enough energy to attain the aims he has set before himself?" (ISM 179). In the word "Kimalu" we can recognize the word "aim": Fisher's Buwongo dialect can be read as Gurdjieffian terminology. Thus "timwe" is "time," and the name of the ritual, Malindo, holds "la" and "do"—two notes in the "food" octave that the "three-storied" concept describes. Alternatively, Malindo may be read as the important Gurdjieffian formula "I am." Man is a three-storied factory because "The upper story of this factory consists of a man's head; the middle floor, of the chest; and the lower, of the stomach, back, and the lower part of the body" (ISM 182). This is the "large square chest" (CMD 220), which is placed in the center of the circle. In Search of the Miraculous, Ouspensky's study of the Gurdjieff work, contains a detailed discussion of this entire subject. It is illustrated with fifteen diagrams that consist of squares containing circles and lines. The numbers given by Fisher may be found in these circles.

Thus, Fisher's "legominism" is a presentation of an extremely abstruse part of Gurdjieff's system. To provide some small indication of the significance of this concept, I briefly quote from Kenneth Walker's A Study of Gurdjieff's Teachings:

Ouspensky then drew on the blackboard a new diagram which he said represented man as a three-storied chemical factory. The work of this factory was to convert coarser matters into finer matters, the coarser matters being the various materials we required for the maintenance of our machinery and for the fuel consumed in running it. Ouspensky said that one of the reasons we were unable to remember ourselves and why the Higher Centres [sic] in us did not function was that we possessed insufficient [amounts] of the finer fuels. Hydrogen 12 was needed by both Emotional and Higher Emotional Centres, and we were invariably short of this high-octave spirit, so that Emotional Centre in us usually had to work with Hydrogen 24. There were two ways of obviating this shortage: first by ceasing to waste Hydrogen on useless projects, and second, by producing more of it. It was about the manufacture of finer hydrogens that he now wanted to speak. (136)

Walker shows that two of the numbers in Fisher's ritual, twelve and forty-eight, can be understood as the key to the entire concept of man as a three-storied factory. Walker rapturously concludes: "And if things were seen pure and uncontaminated with associative thoughts what a resounding *doh* 48 impression would strike in the inner chambers of our minds, a note which would pass without any difficulty to *mi* 12" (148).

The Buwongo ritual symbolizes the birth of a new man, the higher type of man symbolized by "the unharmed infant at our feet" (CMD 223). The goal of Toomer and his followers was to produce as many individuals of this new type as they could in the time allotted to them. In a sense, an "objective" novel such as *The Conjure-Man Dies* was a device designed to apply the necessary shocks to American culture to move certain historical events (octaves) in the desired directions. The "objective" view of time and space described by Frimbo also applies to the literature of the Harlem group; and we may understand Fisher's novel as a popular work of art through which he introduced the idea of the superman and the perfection of the will to African-American culture at a particular time in history. Therefore, we find the word "time" ciphered in the Buwongo ritual as "timwe."

Gurdjieff stated that "The evolution of large masses of humanity is opposed to nature's purposes. The evolution of a certain small percentage may be in accord with nature's purposes" (ISM 57–58). In the figure of N'Gana Frimbo we see the result of human evolution to a higher will; here we must confront the gap between Frimbo, the superman (man number seven), and Dr. John Archer, the emblem of mass man (men numbers one, two, and three). Through Frimbo, Archer learns that man has more powers than he has ever imagined. Yet, Frimbo is murdered, leaving Archer without the means to reach higher levels of consciousness. Archer has seen the higher man, but he does not know the methods by which he can become the higher man. We are told by Gurdjieff that such gaps are a part of the natural order.

The process that Fisher traces in *The Walls of Jericho* takes Joshua Jones from being man number one (physical man—a piano mover) to man number two (emotional man). This is not a very big step, because the first three steps are on the same level; however, it is an important one, as it is the beginning of evolution. Jones's fiancée, Linda, symbolizes the faculty of conscience; as long as Jones has conscience, he will continue to evolve. By contrast the comic characters Bubber and Jinx, who are carried over from *The Walls of Jericho* to *The Conjure-Man Dies*, represent men who exists at the instinctive level and do not develop their emotional and intellectual faculties. Therefore, we may assume that in being confronted with Frimbo (Gurdjieff) John Archer is man number three being given a view of man number six or seven. In meeting this higher man, Archer learns that he, as an educated professional, does not possess certain properties that he assumed he had gained through his scientific education. Helplessly, he sees that there is a potentiality for him to develop far beyond his preset level. The esoteric reading of his name, John Archer,—"no race"—is a testimony to the possibilities that are inherent in his being.

Nella Larsen
The Anatomy of "Sleep"

From the purview of literary criticism, Nella Larsen is an exceedingly troublesome author. George Hutchinson observes that, in part, both *Quicksand* and *Passing* are "satire[s] of black and white obsessions with 'racial integrity'—though this critique has yet to be recognized in the scholarship surrounding the novel[s]" (344). According to Jonathan Little, her work has been consistently underrated because it lacks "triumphant characters or affirming political messages" (173). Little notes that this view has caused critics to "miss some of the insights that Larsen's pervasively ironic vision offers" (173). Little's discussion of Larsen's use of irony makes two points that bear on this study: that Larsen's irony was rooted in her general skepticism (174) and that she "remained uncommitted to any predictable or traditional racial ideology" (175). Moreover, Little recognized her novels as psychological studies; he assigns Larsen's fiction a Freudian locus and states that *Passing* explores "the complex psychological dynamics of denial, transference, and self-justification" (173). These Freudian elements are undeniably part of *Passing;* Irene Redfield does exhibit denial, transference, and self-justification. However, we must consider that for contemporary readers, Freudian psychology is almost synonymous with inwardness in modernist literature. Given the covert nature of the Gurdjieffian esoteric school and the tendency of most critics to see Freud wherever psychology is in evidence, it is not surprising that critics have not recognized Larsen's novels as explicit demonstrations of the dynamics of Gurdjieff's psychology—a psychological system that differs fundamentally from Freudian psychology.[1]

Thadious Davis's biography *Nella Larsen, Novelist of the Harlem Renaissance: A Woman's Life Unveiled* (1994) goes beyond Freudian readings of Larsen's texts. Its discussion of the beginning of Larsen's career as a writer supplies a particularized chronicle of her activities in the Gurdjieff work. Davis constructs an unusually intimate and detailed record of a relatively brief period about which few facts have been available. She states that

Late in the spring of 1925, [Nella] Larsen Imes became part of a mainly literary group of blacks that Jean Toomer organized for lectures and demonstrations in Gurdjieffian philosophy. Dorothy Peterson, attracted to the handsome Toomer and no doubt also to his "admixture of physical and spiritual drives," was one of the principal students. Some observers believed that the "intense devotion he generated in individuals as disparate as Margaret Naumburg [wife of author Waldo Frank], Dorothy Peterson, and Mabel Dodge

Luhan was the result of his physical attractiveness." Peterson encouraged Larsen Imes's attendance, because she agreed with Toomer's belief that "those who were most likely to become absorbed . . . would be educated, relatively successful people who were seeking a remedy for their "incompleteness." In recruiting Larsen Imes, along with Wallace Thurman, Harold Jackman, and Aaron Douglas, Peterson identified those she considered most open to self exploration. (167)

Davis states that most of the Harlem literati "came to one meeting and did not return" (167), and cites Langston Hughes's often-quoted assertion that Toomer failed to "drop the seeds of Gurdjieff" in Harlem. Davis provides more on Larsen Imes's Gurdjieffian adventure:

Like her two friends, Nella Larsen Imes was attracted to Toomer's teachings. She was searching for something, and the group validated the legitimacy of her search. The idea of self-regeneration had a special appeal to her, given the self-fashioning that she had accomplished. Unlike the two Dorothys, however, she was too practical-minded and materialistic to give herself over to the spiritual base of the philosophy or to Toomer's mysticism.

Her two friends were another matter. She found their involvement with the Gurdjieffs [sic] unreasonable and frequently joked about Dorothy Harris' being "pseudo-religious," though she found Harris "charming" and a good bridge partner. She also humorously conveyed to Dorothy Peterson, who was in Europe and on her way to Gurdjieff's institute at Fontainebleau, Elmer Imes's message: "Remember Katherine Mansfield." (Mansfield had died at Fontainebleau in 1923.) The warning was intended to caution Peterson against putting too much faith in the healing potential of Gurdjieff's philosophy. (167–69)

Davis constructs Larsen's separation from the Gurdjieff movement by positing that Larsen's desires for "attaining significance through writing," "individuation," and "the expression of her creativity" contradicted the Gurdjieffian goal of "redirecting an internally aimless life" (169).

Hutchinson believes that Davis's treatment of Nella Larsen's biography is of limited use: "Despite the many valuable facts the biographer ha[s] managed to recover, the stor[y] [she] tell[s] [is] fundamentally flawed, reproducing the bipolar structure of American black/white racial culture at the expense of the interracial subject" (345). As an offshoot of Davis's "tendency to scapegoat or repress interracial communion" (Hutchinson 345), Davis asserts that Larsen's fiction was possible only because of her separation from the Harlem Gurdjieffians. On the contrary, Nella Larsen began her career as a writer by drawing closer to Gurdjieffians and by using the methods that they innovated in common to produce "legominisms," or texts with a coded content.

Larsen's involvement with esoteric concepts first appears in her short fiction (e.g., "The Wrong Man" and "Sanctuary"), however, the focus of this chapter is restricted to her two novels. Larsen's novels *Quicksand* (1928) and *Passing* (1929) are cautionary tales. Her approach to the creation of "objective" literature was to allegorize the chief danger that faces humans: unreflective immersion in ordinary living. According to Gurdjieff, "Everything in the world, from solar systems to man, and from man to atom, either rises or descends, either evolves or degenerates. *But nothing evolves mechanically.* Only degeneration and destruction proceed mechanically. That which cannot evolve consciously—degenerates" (ISM 70). That is, because the opportunity for evolution rarely comes to individuals, the common path of human life is rapid and unrecognized degeneration.

Larsen's approach to the "objective" becomes explicit once we realize that she adopted a devolutionary strategy in common with *Infants of the Spring, Jonah's Gourd Vine, Black Empire,* and *Slaves Today* and antithetical to the evolutional strategy used in *The Blacker the Berry, The Walls of Jericho, Black No More,* and *Their Eyes Were Watching God.* Evolutional texts enact and embody the integration of the three centers (mind, body, emotions), and the protagonists achieve psychological wholeness. The alternative approach (the devolutionary strategy) used by the "objective" artist would be to shock or wake up readers by showing what will happen if there is no cultivation of the "real self." To describe the path of devolution, Larsen presents two harrowing accounts of the dangers of blindly pursuing the goals of a largely pathological American culture.

Larsen's *Quicksand* is often read as a feminist censure of marriage, patriarchal oppression, and imprisoning constructions of gender.[2] What is overlooked in these sociological readings is the psychological signification of symbols in the text. Ann E. Hostetler comes close to this psychological approach: "The object of desire, she fails repeatedly to come to terms with her own desires. . . . The narrative surface of *Quicksand* is richly encrusted with symbols chosen from the object world of haute-bourgeois culture; black folk culture is significantly absent. In fact, the text is iconic of Helga's dilemma: Helga is the text—an aesthetic experiment, an isolated gem on the margins of the African American literary heritage" (35–45). To give Hostetler's words a Gurdjieffian reading, the "objective" and psychological level of *Quicksand* is synonymous with the symbolic (or iconic) level of the text. The green and gold negligee that Helga wears at both the beginning and end of the novel, when "she abandons her restless search for identity through clothes" (Hostetler 44), represents her neglect of her inner self to fulfill her desires for pleasure (green) and material possessions (gold). By neglecting her mind and emotions, Helga is dominated by her instinctive self—possibly by her "sex center." Hostetler indicates that Helga "is unable to reconcile her sexual awakening with her developing sense of identity as a black woman" (43); Helga's love affair with Anderson, a mulatto, fails because she cannot resist the slide into objectification, and she comes to see herself as "a sensual creature devoid of self" (43). In *Quicksand* Larsen has chosen to portray Helga's "sex center" as the primary motivating force in her inner life because this theme is an important one in Gurdjieff's psychology: "Sex plays a tremendous role in maintaining the mechanicalness of life.

Everything that people do is connected with 'sex': politics, religion, art, the theater, music, is all 'sex' " (ISM 254).

Throughout *Quicksand*, Helga is concerned with her clothing as she attempts to alter her persona (or "false personality") to satisfy her desires by manipulating those around her. Helga Crane lives her life in a condition of "sleep," never realizing what has value and what are evasions. Her regard for finery, her opinions on race, and her dealings with men are directed and determined externally by debased transitory and negative influences. The "green" of her husband's name—Pleasant Green—is the unopposed, instinctive green of her negligee. Both her husband and her outer shell or "false personality" are manifestations of neglect of the "true self " or the "essence" (Gurdjieff's term). Because Helga has pursued a course of negligence, which Larsen has symbolized by the color green, her intellectual and emotional impoverishment results. Helga comes to realize the "oppression, the degradation, that her life had become" (161) after delivering her fourth child and being "beset by the insistent craving for sleep" (159). With time to think, she resolves to reclaim her life and her will. However, what she wishes to reclaim is merely the gold, the "false personality" that is not her true self. Helga has no knowledge of a self beyond poses and surfaces—the colored clothes and the exotic sheath of her Negroness. Helga is so removed from her essence that she cannot realize that now she is too weak even to reclaim the misdirected will that she once exercised: "So she dozed and dreamed in snatches of sleeping and waking, letting time run on. Away" (135).

Thus far we have been concerned only with the novel on a literal level. Admission to the esoteric level of the novel is gained through various clues provided by Larsen. Perhaps the most accessible clue of the novel was discussed by Deborah E. McDowell in her 1986 edition of *Quicksand and Passing*, where she suggests "the possibility that Larsen used the Naxos allusion as an anagram of 'Saxon,' to suggest the school's worship of everything Anglo-Saxon" (243 n. 2). Although McDowell recognized the southern setting (Naxos) in the beginning of *Quicksand* as an anagram of Saxon, there is a further implication that the "doubleness" might point not to Helga Crane but to "the double door" of anagramic wordplay. Both *Quicksand* and *Passing* are texts that expand upon reading the text twice. Both narratives commence with the protagonists absorbed in the act of reading, although there is a difference in how the competency of the protagonists is addressed. In *Quicksand* the distraught Helga's attempt to read a novel is largely an exercise in breakdown, and the act of reading dissolves; the chapter ends as Helga goes to bed "leaving her room disorderly for the first time" (44). In the morning the girl who comes to awaken Helga finds "books and papers scattered upon the floor" (44). By contrast, *Passing* is divided into thirds, with the entire first third devoted to Irene Redfield's attempt to read a letter from Clare Kendry.

Helga Crane's choice for escape from the unceasing pressures and acute dissatisfactions of school life is a novel, Maurice [Marmaduke] Pickthall's *Said the Fisherman:* "She wanted forgetfulness, complete mental relaxation, rest from thought of any kind" (36). McDowell's note on this novel discloses a degree of uncertainty about Larsen's intentions: *"Said the Fisherman* (1903) has Eastern color, movement, and sharp authenticity. Perhaps Larsen intends an ironic contrast to the dull sobriety and sterility of Naxos" (243 n. 3). McDowell interprets Helga's choice of reading material as indicating Larsen's investment in irony, not as a comment on the reading itself. However, the context establishes the subject of the passage as Helga's feelings and her wish to escape from them through reading. Moreover, at this early point in the novel we are given little sense of the quality of the life from which Helga seeks escape; further, Helga never gets any reading done, and thus a comparison of Pickthall's "color, movement, and sharp authenticity" to life at Naxos could not be appreciated by Helga. In fact *Said the Fisherman* only constitutes a contrast to Naxos in so far as Helga Crane constructs such a contrast through her misreading of the previously read text. Helga refers to the pleasures of Pickthall's *Said the Fisherman* as deriving from "Said and his audacious villainy" (38), a reading that says much about the failings of her character.

In another reading of this episode in *Quicksand,* Davis underscores the inappropriateness of Helga's interpretation: "The book is not 'light' reading. Set in Egypt, the novel traces the life of a simple, spiritual man from 1871 to 1882" (259), which markedly contrasts with Helga's enjoyment of Said's "villainy." Davis accounts for Larsen's choice of this novel by stating that "the use of Pickthall's novel accentuates Helga's fashionable, wide-ranging tastes and her discerning intelligence about the relationship between subjects in books and concerns in mundane life" (259). In other words, Davis sees Helga's choice of *Said the Fisherman* as an indication of her intellectual sophistication and artistic sensibility. However, Davis does not resolve the contradiction of Helga's enjoyment of Said's "villainy" with what Davis sees as Said's simplicity and spirituality. Davis reads *Quicksand* as tragedy: "Helga's tragedy is personal but far-reaching in its implications. Her female perspective intensifies the psychological dualism inherent in her obsessive awareness that she is a product of both white and black cultures" (274). Davis also sees the novel as "a cautionary tale of the creative process, with the life of the female struggling to become an artist expressive of her matrilineal heritage as the central idea" (275).

Neither McDowell nor Davis have accurately appraised *Said the Fisherman,* and the result is that neither reading sheds much light on the nature of *Quicksand.* Said is not, as McDowell says, either simple or spiritual; he is as Helga Crane states, "villainous." Said is a complete fool, a man of no understanding who steals, cheats, kidnaps, distrusts the honest, trusts the criminal, and never sees a situation correctly. *Said the Fisherman* falls into the category of Sufi teaching stories, a genre that was of major influence on Gurdjieff's *Beelzebub's Tales,* the urtext for *Quicksand.*

Pickthall's character, Said, resembles the famous Mulla (Master) Nasrudin, the unenlightened man about whom there are thousands of jokes and comic stories and who is referred to many times in *Beelzebub's Tales*. Pickthall, an Islamic scholar and Arabic translator, formulated his novel out of this traditional body of Islamic religious lore, although with Pickthall's Said there is not the ever-present "Sufi attitude towards life" (Shah *The Sufis* 64) whereby mystical experience is brought close to the surface.

Said is a young, impetuous, amoral, cowardly, egotistical, unfaithful, and lazy person—in short, a fool. (At the conclusion of *Quicksand*, Helga Crane emphatically pronounces herself a fool: "She had, to put it as brutally as anyone could, been a fool. The damnedest kind of fool. And she had paid for it. Enough. More than enough" [159].) Nevertheless, at times Said prospers, although he never seems to know why he does so; the enjoyment that comes from reading his story is in witnessing his losses become successes only to see them reversed by his relentlessly stubborn foolishness. That Helga Crane enjoys Said's "villainous" character demonstrates Larsen's satirical use of this intertext to frame her narrative about Helga Crane: Like Said, Helga never sees anything clearly. Thus, an important function of the intertextual pairing of *Said the Fisherman* and *Quicksand* is to undercut, even eradicate, the possibility of a tragic reading of *Quicksand*. *Said the Fisherman* belongs to the genre of wisdom literature that applies its satire against the protagonist; although the genre resembles the picaresque, it is not the larger society that is in question but the protagonist's failure to develop self-awareness. Said's most telling encounters are his meetings with the "saint" Ismail Abbas, who gives Said wise counsel. Said never grasps the wisdom of Abbas's advice, and his reaction is to do the opposite of what the sheriff suggests. Said's relationship with the wise and holy Ismail Abbas parallels that of Helga Crane and her lover Robert Anderson, although Helga's reaction to Anderson's advice is instantaneous and violent.

Once we see that Helga reads Pickthall's novel without grasping that she herself is Said, we cannot take her any more seriously than we take Said (although to say this is to immediately feel the need to retract the statement). Said teaches by means of his negative example, for like Sufi teaching stories, *Said the Fisherman* is serious comedy. Idries Shah states that "it is inherent in the Nasruddin story that it may be understood at any of many depths. There is the joke, the moral—and the little extra which brings the consciousness of the potential mystic a little further on the way to realization" (63). Having grasped the intertextual method of Larsen's satire, we begin to see that *Quicksand* has much in common with *Said the Fisherman*. Characters begin to give way and not to seem solid constructions; the very furniture begins to mock the protagonist. The elaborately decorated surroundings and the exquisite costumes reveal themselves as the trappings of a mechanical level of consciousness, one of the props by which Helga Crane convinces herself that she is an artist and a sophisticate, when, in Gurdjieffian terms, she is wholly in a state of "sleep."

The story of Helga Crane is bracketed by two texts, Pickthall's novel and Anatole France's short story "The Procurator of Judea." Helga throws Pickthall's novel to the floor and never rereads it. France's story is read to Helga by her nurse as she attempts to recover her strength after giving birth. The prominent placement of these texts establish reading itself (along with misreading and unreading) as the narrative's central activities—not the simple act of "reading," but a twofold (sylleptic) or hermeneutic type of reading through which the esoteric labyrinth of the subtext can be negotiated. We are presented with both the mimetic dyad of the texts that enclose Helga Crane's narrative and the surreptitious ironies that belong to Pickthall and France. Of more concern to us is Larsen's intertextual treatment of these texts.

Pickthall's and France's texts introduce a religious countertext to the "relaxation" initially sought in *Said the Fisherman* by an "unnerved" (37) Helga and finally the "irony" that a "disillusion[ed]" (57) Helga hoped to derive from hearing "The Procurator of Judea" read to her. The relationship of the framing texts to the act of reading becomes explicit when they are read with care. From *Said the Fisherman* we learn that

He [Said] had a very large and precious copy of the Coran, so exquisitely written that each word was a monogram for a learned scribe to decipher; for Said it was quite illegible. This manuscript, bound in finely-chased leather, was carried every Friday by a servant to the mosque, together with a cushion. It was a small place of worship frequented by poor people, to whom a merchant was a great men. As soon as Said was comfortably seated on a cushion, the volume was placed in his hands. Opening it at random, he would recite some passage which he knew by heart, in a very loud, nasal voice, and to the edification of all who sat there on the bare stones, waiting for the coming of the preacher. (216–17)

This passage directs us to the subject of "reading" and the means by which a text must be deciphered. If Said cannot read the exquisitely written monograms of his Koran and Helga Crane cannot read Maurice Pickthall's *Said the Fisherman*, is not the text of *Quicksand* illegible to casual readers?

The story told in "The Procurator of Judea" also turns upon an act of reading, although it is more accurate to say that in France's story reading resembles Helga Crane's nonreading of *Said the Fisherman*. In the concluding half of Larsen's textual frame, L. Aelius Lamia, a student of philosophy and of whom the narrator states "His misfortunes had made him wise" (France 1), goes up into the hills to read an Epicurean roll, the "Treatise on Nature" (Lucretius's *De Rerum Natura*). He is then interrupted by an approaching slave-borne litter and Lamia recognizes his benefactor from the days of his exile, Pontius Pilate. The remainder of the story is occupied with conversations that pass between Lamia and Pilate; the

Epicurean text is never again mentioned. Like *Said the Fisherman*, France's text is an objective correlative of the state that Helga Crane has reached in her path of dissolution. Helga is bedridden and must have the second text read to her. Surrounded by the rejoicing Christians who she has now come to despise, Helga falls asleep before she can hear "the superbly ironic ending" (159), wherein Pilate cannot remember Jesus Christ: "Thus all the previous ironic implications are topped by Pilate's unawareness of his key role in the most significant historical event of his era" (Bresky 101). Larsen uses France's story to comment on Helga's similarly obstructed awareness of where significance and vitality are to be found in her world.

Like Pilate, Helga Crane has ignored the inner meaning of the events that have confronted her, and she lives purposelessly, giving no thought to anything beyond the accidental, sensual, and subjective. Helga only wants to hear the story because it confirms her rejection of the world and the potentialities of larger meanings. Yet, on another level, we recognize that because France's story is about Pilate, it raises questions of religious meaning. Helga is read to by Mrs. Hartley ("heart lie"), whose interpretation of Christianity would not be unsympathetic toward Gurdjieff and his brand of esoteric Christianity. This reading is supported by the way in which Larsen has introduced France's story into her text and by the fact that Mrs. Hartley finishes the reading without Helga, who has fallen asleep.

On discovering that Pilate cannot remember Christ, Mrs. Hartley is puzzled and pronounces this "Silly" (159). Mrs. Hartley's reaction serves only to obliterate "the superbly ironic ending" that Helga had sought. We now witness not Helga's informed, ironic, and antireligious reading of the text but Mrs. Hartley's incomprehension in the face of France's Epicurean historicism. Mrs. Hartley's failed reading parallels Helga's misreading of *Said* at the opening of the novel in which "villainy" is substituted for spirituality; here "silliness" is substituted for "irony." Because neither Helga nor Mrs. Hartley can legibly read a text, we come to realize that in Larsen's view what is wanted are not villainy and irony but "service" and "sacrifice" (54), the virtues advocated by Dr. Anderson early in the novel and violently rebuffed by Helga in her exit interview from Naxos. Thus Helga's intention to read Pickthall for Said's "villainy" and France for Pilate's "irony" are wholly undermined by the spiritual nature of the texts.

Realizing that it is now too late to remedy her situation, Helga wishes to enjoy France's ironic, historic obliteration of Christ, for she has come to despise the fervid, ineffectual Christians who surround her. However, in contrast to Davis's assertion, Helga does not require France's story because she wishes to return to her "blunted perceptions," but because she wishes to reinforce her antireligious posture with an infusion of Epicureanism. It was a principle of the Epicurean philosophy that "The source of most, if not all, human ills is religion" (G. H. Clark 5). This view delights Helga in her hatred of her surroundings: "And this, Helga decided, was what ailed the whole Negro race in America, this fatuous belief in the white man's God, this childlike trust in full compensation for all woes and privations in 'kingdom come'" (160). Helga remembers her favorite story, and falls asleep without hearing it read to her. In the days that follow, with too much time to think, Helga comes to realize the mistake that she has made in turning away from self-fulfillment to embrace the "illusions" and "blunted . . . perceptions" (159) of religion. Although it is still her hope "to think out a feasible way of retrieving all these agreeable, desired things" (clothes, books, social life) and "sophisticated tuneless music" (161), she cannot summon sufficient energy to "work out some arrangement," and she cannot escape the confines of her mechanical existence. The novel ends with her condemned to a life of timeless, meaningless repetition: "And hardly had she left her bed and become able to walk again without pain, hardly had the children returned from the homes of the neighbors, when she began to have her fifth child" (162).

Despite Davis's repudiation of Larsen's lasting interest in Gurdjieff and the influence on Larsen's fiction by the ideas that Jean Toomer taught in Harlem, Davis accords *Quicksand* a thoroughly Gurdjieffian reading—although it is not clear that this was intended. This reading became unavoidable, because in applying a feminist construct to the novel, Davis's interpretation of the novel became centered on the role of Audrey Denny, "The only character with whom Helga never directly interacts, [who] represents an element of Helga's own self that she does not allow herself to become" (272). In recognizing that she has lost her chance to develop herself, "ruined her life" (159), Helga has come face to face with what Larsen calls "terrible reality" (159), namely, Gurdjieff's "The Terror of the Situation"—man's incapacity to identify and correct his weaknesses (Waldberg 5). Audrey Denny reemerges in the closing chapters of Larsen's text because she is another representation of Helga's possibilities: Her name is an anagram for "Deny I erred." This complicated wordplay is related to the pen name Allen Semi—Nella Imes in reverse—that Larsen Imes used in publishing stories in 1926 (Davis 173). It also uses the convention of reading a y for an i invented by Thurman for *Infants* and used by Hurston in her novels. The meaning of the anagram is transparent: Helga is able to support her actions by never going near Audrey Denny, for to do so would cause her to stop avoiding the dissipation of her will, energy, and attention.

If the reader is interested enough to recognize the Naxos/Saxon anagram, which serves as a strong clue to the Gurdjieffian subtext, one will also penetrate the actual hidden level in which the words may be read as patterns of sound. Helga Cranes's name is repeated in full throughout the text; thus, the reader is repeatedly invited to read "race hell" in Helga Crane. We also read "cry [of] regret" in Margaret Creighton, "reason robber" in Robert Anderson, "angry" in Anne Grey, and "jail" in James Vayle. However, these distilled descriptions reveal nothing about the characters that is not evident from the text in which they have corresponding effects on Helga Crane. For example, we are told about an "angry" Anne Grey that "She talked, wept, and ground her teeth dramatically about the wrongs and shames of her race. At times she lashed her fury to surprising heights for one by nature so placid and gentle" (79). The anagrams that compose the names do nothing to illuminate the characters' qualities, they only point to Larsen's system for creating progressively more difficult anagrams. Thus, if Anne Grey, an easily read anagram that is only slightly more difficult than "Saxon/Naxos," opens the reader to the more obscure anagrams, we then see in James Vayle a more loosely constructed anagram, "jail." By the time we discover "race Hell" in Helga Crane, we realize that certain letters should be ignored and that we have license to arrange the letters according to need.

In addition to Helga Crane's inability to conduct the reading of Pickthall's *Said the Fisherman*, we are also treated to an additional failing of Helga Crane. We learn that the night is "eerily quiet" (36), and that in this silence Helga discards her book and darkens the room, being content to sit motionlessly for hours. Curiously, the narrator begins to catalog the sounds heard as the night comes on: "The minutes gathered into hours, but still she sat motionless, a disdainful smile or an angry frown passing now and then across her face. Somewhere in the room a little clock ticked time away. Somewhere outside a whippoorwill wailed. Evening died. A sweet smell of early Southern flowers rushed in on a newly risen breeze which suddenly parted the thin silk curtains at the opened windows. A slender frail glass vase fell from the sill with a tingling crash, but Helga Crane did not shift her position" (38). It is not readily apparent from this passage that the subject continues to be reading, for there has been a nearly imperceptible shift of subject from Helga Crane's misreading of *Said the Fisherman* to the reader of *Quicksand*, who is actively misreading Larsen's text. However, Larsen, directs the reader toward the method that will allow the "curtains" of the text to be drawn apart by restating the motif in the paragraph that follows; Helga, having risen, "paused before the old bowlegged secretary that held with almost articulate protest her schoolteacher paraphernalia of drab books and papers" (38). Her reaction to the tangible signs of her frustrated attempts at teaching is physical: "Frantically Helga Crane clutched at the lot and then flung them violently, scornfully toward the wastebasket" (38). Similarly, the reader is to dispose of old methods of reading.

These actions establish that Helga Crane has refused to read and refused to listen; our attention is thus directed toward reading and toward listening. In effect, we are being told that to gain access to the "text," we must practice a new kind of reading, one that requires listening to the sounds in the world of the novel and in the experiences created by Larsen's prose. If we are attuned to the sounds made by the "newly risen breeze which suddenly parted the thin silk curtains" (38), in the "text" that opens beyond the parting curtains we can learn what is divulged by the "tinkling crash" of the syllables. The first paragraph ends by sounding Orage's

name; we cannot miss the emphatic "or" in the musical tour de force of its concluding sentence: "To the rapping of other teachers, bearing fresh scandals, or
seeking information, or other more concrete favors, or merely talk, at that hour
Helga Crane never opened her door" (36). Because this method of reading operates bidirectionally, the sound of "age" (in "rigidity" and "huge") is located two
sentences above the occurrence of "or."

Larsen innovated an additional technique for "objective" writing by using the
material on the literal level of the text to comment on the personality whose name
was hidden in the syllables. This technique was not used as explicitly by Hurston
or Schuyler, in whose texts there seems to be little or no relationship between the
literal text and the coded syllables of the subtext. Larsen's integration of the
mimetic and hermeneutic levels of *Quicksand* is extraordinarily well coordinated;
her novel has taken to a new height of complexity the technical problem of controlling the form of the novel while simultaneously concealing and revealing its
Gurdjieffian contents.

The most unusual aspect of the subtext of *Quicksand* is the manner in which
Larsen has inserted Gurdjieff into the narrative. We encounter Gurdjieff when
Helga Crane is in grave financial difficulty and must take a position as secretary to
a Mrs. Hayes-Rore, a lecturer on the race question. Mrs. Hayes-Rore is a decidedly
odd minor character, who Anne Grey calls Aunt Jeanette. She is described as "a
plump lemon-colored woman with badly straightened hair and dirty fingernails.
Her direct, penetrating gaze was somewhat formidable" (68). On the following
page we learn that Mr. Hayes-Rore, a crooked politician, died mysteriously and
left his wife a considerable sum of money. What Helga notices about this figure is
confounding. Helga registers a "humorous gleam, and something in the way she
held her untidy head gave the impression of a cat watching its prey" (70). Further,
she learns that Mrs. Hayes-Rore is "interested in girls" (71), that she never lies
(74), and that she has the run of her nearly divine niece's house (73). If we assem-
ble the clues, we can solve the riddle: She is actually Mrs. Hayes-Rore's unnamed
husband disguised as his own wife. Mrs. Hayes-Rore can truthfully state that she
never lies, because her name declares her identity: "her" name is an homophone
for "he's Rore."

On the hermeneutic level, Mrs. Hayes-Rore is further revealed to be another
man, Gurdjieff himself. This is evidenced by the subtext and again by the physical
description of Helga's new employer. Gurdjieff's name is sounded out by two
syllables in the paragraph following her description (70) combined with a single
syllable from the actual description: "girl," "or'd," "effective." In particular, the
unusual contraction "or'd" calls attention to sounds on the syllabic level. This obscure presentation is compensated for by the exactitude of Mrs. Hayes-Rore's
physical description: "a . . . lemon-colored woman with badly straightened hair . . .
Her direct, penetrating gaze was somewhat formidable." Solita Solano, who later

became Gurdjieff's secretary, describes her first sight of him as "this 'strange' ecru man about whom I could see nothing extraordinary except the size and power of his eyes. . . . I rejected his language, the suit he was wearing and his table manners" (Webb 326). Larsen has presented her version of Gurdjieff in a disguise, a characteristic often associated with him. Ouspensky states that on first meeting Gurdjieff, he saw "a man of an oriental type . . . with a black moustache and piercing eyes, who astonished me because he seemed to be disguised and completely out of keeping with the place and its atmosphere" (Wilson *War* 36).

The mysteries that follow now fall into place. Anne Grey, who we are told twice is "too good to be true" (76) is indeed so; she is Mrs. Hayes-Rore's mistress. It is for this reason that the seemingly refined Anne Grey states that "The most wretched Negro prostitute that walks 135th street is more than any President of these United States" (79). Another description of Anne Grey is also loaded with markedly erotic insinuations: her reading is "lurid," and her beliefs habitually occasion an "orgy of protest" (79). We should also note the sadomasochistic implications of the following: "At times she lashed her fury to surprising heights for one by nature so placid and gentle" (79).

Larsen includes much of Gurdjieff's and Orage's vocabularies, which she employs by seeming to talk about the school at Naxos while actually commenting on events in Harlem after 1925.[3] Thus, we read about "the method" and "the general ideas behind the system" (38). Gurdjieff taught that man in his unevolved state is a machine; Helga Crane refers to the "community" as "a machine" (39), a particularly interesting assessment, because Larsen is presumably commenting on the entire Harlem Renaissance.[4] Larsen also uses the word "work" a number of times (e.g., 42, 53, 53, 65, 73). Although "work" is a common word and is appropriate to a narrative in which a character is searching for employment, the overuse is a device used by Larsen to suggest the presence of a subtext.

Other concepts from the Gurdjieff work appear throughout the novel, the most frequent being man's machinelike nature: Helga Crane gets out of bed "mechanically" (45), the students are "automatons" (47), Helga moves "automatically" (49), and Dr. Anderson commands a "cruel educational machine" (50). The novel is written about man in his ordinary state of consciousness, called in Gurdjieffian terms "man number one" or instinctive-moving-centered man. The novel reflects this by the use of "instinctively" (40, 42) and by portraying man number one: "The essence of life seemed bodily motion" (89). We are shown several other examples of Gurdjieffian concepts: "masks" are slipped on (72); Anne Grey reveals her "buffers" through her "inconsistencies about race" (80); as a child, Helga develops her "false personality" (66); and one of Helga's "subpersonalities" continually overreacts to Dr. Anderson's kindness, which leaves her to face the tragic consequences, first when she leaves Naxos (55) and later when she slaps his face (136).

Following closely upon the publication of *Quicksand*, Nella Larsen's second novel, *Passing* (1929), was dedicated to Carl Van Vechten and his wife Fania Marinoff. With *Passing*, Larsen continued much of what she had initiated in *Quicksand*. The prevailing critical opinion is that this novel is flawed in execution and fails to develop the conflict in outlook toward race that exists between Irene Redfield and her husband Brian; Larsen instead concentrates on the repressed lesbian relationship between Irene and Clare Kendry, an African-American whose passing for white allows her to marry a wealthy, bigoted white man.[5] Jonathan Little's defense of Larsen's ironic methodology, a mode that was rejected by such critics as Davis, McDowell, and Mary Mabel Youman (Little 173), is grounded in his appreciation of Larsen's willingness to avoid the trap of racial thought. Because he reads Larsen as "uncommitted to any predictable or traditional racial ideology," Little comes as close as any critic can to assessing Larsen's textual "attacks on race" without placing Larsen in the Harlem group. He states that

Larsen does not provide the inspirational models of human behavior that some critics seem to demand. Her pervasive irony negates that possibility. However, to fault Larsen for remaining true to her preferred mode of literary expression seems unfair. In *Passing* Larsen brilliantly deploys irony to delve into the often ambiguous, ambivalent, and self-deceiving nature of human behavior and expression. Because of this sophistication and artistic mastery, the internally consistent text resonates on deeper levels than many novels and certainly more than any passing-for-white novel yet written. (182)

The narrative's treatment of what purports to be its major theme, race, is developed out of the different qualities belonging to Irene, Brian, and Clare—emotions, mind, and body/instinct/sexuality, respectively—that are matters of essence (or heredity) and personality. Irene has never really felt passionate love or ecstasy, and she clings compulsively to her fetishistic dream of the importance of race out of a misplaced sense of duty. At the same time, her racial obsession is a burden that "bound and suffocated" (258) her: "For she would not go to Brazil. She belonged in this land of rising towers. She was an American. She grew from this soil, and she would not be uprooted. Not even because of Clare Kendry, or a hundred Clare Kendrys. Brian, too belonged here. His duty was to her and to his boys" (267).

Because Irene is, in every aspect of her being, a conventional person, she believes that her being consists of her social definition and her racial integrity. Her "false personality" or "mask" is that of a Negro; she believes in this "mask" and sees no way to abandon it. ("Mask," a term used many times in the narrative, supports both denotative and esoteric meanings.) Irene's fear that her husband will force her to violate her self by moving his family to Brazil, a multiracial society, has already driven a wedge between them. Her obsession with "outer layer[s]" is referred to several times (e.g., 250, 253, 254, 257, 266, 268), and there are references to Irene's inability to penetrate the expressions—the outer layers—of Brian and

Clare and of their ability to penetrate her thoughts (e.g., 196, 212, 266). These instances establish Irene's inability to separate the inner self ("essence") from the outer self ("false personality") and thus to realize that she is not merely what the world has given to her.

Clare has married a white man to make her way in the world. At the same time, she cannot leave behind her connection to the African-American subculture, thus endangering her position in the professional world. Ironically, she is married to a white racist. Because she cannot entirely abandon her life as a black person, she thrusts herself into Irene's life, threatening not only her own vulnerable situation but the stability of the Redfields' marriage. Clare symbolizes the complex of qualities that Irene lacks or denies; Clare's life as a Negro passing for white allows her to reify the falsity of the idea of race and to enact the separation of the true self from the "false personality" that Larsen calls the "outer layer" (266) and "outward self" (257). Clare is not a Gurdjieffian, but her role-playing has allowed her to make discoveries about people that approximate the fundamental ideas in Gurdjieffian psychology. When Irene mentions Clare's children, Clare tells her, "Children aren't everything. . . . There are other things in the world, though I admit some people don't seem to suspect it" (240). By removing herself from the expectations of society, Clare has been able to come closer to the truth of the human situation than has her psychically castellated friend, Irene.

Larsen has represented a spectrum of attitudes toward race through her characters and allowed the resulting events to proceed to their logical outcomes to demonstrate the pathology of racialist thinking. John Bellew's case is clear-cut; belatedly, he discovers that he is in love with a woman who he feels he must hate. Irene finds that her fear of the unknown, masked as loyalty to the artificial and delusional concept of race, has utterly destroyed her reason and turned her into a murderer. Brian Redfield is a skeptic who sees sex as a great joke (220) and race as a hoax. He wants to go to Brazil to escape American racism. However, we see his ideas only through the distortions of Irene's emotional turbulence, and, therefore, do not learn much about Brian's thoughts and plans. Brian is forced to confront his mistake of marrying a woman who is irrevocably chained to the concept of racial loyalty. He is closer to Clare's position, in that he is able to see through the sociopathological strictures of his society, however, he cannot free himself from their power over him. His vaunted freedom, pursued through a fantasy of escape to a utopia that he identifies with Brazil, is only an intellectual and attitudinal indulgence.

Passing is an effective and thorough attack on the institution of racialization. It was designed to strip away the reader's defense of race, whether tacit or unconscious, by graphically showing the destruction that results from the blind acceptance of racially based thought and behavior. Although Larsen's satire is so elusive as to have been identified as "irony" by Little, her satire has been noticed by other critics: Bernard Bell observes that *Passing* satirizes Clare Kendry's "color fantasies" (112) and McDowell states that "Not only does Larsen undercut Irene's credibility as narrator, but she also satirizes and parodies the manners and morals of the black middle class that Irene so faithfully represents" (xxv). By allowing her readers access to the psychological functioning of characters shaped by the race-dominated American culture, Larsen exposes them to the negative and destructive effects that the culture causes. Usually these effects are not realized because of the "buffers" that allow humans to live in their own illusions. The power of *Passing* is derived from its ability to bypass the reader's defenses by allowing the reader to identify with the characters. In the Gurdjieffian view, it is identification with external conditions that principally causes the difficulties of human life, for these identifications are the source of illusions. The illusion in *Passing* is the identification of Irene with her role as a "Negro." By being drawn uncomfortably close to Irene's damaged psyche, the reader comes face to face with the unpleasant consequences of a resolute belief in race.

Because Larsen presents the world through Irene's mind and emotions, the reader is forced to recognize the fundamental dialectic that comprises the novel, namely, that Irene feels she is "good" and Clare is "bad." Clare even goes along with this assignment of good and bad roles: "You are so good. . . . It's just that I haven't any proper morals or sense of duty, as you have, that makes me act as I do" (240). At the same time, the reader sees that Irene is not "good": It is she, not Clare, who is willing to do anything to get her own way. It is Irene who passes when she needs to; it is Irene who will accept an empty marriage—to live a lie—just to "keep her life fixed, certain" (268). It is ultimately Irene who decides to murder Clare: "The epiphanic realization results in Irene's desire to be rid of Clare in her and Brian's life and brings out an ugly, calculating side of her character" (ID 85). By identifying with Irene—a Negro woman—the reader is forced to participate in her mental deterioration, self-destruction, and, ultimately, to identify with the motivations of her *racially determined* crime. Presumably, this entirely negative experience forces the reader to become aware of the deleterious role of the institution of race in American life.

The chief departure from the structuring of *Quicksand* that Larsen made in coding *Passing* was to abandon an intertextual reference: Where *Quicksand* depended upon the hermeneutic investigation and incorporation of the intertextual frame of *Said the Fisherman* and "The Procurator of Judea," on the mimetic level *Passing* is a self-contained narrative that projects no direct references to outside texts. The Gurdjieffian subtext, however, is present throughout *Passing*. However, the subtext is not mediated by another intertext that would fulfill the role of *Said* and "The Procurator" in *Quicksand*, instead, *Beelzebub's Tales* is the major countertext to *Passing*. In other ways *Passing* has much in common with *Quicksand*, being no less dependent on such sylleptic devices as emblematic character names.

Also, despite Larsen's abandonment of a mimetic intertextuality, *Passing* is intimately involved with the process of reading, an activity that occupies much of the novel.

The narrative of *Passing* is set in motion by the arrival of a letter:

After her other ordinary and clearly directed letters the long envelope of thin Italian paper with its almost illegible scrawl seemed out of place and alien. And there was, too, something mysterious and slightly furtive about it. A thin sly thing which bore no return address to betray the sender. Not that she hadn't immediately known who the sender was. Some two years ago she had one very like it in outward appearance. Furtive, but yet in some peculiar, determined way a little flaunting. Purple ink. Foreign paper of extraordinary size." (171)

Passing performs an "attack on reading" by undermining the normative method of critical reading, and at the same time the novel is a course in the proper reading of both text and subtext. We see that Irene Redfield does not actually read the letter that she has received: For her, the primary attribute of the letter is its indecipherability. Tellingly, Irene's initial reaction is to begin to remember Clare Kendry. The nine paragraphs that follow the opening paragraph quoted above recapitulate the most outstanding characteristics that distinguish Clare Kendry. It is only in the tenth paragraph of the novel that "Irene brought her thoughts back to the present, to the letter from Clare Kendry that she still held unopened in her hand" (173). Only at this point does Irene open the letter and begin to read, yet she finds that she is unable to read the letter: "She ran through the letter, puzzling out, as best she could, the carelessly formed words or making instinctive guesses at them" (174).

The narrator informs us that Irene can read Clare Kendry's letter but only by a process of puzzling out the words: It is not necessary to treat a text as a puzzle unless the text is bewildering, as in the case of Clare's "carelessly formed words" (174). The text of *Passing* offers itself as a puzzle through a declaration that is intended to open into the subtext. Thus, the opening section concludes with a trenchant annunciation: "The words stood out from among the many paragraphs of other words, bringing with them a clear, sharp remembrance in which even now, after two years, humiliation, resentment, and rage were mingled" (174). In accord with Larsen's directions, we find that the text of *Passing* offers the reader carefully formed words that nevertheless stand out in their insistence to be reformulated as other words. A degree of confusion is, perhaps, introduced by the inadequacy of Larsen's analogy: The text of Clare's letter is of a different order of obscurity than the text of Larsen's novel. *Passing* is a text that gives the appearance of legibility, that is, of being accessible to the normative means of interpreting a novel; it even reads as though it were intended to be a reasonably good novel. Clare's letter, we presume, was meant to communicate clearly. However, her emotional pitch has intervened and she has produced a text of "carelessly formed words" (174). To read Clare's letter, Irene is forced into a mode of "puzzling out" the meaning of the text because she cannot read it. On the subject of the racial and psychological subtext, Davis states that *Passing* reads "like a novel operating in codes, whose meanings the author is thinking through in the process of writing" (308). That is, Davis assumes the author's "thinking through" has been successful, as witnessed by the production of the text, that the writing process is a type of code-breaking. This process is pictured in the text as the protagonist deciphering the peculiar letter that is nearly illegible. The reader only indirectly confronts Clare's letter as it is being successfully decoded by Irene, the reader within the narrative. It is obvious to both the reader of *Passing* and to Irene that the reading of Clare's letter presents a certain difficulty. Yet the reader of *Passing* has no reason to doubt Irene's capacity to negotiate the difficulties of this strange letter.

The reader's ease in unraveling the novel's seemingly facile and transparent text is a problem in attempting to decipher the codes to which Larsen alludes. By invoking the theme of an inner or hidden reality, Larsen reinforces the idea that the mimetic level of the narrative is but a simulacrum: The list of self-referential devices of concealment includes "mask(s)" (186, 250, 253, 266), "clue" (180), "secret joke" (240), "outward self" (257), and "outer shell" (268). The key that Larsen provides is that through her protagonist she imitates the process of reading an illegible text. However, there is no reason for the reader to suspect that the mimetic level of the text is but "the outer shell" of the text, and Larsen's architecture has proven inadequate.

Properly deciphered, the opening paragraph of the novel contains the names of Orage ("ordinary," "morning," "illegible," "extraordinary"); Ouspensky ("mysterious," "address," "sender," "sender," "ink"); and Gurdjieff ("furtive," "furtive," "purple"). The rationale for the curious duplications of "sender" and "furtive" becomes apparent once we notice that it is through similar repetitions that the authors using this coding system divulge the existence of their ciphers. Such wordplay is found throughout the text and constructs the mimetic level of the novel. Here it is only possible to provide a minimal sense of Larsen's procedures. In the fourth paragraph of the text she gives Orage's name in a revealing list of words: "for," "ragged," "raged," "for," "part," "manage," "edged," "poor," "farthermost," "corner," and "work" (172). The paragraph that follows gives a similar effect: "portion," "dollar," "wage," "errands," "floor," and "janitor." Halfway through the paragraph, Larsen gives Toomer's name: "She wanted *to* go *to* h*er* school's picnic, and she had *m*ade up h*er* *m*ind *to* wear a new dress." We also recognize that the concluding sentence of the paragraph provides Ouspensky's name: "d*ress*. So, in *spi*te of certa*in* unpleasantness and po*ss*ible danger, she had ta*k*en the mon*ey*" (172). The method of Larsen's construction is that the sound is the guide to the reading ear and eye; in this case the clue is remarkably compact. In the concluding sentence of section one, we find a repetitive pattern of syllables "ar" ("paragraphs," "clear," "sharp") and "or" ("words," "words") that run against "rage" and combine to form the name A. R. Orage.

Although the narrative of *Passing* has little in common with Hurston's *Their Eyes Were Watching God*, the design of their subtexts shares many common features. Both novels divide into three parts, although the twenty chapters of Hurston's text do not declare this feature of the novel's plan. The threefold division of *Their Eyes* is a narrative feature and is contingent on the marriage of the protagonist to three different men; this division corresponds to the Gurdjieffian idea of man's threefold composition—body, emotions, intellect.

In *Passing* Larsen has worked out a much more refined scheme: "Neat and symmetrical, *Passing* is composed of three sections, with four chapters each. The order and control which that tight organization suggests are a clever cover for the unconventional subplot in the novel's hiding places" (McDowell xxx). The plan of *Passing* can be related to the Gurdjieff work because in the full exposition of the system there were not three centers but five—mind, body, emotions, instinct, and sex. In the Oragean version taught by Jean Toomer and C. Daly King, the "three centers" locution became a matter of doctrine. The "three" centers were further divided by Gurdjieff: "each center was divided into three parts or *three stories* which, in their turn, were also divided into three" (ISM 56). Larsen's division of *Passing* into three sections with each section further divided into four sections approximates the structure of man's psychological composition.

Beginning with the novel's plan, Davis is able to relate the structure of *Passing* to its subject: "Divided into three parts, 'Encounter,' 'Re-encounter,' and 'Finale,' introducing the structure of replications and ritual returns, the novel begins in the narrative present but immediately proceeds with the retrieval of memory that is one of its main concerns" (309). This shift away from the present and into memory traps the reader within the obsessive consciousness of Irene Redfield, a device that forces the reader to evaluate the quality of the consciousness that perceives reality. Also, we soon realize that it is consciousness itself that is the subject of the novel—not Clare and her fate (ID 82), passing (Fuller 14), race (Bone 98), lesbian sexuality (Davis 325; McDowell xxxi), or marital stability (ITD xv). In *Passing* we do not receive information about these themes so much as information about how consciousness obtains information organized around these themes.

In the first part of *Passing* ("Encounter") the words "feeling" and "felt" occur twenty times. Larsen's interest in Irene's feelings suggests that the first section evokes the work of the emotional center. Much of the text consists of descriptions of Irene's emotional states: These are mostly "negative" states—fear, humiliation, resentment, rage, dread, isolation, annoyance, contempt, and embarrassment. At times we are told that Irene has no explanation for these states (e.g., 195). The word "think" occurs twice in "Encounter," when Clare announces herself to Irene (171) and when Irene thinks of never seeing Clare again (191). The parallelism of these two occasions of mindless "thought" signals the irrational quality of the "thinking" that they circumscribe. Although there is one reference to Irene's "reason" (201), it is not clear that it is actually her reason that has come into play. It is more likely another faculty (e.g., one of her subpersonalities) that appears to be reasonable because it does not concur with the "sense of dread" that she experiences prior to taking "thought." Irene's reason functions in a way that is surprisingly similar to her instincts: "The next morning, the day of her departure for New York, had brought a letter, which, at first glance, she had instinctively known came from Clare Kendry, though she couldn't remember ever having had a letter from her before" (207). There is also one mention of Irene's "mental calculation" (181). However, this hyperbolic designation seems to be ironic; Irene is merely calculating that it has been "all of twelve years since she . . . had laid eyes on Clare Kendry" (181). Thus, the first section of *Passing* is devoted to acts of feeling; the few instances of thinking are dubious, trivial, and undermined by irony and artifice.

In the first section Larsen also illustrates a central tenet of Gurdjieffian psychology, namely, that the essential characters of the genders are fixed: Women are emotional and men are intellectual.[6] When men work on themselves, they must do so emotionally. Conversely, the development of women must emphasize the intellectual, because they are already emotionally one sided. In the normal state of consciousness, what Gurdjieffians call the state of "sleep," the three divisions do not attend to their proper functions, but perform the tasks that should be assigned to other centers. In dividing *Passing* into three sections that correspond to the three "centers," Larsen reflects the Gurdjieffian principle that often "thoughts" (more properly "pseudothoughts") are felt, not thought, and "emotions" ("pseudoemotions") are thought, not felt. Thus, men often do not feel but rather think their emotions, whereas women asked to make a decision will not reason but will feel their responses. The interactions between the characters in *Passing* are rooted in the principle of the wrong work of centers. According to Gurdjieff, "The emotional center working for the thinking center brings unnecessary nervousness, feverishness, and hurry into situations where, on the contrary, calm judgment and deliberation are essential" (ISM 110). This is also a good description for the psychic deterioration of Irene Redfield. Brian Redfield can be summed up by Gurdjieff's statement that "The mind cannot understand shades of feeling. We shall see this clearly if we imagine one man reasoning about the emotions of another" (ISM 110). As we shall see below, this is exactly what Brian does in trying to understand the practice of passing. Finally, Gurdjieff states that "Moving center working for thinking center produces, for example, mechanical reading or mechanical listening, as when a man reads or listens to nothing but words and is utterly unconscious of what he is reading or hearing" (ISM 110).

In the second part, "Re-encounter," Irene proceeds with her feelings, until she begins to interact with her husband: "Brian, she was thinking, was extremely good-looking" (214). As soon as Brian makes an entrance, appearances of the word "think" increase; in a discussion of passing, Brian manages to use the word twice in one paragraph (216). Thus, the second section is a demonstration of the work of the intellectual center. As with Irene's name, Brian's name is an emblematic anagram. His name points to the conventional idea that the "brain" is the seat of the intellectual function; we have already seen that Brian is associated with the introduction of "thought" into the text, if only because he causes Irene to "think" about him.

On the following page, Irene thinks yet again and then plunges into her habitual mode of feeling things. It is as though the presence of Brian has summoned a group of "I"s (or subpersonalities) that are interested in thinking. However this thinking "I" is weaker than the dominant "I," which fears Brian's threat to take her to Brazil, and the passage rapidly gives way to her feelings of fear. Irene does not want to be free, we learn, but to be free of fear. Thinking about Clare's practice of passing, Irene concludes that "She [Clare] couldn't have had an entirely serene life" (233). The evident wordplay (Irene/serene), an eye rhyme, emphasizes Irene's overdetermined emotionality; the desire for peace of mind implied by the wordplay points to Irene's tendency to project her own feelings onto Clare. Irene Westover, the name by which Irene is identified by Clare, is an anagram for "I never rest." Clare's initial inquiry, "Pardon me but I think I know you" (179), is replete with double meaning and calls attention to itself. Not surrendering after Irene's initial rebuff, Clare ripostes: "Why, of course, I know you! . . . Don't tell me you're not Irene Westover. Or do they still call you 'Rene?'" (179). If we bring Gurdjieffian psychology to bear on this episode, it can be easily decoded. Larsen's innovation here is to have shifted not into the past but into Irene Redfield's psyche. McDowell confirms this observation in her introduction to the 1986 edition: "It is largely through her eyes, described appropriately as 'unseeing,' that most of the narrative's events are filtered, significantly, in retrospect and necessarily blurred. The classic unreliable narrator, Irene is confused and deluded about herself, her motivations, and much that she experiences. It is important, therefore, to see the duplicity at the heart of her story" (xxiv). We may think of Clare as a component of the narrator, but there is no single narrator, for there is not a single "I" that can legitimately call itself Irene Redfield. Thus, in being identified, Irene's mask has been penetrated. Through Clare (who Irene feels is able to read her mind [266]), we are alerted by the changed spelling that in her essence she is 'Rene, a woman who lacks an "I." Irene Redfield is 'Rene Westover's "false personality." In Gurdjieffian terminology, "Man has no individual I. But there are, instead, hundreds and thousands of separate small I's, very often entirely unknown to one another, never coming into contact, or, on the contrary, hostile to each other, mutually exclusive and incompatible" (ISM 59–60).

The name Irene is a pun. Pronounced in its original Greek, Irene is a homophone for "irony." Irene's name also suggests her emotionality, because it contains "ire." This reading suggests that Irene has an overdeveloped emotional center, which has thus resulted in the underdevelopment of her instinct and intellect.

Although Irene desires serenity, she is emotionality itself, an agitated personality whose nerves stretch progressively tighter as the narrative proceeds. Similarly, Clare is identified with one center, the body, the instinctive or moving center. In contrast with Irene's desire for serenity, Clare and Brian are restless souls aimed toward freedom and expanded selfhood. In a particularly important episode, Brian and Irene share one of the few intimate interactions that they are allowed in the novel. In answer to Irene's attempt to form some thoughts about passing—they are speaking somewhat abstractly about Clare—Brian ("brain") replies "Instinct of the race to survive and expand" (216). Not only does Brian think while trying to explain an emotional complex, he casts his answer in terms of instinct, the third center. This center is the symbolic provenance of Clare, who figures largely in the third section of the novel, "Finale," and who reifies the moving center, sexual function, and instinctive functions. Clare Kendry's name deciphers as "declare kin," which is reinforced by a passage that broaches the subject of passing: "Feeling of kinship, or something like that?" (237). Clare is "catlike" (172), and "without feeling at all" (172). Instinct is also associated with Clare when Irene receives a letter that "she had known instinctively came from Clare" (207). The tension between Irene and her perception of Clare as a rival for Brian's love illustrates the rivalry between the three centers.

On the hermeneutic level of the text, Larsen's goal is to reify the chaos that Gurdjieff addressed in his rhetorical question "In what chaos is the being we call man?" (*Views* 49). To do this, she dissects Irene's inner mechanisms as their disintegration becomes increasingly visible in "Re-Encounter," the second section of her novel. Irene, convinced that Brian has fallen in love with Clare, hosts a tea party and struggles to maintain a calm exterior. Her despairing reaction to the belief that her marriage has been threatened has drained her of energy: "She had no thoughts at all now, and all she felt was a great fatigue" (254). Irene watches Clare charm another guest, and her defensive frame of mind forces her to conclude that such wiles must have also worked with Brian.

The following paragraph is a concise summary of the theoretical idea of man's three centers. Larsen draws forth the rapid shift from one state to another, which is brought about "automatically" by the suggestion of one center to another, by naming all three centers in a brief passage: "Her *mental* and *physical* languor receded. Brian. What did it mean? How would it affect her and the boys? The Boys! She had a surge of relief. It ebbed, vanished. A *feeling* of absolute unimportance followed" (254; emphases added). In the one-sentence paragraph that follows, we learn that "Rage boiled up in her." Thus we see Irene rapidly move from fatigue to rage, as we witness that all of her inner turmoil is not only without basis in reality but accomplished without rational thought. Her feelings dominate her perceptions, and they are not consistent or controllable. At the same time, we are given an impression of the division of Irene into mutually supporting and opposing functions. Here the languor Irene experiences is both mental and physical; however, her fatigue gives way when the emotional center shifts her to rage, and she strikes out, breaking a cup. Moreover, we see that Irene's states are illusions: One minute she is enervated; in the next minute she is fierce with rage and able to strike out forcefully.

In the final analysis, *Passing* proves to be a novel about Irene's emotions; we can diagnose the force that drives her emotions as a race complex. In Gurdjieffian psychological terms, Irene's problems stem from her willingness to identify with outside determinations of her identity; such a diagnosis is as close as the Method comes to treating the subject of race. Were she able to separate her racial role from her internal functioning, Irene would be able to free herself from her emotional fixations. In *Passing*, the psychological fragmentation that Irene represents is given its most comprehensive development on the symbolic level. Clare's letter is torn up by Irene at the end of the first part "with an unusual methodicalness" (208). Irene then gathers up the "tiny ragged squares" and drops them over a railing. A similar fragmentation occurs when Irene drops a cup of tea at a party. Zulena, the maid, gathers up the white fragments. The broken cup foreshadows Clare's climactic destruction: She is shown standing at the window from which she will presently plunge "as if the whole structure of her life were not lying in fragments before her" (271). It is apparent that Irene is undergoing some sort of mental crisis at the time; by describing Irene's crisis during the cup-breaking incident rather than at any other place, the structure of the text more clearly signals the importance of the shifting and successive appearances of Irene's different "I"s. Little accurately notes that because Irene is projecting her feelings onto Clare, it is not Clare's life that is in fragments but Irene's (180). Because of what Gurdjieff calls "buffers," Irene cannot see that it is her own life that is fragmented.

Larsen has other means for presenting the Gurdjieffian material besides embodying concepts in the characters' thoughts and actions and through symbols and wordplay. She works the material into the fabric through syllepsis, so that key Gurdjeffian words appear in the novel in unremarkable usages. In addition to "thinking," "feeling," and "instinct," these terms include "fragments," "the book," "the method," "mask," and "outward self."

Apart from the emblematic names are the names that declare the artificiality of the narrative's mimesis. These names seek to undermine the language of the text to make the reader aware of the hermeneutic subtext and its Gurdjieffian metalanguage. John Bellew's name may be read as "join—be well," a derisively ironic name attached to Clare's bigoted husband, who is unaware that he is married to a black woman. Similarly, Hugh Wentworth may be read as "work wants you." Both of these names are comparable to Schuyler's John Kitchen, "join in it."[7]

Another category of divulgent names are those that are an attack on the reading of the novel. Both titles of Larsen's novels belong to this category in that "quicksand" and "passing" signify what Davis calls the dependency of both texts on "silence, concealment, and secrecy" (324). However, it is the Gurdjieffian aspect of the text that is not truly silent, half concealed, and unwillingly secret. Larsen chooses every opportunity to announce the "inward" and esoteric nature of her text: With "unseeing eyes" (177–78; 250) the reader follows Irene as she searches for "the drawing book" (175)—"drawing" is an anagram for "inward." Likewise she confronts the reader with catalogs of meaningful sounds (183, 189, 194, 196, 201, 251); the "attack on reading" is pursued not only through calling attention to the unseen and the unrecognized, but also to what remains consciously unheard.

One potentially disruptive name is that of Irene's maid, who intervenes between Irene and an importunate Clare Kendry. Clare telephones repeatedly, and the maid meets with Irene's response, "Not in, Liza, take the message" (193). The temptation is to read Liza's name as a distinction of class (Fuller 19). However, the action of lying is described in the text, which establishes the homophonic equivalence of "Liza" and "lies." Having discovered that one maid, Liza, lies, it is not difficult to discover that the names of the other maids carry an equal significance. When Zulena and Sadie are reversed they read "aneluz" and "eidas," and instruct the reader to "analyze ideas." Because *Passing* presents Gurdjieffian ideas in a tightly organized scheme of thematic chapters, the invitation to "analyze ideas" indicates that Larsen's ultimate purpose was to construct a "legominism," or a text in which esoteric teachings have been preserved.

In keeping with Larsen's frequent reversal of names and roles (Davis 327), Gurdjieff himself makes a passing appearance as a woman, Gertrude Martin. In *Passing* we are provided with a more straightforward indication of Gurdjieff's presence: Gertrude Martin is to be read as "Mr. G" and "gert" represents the homophone "gurd." Additionally, there is a brief and indistinct allusion to Gurdjieff's famous eyes in Gertrude Martin's "staring" and "eyelids" (194). Gertrude Martin shares Mrs. Hayes-Rore's (Gurdjieff's) habits of poor dress and slovenly grooming: "Her overtrimmed georgette crepe dress was too short and showed an appalling amount of leg, stout legs in sleazy stockings of a vivid rose-beige shade. Her plump hands were newly and not too completely manicured—for the occasion, probably" (196). As more evidence, Larsen includes the word "georgette" to emphasizes the identification of George Ivanovich Gurdjieff.

A further, direct indication that we are to find Gurdjieff secreted behind this persona is Clare's assertion that she found Gertrude Martin "in the book" (196), a seemingly commonplace reference to the telephone book that also reads sylleptically as the name given to *Beelzebub's Tales*. In describing the arrival of *Beelzebub's Tales* in New York in 1925 and its adoption by Orage's groups, James Webb states that "copies of what became known simply as THE BOOK [sic] were highly prized, and a complete copy was a rarity to be treasured. . . . References to THE BOOK [sic] became common in some intellectual circles as dark hints about the Method" (311).

A more comprehensive allusion is located in a passage that describes Irene's concern with purchasing a present, a particular drawing book that her son Ted wanted. Significantly, one son, Junior, had wanted a "mechanical airplane," which she had acquired "without too much trouble" (175); this is an understated indictment of Irene's machinelike personality. Irene's quest for Ted's drawing book caused her to travel all over town in the heat. She then suffered heat prostration, which, in turn, required that she pass as a white woman to visit the tea room atop the Drayton Hotel. There, the circumstances initiated by her search for Ted's drawing book, "for which Ted had so gravely and insistently given her precise direction" (175), result in her initial reencounter with Clare. Larsen's description of Irene's search for Ted's book (The Book) delivers a strong intimation that the episode may be read as a parable:

Without too much trouble she had got the *mechanical* airplane for Junior. But the drawing book, for which *Ted had so gravely and consistently given her precise directions*, had sent her in and out of *five* shops without success.

It was while she was on her way to a *sixth* place that right before her smarting eyes a *man* toppled over and became an inert crumpled heap on the scorching cement. About the lifeless figure a little crowd gathered. *Was the man dead or only faint* someone asked her. But Irene didn't know and didn't try to discover. She edged her way out of the increasing crowd, feeling disagreeably damp and sticky and soiled from contact with so many bodies. (175; emphases added)

The passage above contains important work ideas related to the nature of man. Man is asleep, but can awaken. Man number six embodies this most conscious form of man. Larsen alludes to these concepts in the passage quoted above. The book for which Irene searches gives "precise directions" for evolving to the "sixth place" on the scheme of man's possible evolution. We are shown that Irene is not interested in man's condition, for she cannot tell whether the fallen man is dead or only faint. When she herself begins to approach an unconscious state, she grows no more aware of the importance of the unanswered question. However, faced with the task of evolving beyond her mechanical nature, Irene only wants to withdraw to a place of "immediate safety": " 'I guess,' she told her Samaritan, 'it's tea I need. On a roof somewhere' " (175). In the safety of a taxi, Irene has forgotten that she has not found Ted's book, and she turns her attention to repairing her "false personality": "Reviving under the warm breeze stirred up by the moving cab, Irene made some small attempts to repair the damage that the heat and crowds had done to her appearance" (175).

Passing can be viewed as a constructive reworking of the "tragic mulatto" theme, because "parody need not include humorous effect or ridicule" (Palmeri 20). Larsen subverts the tacit racialism of this tradition by making her points dialogically. By opposing characters with differing views, Larsen strips away the illusion of authority from each posture. Additionally, *Passing* exposes the absurdities inherent in the culture of American racialism through caricature and the narrator's mocking tone and ironic selection of details. The novel depicts a catalog of racialist absurdities. Clare Kendry successfully manages to pass for white, yet endangers her situation through a compulsion to socialize with African-Americans. Claude Jones has chosen to deal with his blackness by becoming a black Jew; his strategy contrasts with both Clare's passing and Irene's refusal to pass. Brian Redfield is paired with Irene: He wants to escape to the racelessness that he imagines exists in Brazil; Irene, however, rejects his plan to emigrate and will not give up her identity as a Negro, although she passes for white when it is convenient. Clare, too, has a foil, and is paired with Gertrude Martin, a Negro who is fair enough to pass and is married to a white man who is aware that Gertrude is a black.

Larsen's satirical "attack on race" is aimed at establishing the meaninglessness of Irene's question about "what race is" (216). This question is made explicit in a dialogue between the Redfields, whose tense relationship—the very fabric of Larsen's satire—is being destroyed by Brian's wish to relocate his family to a multiracial Brazil and Irene's determination to cling to the life she knows in a race-obsessed New York. Brian Redfield's Brazil hovers over Irene's life as a threat to her "identity"—the nearly tangible extinction of everything that she feels is her essence—although she does not use that term. As the rekindled relationship between Irene and Clare develops, Irene increasingly associates Clare with the threat of losing Brian to Brazil. Brazil exists within the narrative as both a symbolic and an actualized racial utopia. The image of Brazil that sustains Brian's dream of an escape from racialism reifies Toomer's idea of a "new race." Little's point that "By the time she wrote *Passing* in 1929, Brazil symbolized a deflated and ironic hope for an alternative community that was more a romantic dream than a reality" (174) helps to clarify Larsen's use of Brazil. Again, *Passing* describes the course of devolution. Although Brian has the insight to see through the fiction of race, his means for a remedy are inadequate. His wish to escape to a place where problems have already been solved violates the facts of the human condition, for "We live in a world subject to forty-eight orders of laws, that is to say, very far from the will of the absolute and in a very remote and dark corner of the universe" (ISM 81). Thus, Brazil is both an ironic version of Toomer's "new race" and a reminder that only a few escape the forces that determine destiny.

Despite its ironic meaning, Brazil is firmly established in the background of the action in *Passing*. There it haunts Irene as an alternative to a racially divided society, exactly as though Brian's utopia without racial problems can be visited. Because Brazil inhabits the text as an actualized antiworld, the satire in *Passing* delicately but effectively strips away the illusions of modern American life by showing its pervasive and unsuspected spiritual emptiness. Irene's inability to free herself of her psychological dependency on race—virtually an addiction to racially oriented thought—to establish a "real" identity finally leads to a paranoid condition that causes her to kill Clare Kendry.

The theme of "mental freedom" is much more important to the meaning of *Passing*. This fundamental Gurdjieffian concept answers Irene's questions of "what race is," not Brian's yearning for Brazil. In the Gurdjieffian conception of man's possibilities, the utopian state is only reached through universally applied mental freedom. The word "free" occurs many times in *Passing* (217, 227, 246, 260, 263, 268, 271). In the novel's final pages, Dave Freeland, more a name than a character, appears as a voice that Irene recognizes (272), then as the announcer of Irene's approach to Clare's mutilated body (273), and finally Freeland places Irene beside Clare in the moment before Clare's fatal fall (274). What Larsen points to is that the lack of freedom portrayed in *Passing* is *mental freedom*, the product of "identification." If Irene, Brian, Clare, and Jack Bellew were free of their identifications with socially prescribed roles—wife, woman, man, white man, mother, Negro, father, husband—then they could, presumably, live fulfilling lives, harmoniously discovering new horizons of love, compassion, and service.

5 George Schuyler
New Races and New Worlds

There is a notable disparity among the literary careers of the Harlem group. Wallace Thurman and Rudolph Fisher died in 1934. Thurman had published two novels and collaborated on another novel and a play; he also authored some unpublished plays and two screenplays. Fisher published two novels and more than a dozen short stories, had one play produced, and wrote on medical topics. Like Jean Toomer, after some initial success, Nella Larsen found herself without an audience for her work, although she continued to write for several years. Whereas Toomer preserved his unpublished manuscripts, Larsen destroyed her unpublished novels, and subsequently pursued a long career in nursing. Although Zora Neale Hurston published four novels, a collection of folklore, a travel book, and an autobiography, she gradually fell into obscurity and published her final novel, *Seraph on the Suwanee*, in 1948. At the end of her life, she was still writing a historical work, "Herod the Great." In contrast, George S. Schuyler (1895–1977) had a long career as a successful writer and was considered the premiere black journalist and essayist of the first half of the twentieth century. He was a prolific writer who found a market for nearly everything that he produced, including his biography, *Black and Conservative* published in 1966. Although Avon contracted for Schuyler's voluminous *The Negro in America*, it was never published (Talalay 224–25).

Schuyler stands apart from the Harlem group as being the most like Gurdjieff. Gurdjieff was not an objectionable person; his habit was to intentionally generate situations that provided people the "impressions" that they required after he had "objectively" assessed their characters.[1] Of course, the victims of these often psychologically unpleasant or socially embarrassing situations did not perceive the meaning of what was transpiring, nor were they aware at the time that Gurdjieff was manipulating them (Wilson *War* 68–70). Often the results of these situations were not only objectionable but, from a certain perspective, comic. Because of the sense of power and mastery over other people that resulted from these outrageous events, there was a temptation for those involved in the Gurdjieff work to imitate their teacher's outward behavior. Jean Toomer, who knew Gurdjieff better than the members of the Harlem group, at times adopted the persona of a peasant that Gurdjieff used to offend pretentious people, speaking broken English, using poor table manners, and expressing himself through vulgar language (Larson ID 144).

Nevertheless, it was Schuyler who excelled at Gurdjieffian mimicry, although he adopted the Beelzebub persona that Gurdjieff began to use in 1925. For example, when Gurdjieff visited America in 1930, he sent ahead a transatlantic radiogram that he signed "Ambassador from Hell" (Moore 235). Hill and Rasmussen perhaps describe Schuyler's Gurdjieffian persona when they state that "there was a Rabelaisian coarseness in Schuyler's temperament that along with his general misanthropy not only fit his rebellious character but also came to characterize his literary persona" (263).

In 1931 Schuyler traveled to Liberia to investigate the ongoing practice of slave labor. His findings were published in a series of articles in the *New York Evening Post*. The six-part series also ran in the *Washington Post*, the *Philadelphia Ledger*, and several other prominent newspapers (BE "Afterword" 262). The material gathered for the series was further put to use, when George Putnam rushed Schuyler's novel *Slaves Today: A Story of Liberia* (1931) into print to capitalize on the interest raised by Schuyler's disturbing series of articles. Possibly the most revealing aspect of *Slaves Today* is what it suggests about the nature of the texts produced by the Harlem group. Because it was Schuyler's first novel, it parallels the first novels by Thurman (*The Blacker the Berry* 1929), Fisher (*The Walls of Jericho* 1928), and Larsen (*Quicksand* 1928), all of which illustrate a single, important Gurdjieffian concept. For example, Fisher's *The Walls of Jericho* extends one of his short stories that was based on Gurdjieff's parable of the carriage, horse, and driver in relation to their master. Similarly, *Slaves Today* is based on another of Gurdjieff's teaching stories: "No one can escape from prison without the help of those *who have escaped before*. Only they can say in what way escape is possible or can send tools, files, or whatever may be necessary. But *one* prisoner alone cannot find these people or get into touch with them. An organization is necessary. Nothing can be achieved without an organization" (ISM 30).

Slaves Today has a documentary character that served Schuyler's avowed purpose to "arouse enlightened world opinion against this brutalizing of the native population in a Negro republic" in order that "the conscience of civilized people will stop similar atrocities in native lands ruled by proud white nations that boast of their superior culture" (quoted in Talalay 72–73). Perhaps more than any other text discussed in this study, the novel is an "attack on race"; there is little in the text to divert the reader from the theme of the exploitation of blacks by other blacks. Also, the novel viciously deconstructs the romantic depiction of Africa that was the stock in trade of the Garvey movement (Talalay 72). Working close to his journalistic account of Liberian slavery, the plot of *Slaves Today* is based on actual experiences of actual people. Schuyler's text presents a clear portrait of the society that confronted him in Liberia, and he recorded in detail its economy, politics, international relations, religion, tribal culture, health conditions, and environment. Bernard Bell calls the novel "a sober unmasking of the romance of black power in

Africa" (*Afro-American* 145), underscoring the documentary nature of the text by noting the omniscient author-narrator's clarity about "the class nature of the tyranny he sees in Liberia" (144).

Irony is infused into the text by the reversal of the historical situation that engenders the action. Liberia is ruled by the descendants of American slaves who have enslaved the aboriginal population. The narrative immerses the reader in the sordid events that transpire on every level of Liberian society and exposes the illusory nature of the desires that control the lives of the rulers and the ruled. The novel opens and closes with a view of the executive mansion on the principal thoroughfare of Monrovia and concludes with the murder of David Jackson, the director of public works. Between these scenes, we are mainly concerned with the story of Zo, Jackson's killer, a man kidnapped and transported to the island of Fernando Po. There he has had to work for insignificant wages with no chance of returning to the mainland. The novel tells of Zo's attempts to escape from the island. Because Zo is inexperienced, trusting, and overconfident, he encounters many obstacles in his quest for freedom. In this aspect of the text, it resembles a Sufi teaching story, such as Pickthall's *Said the Fisherman* that was discussed in connection with Larsen's *Quicksand*. However, unlike Pickthall's text, the narrative of Zo is too one-dimensional to achieve a similar effect.

Although *Slaves Today* was effective in attracting attention to the abuse of power in Liberia and to the larger issue of the European colonization of the African continent, it is not successful as an esoteric text. One characteristic of texts such as *Infants, Passing,* and *The Conjure-Man Dies* is that they provide enough of an "attack on reading" that even when the reader remains unaware of the subtext, a question is raised as to why certain aspects of the text have been effected. Perhaps the best example of a text that produces this result is Hurston's *Dust Tracks on a Road,* which Robert E. Hemenway pronounces "one of the most peculiar autobiographies in Afro-American literary history" ("Introduction" ix). He states that the text "adds considerably to the mystery surrounding Zora Neale Hurston" and that in it "the paradoxes abound" ("Introduction" ix). The problem with *Slaves Today* is that it provides no such disturbances. Although the text contains the same use of Gurdjieffian terminology, anagrams, and the names of Orage, Gurdjieff, Toomer, and Ouspensky sounded out on nearly every page, there is nothing that offers the reader entry into the subtext. The entirety of the "attack on reading" is delivered early in the text: We are told of a government official that "His state papers were masterpieces because they could be interpreted in many ways, but they seldom contained anything definite" (12). The one episode that comes close to alerting the reader is Zo's seduction by Juan and Marie. Juan brings the other two together so that Zo can be robbed. He pretends to be asleep but occasionally he opens one eye, although Zo misses this: Here "one eye" (188) is a pun on the Gurdjieffian concept "one 'I.'" Marie is even less suggestive; she is described as "light yellow in color" and she has "large black eyes" (183)—two attributes associated with Gurdjieff. However, unlike Larsen's Mrs. Hayes-Rore, there is no mystery associated with Marie to suggest that there is more to the character than is evident.

Published in the same year as *Slaves Today*, *Black No More: Being an Account of the Strange and Wonderful Workings of Science in the Land of the Free, A.D. 1933–1940* (1931) is a novel that stands in strong contrast to the ironic, sober Liberian story. A much stronger literary performance that reflects Schuyler's masterful comic gift, *Black No More* combines irreverent satire and science fiction in one of the most hilarious send-ups of America's culture of racism ever written. V. F. Calverton, editor of the socialist journal *The Modern Quarterly* and *An Anthology of American Negro Literature* (1929), suggested to Schuyler that he write a satire about race in America. Calverton also played an important role in the publication of the novel by the Macaulay Company (Hoyrd 6).

Like *Slaves Today*, *Black No More* has a documentary aspect to it. The novel was inspired by a report in an October 24, 1929, *New York Times* article, "Biologist Asserts He Can Remold Man." In the unsigned article, the *Times* reported the claims of Dr. Yusaburo Noguchi, a Japanese biologist. According to Noguchi, after fifteen years of experimentation he had developed a technique for changing the racial characteristics of human beings, even down to the pigment colorings. With the financial support of the Japanese government, Noguchi had conducted an intensive field investigation in Brazil, where he had been studying jungle peoples. By electrical nutrition and glandular control, Noguchi said he believed he could change an Indian to a darker color with the physical characteristics of a Negro or mold a Japanese to have the same appearance as a Caucasian (Hoyrd 1–2). The strange appearance and disappearance of Dr. Noguchi seemed to have been tailor-made for Schuyler's purposes. Borrowing the outlandish terminology in the article, Schuyler relocated his scientist to Harlem and had him launch a science-fiction attack on race that had a far greater effect on American society than had the real Dr. Noguchi.

Like *Slaves Today*, *Black No More* is primarily designed to attack racialism. Schuyler invested his artistry in writing an entertaining story rather than in creating an elaborate "legominism," a subtext intended to preserve and spread Gurdjieff's esoteric teachings. In *Black No More*, Schuyler forgoes the inclusion of much of the "objective" material that occupied Toomer, who attempted to incorporate all of Gurdjieff's system into his texts. Schuyler's main concern is race, in the sense of categorization by color. He also presents the superman theme, but without being heavy-handed. On the literal level of his novel, Schuyler's targets are surprisingly broad: His satire not only attacks racism and racial thought in general, he ridicules the racist ideology of the era's pseudoscientists (Hoyrd 69). Schuyler also takes deliberate aim at religion, science, politics, certain aspects of black culture, and capitalism, albeit not persuasively (Bell *Afro-American* 144). Although Schuyler treats the esoteric concept of a new American race in *Black No More*, he deemphasizes the esoteric aspect of this concept and ignores the question of evolved consciousness. In keeping with his attack upon racist science, he gives his treatment of race an unconventionally biological foundation.

The pseudoscientific discourse of eugenics and racist anthropology, medicine, sociology, and psychology constructs the background of the Menippean narrative of *Black No More*. Schuyler's satire opposes Dr. Buggerie's racist pseudoscience with Dr. Crookman's futuristic science (Hoyrd 65). Informing the science of Schuyler's futuristic biology ("electrical nutrition and glandular control") is the esoteric myth of Blavatsky's sixth root-race that Jean Toomer brought to Harlem. Toomer welded Blavatsky's evolutionary scheme to Gurdjieff's idea of "reciprocal maintenance," namely, that because lower octaves feed higher octaves, if man did not evolve, he would cease to matter to the cosmos. Thus, the superman theme became important in the texts of the Harlem group because of its relationship to the racial themes—both contemporary and esoteric—that occupied the attention of Toomer and his followers.

The idea of a new race achieved its widest circulation by a member of the Harlem group in Schuyler's *Black No More*. The novel tells a story in which African-Americans are transformed into whites by a process invented by an obscure black scientist, Dr. Junius Crookman. Crookman's black clients so clamor for the metamorphosing treatments that he must operate his machine night and day. Because he has them pay a modest amount for the treatment, he becomes enormously wealthy. The novel's protagonist, Max Fisher, the first subject transformed by Crookman, is a streetwise confidence man who also becomes wealthy. Fisher uses his new racial identity to organize white hate groups, which he then manipulates to his economic and romantic advantage. At the ironic conclusion of Schuyler's satire, the population of America is not white, as might be expected. Realizing that genetics will determine the race of the next generation, Dr. Crookman perpetrates a ruse that causes the entire population to artificially darken itself, so that everyone in America looks like an African-American. Whatever their underlying color, the new Americans are in the end both mentally and biologically raceless. Helen Givens, a former racist, is the wife of Matthew Fisher. After delivering a black baby and discovering that she has remote Negro ancestry, Helen declares, "'To hell with society!' Compared to what she possessed, thought Helen, all talk of race and color was damned foolishness" (193).

In Schuyler's narrative, futuristic, fictional science is victorious over pseudoscience. Taking the subtext into account, however, we can read the narrative as a contest between esoteric science and pseudoscience that takes place in historical time. Toomer taught his group to use the octave (the Law of Eight) and the "neutralizer" (the Law of Three) to analyze and understand their place on the scale of world history. (For example, Tolson's poem "Libretto for the Republic of Liberia" presents the time span of the modern period of history as one octave.) Because the group believed that they possessed the means to become supermen and thus could interpret the laws of history, they set out to manipulate society to conform to their esoteric aims. To do this they adopted "masks," such as the initial phase of Schuyler's Marxism and his later conservatism. Positioned behind their masks, the Harlem group published popular novels seeded with ideas that they wanted to circulate in society.

Black No More demonstrates a unique relationship to other Gurdjieffian texts. In contrast to *Beelzebub's Tales,* which was intentionally written to be impenetrable and therefore has achieved only a tiny readership, or Toomer's novels, which were artistic failures, *Black No More* is an example of overwhelming literary success. But when we look beyond the differences in style to method, an unexpected likeness emerges. Orage noted that, in *Beelzebub's Tales,* Gurdjieff created parables: "In fact many of the chapters are cartoons in the religious sense. A cartoon here is a picture of an aspect of a man's life on this planet, exaggerated in a certain way in order to draw attention to it, to make one ponder as so arrive at the truth. This is a satire on the various religious cults, sects, rituals, mysteries, systems of breathing, fasting, and so on" (Nott *Teachings* 129). Schuyler also used cartoons in *Black No More,* and we see a similarly exaggerated treatment of anthropology, lynching, the Ku Klux Klan, national politics, black urban culture, the NAACP, the Garvey movement, and romantic love. *Beelzebub's Tales* and *Black No More* also share a genre: Both are Menippean satires characterized by an extraordinary freedom of plot and philosophical invention, exaggerated situations, slum naturalism, moral-psychological experimentation, scandal scenes, mesalliances, inserted genres, and presentations of current and topical issues (Hoyrd 10–11). Because it is a Menippean satire, *Black No More* cannot usefully be described as a satire of "simple effects" (Bell *Afro-American* 138).

In contrast to Toomer's failed attempts at writing Gurdjieffian satires, *Black No More* has remained in print for sixty years, and although a classic of African-American literature, it is still enjoyed as a popular book. This success is partly due to the novel's unfaltering comic attacks on excesses and taboos that still inhabit American society. However, the novel is neither simplistic nor reductive and it equally attacks blacks and whites for their attitudes toward race. Schuyler's message is that salvation for America, and perhaps even for the world, will arise if the populations become "mulatto-minded" (quoted in Singh *Novels* 61). Schuyler's views on race were also aired in newspaper columns, where he suggested that massive miscegenation is the only solution to America's race problem (Singh *Novels* 145). Given the unacceptability of miscegenation to both races, it would seem that *Black No More* is popular in spite of the radical program of social engineering that it advocates.

Ironically, *Black No More* is more often read as a condemnation of white racism or of black intraracial elitism than as a condemnation of the concept of racialism. What can be extracted from the text is further complicated by Schuyler's discourse: In *Black No More* "what Schuyler espouses is not always readily distinguished from what he condemns" (Talalay 95). Given the shift in values that has shaped thought about race since the wider acceptance of black nationalist militancy by African-American intellectuals after the death of Martin Luther King, it is doubtful that the contemporary reader can any longer successfully extract Schuyler's message about race from the literal level of the novel. For example, in the introduction to the 1971 edition of *Black No More*, Charles R. Larson has so misconstrued Schuyler's intention to write "a satire on Colorphobia" that he states that "the thesis of Schuyler's book appears to be that the New Negro will be white or nothing at all" (BNM 10). Larson laments that Schuyler's "chromatic emancipation" is "a plea for assimilation, for mediocrity, for reduplication, for faith in the (white) American dream" (BNM 12).

If we consider how *Black No More* fits the requirements for "objective" literature, we see that Schuyler did not depict a new race endowed with a higher level of consciousness. Capitalizing on the "Negro-art hokum" that he sardonically disparaged in his 1926 essay, Schuyler set his novel in Harlem and peopled it with customary Harlem types. In that way he assured himself an audience, for the Negro fad had not quite died in 1931. Indeed, the novel was a critical success, and even W. E. B. Du Bois, the subject of some of Schuyler's lampooning, was broadminded enough to accord it a good review. The esoteric aspects of *Black No More* come more sharply into view when it is compared to Edward Bulwer-Lytton's novel *Vril: The Power of the Coming Race* (1871), the source of Blavatsky's ideas on race. *Vril* is an dystopian novel, a quest narrative, a tale of science fiction, a satire on liberalism, and an allegory illustrating man's limitations. The novel's broad satire ridicules democracy, attacks socialism, condemns women's equality, and derides Darwinism. The novel's thesis is that should we ever achieve a material paradise, our competitive nature would prevent us from long enjoying a perfected polity (Campbell 126). Radically departing from the complacency of Bulwer-Lytton's mid-Victorian materialism, the implication of Blavatsky's *The Secret Doctrine* is that the present form of man is about to end; in contrast with Bulwer-Lytton's embrace of the status quo, her text looks prophetically toward the coming of the race of new men.

Rather than dwelling on the coming race, in *Black No More* Schuyler marked the transition from the dominance of one racial phase (racially divided mass man) to a modern racial phase (universal or synthetic man). In other words, Schuyler subordinated the esoteric content of his novel to the comic content and conventional form of his Menippean satire. Schuyler reached a large audience with his fiction because he moved away from direct Gurdjieffian influence and wrote works that looked conventional. Schuyler demonstrated a marked literary ambition; he appears to have been a modernist experimenter who could also tell a story compellingly. There are, of course, "objective" aspects to *Slaves Today* and *Black No More*, but these nearly undetectable elements were not allowed to interfere with the easy absorption of his narratives.

Schuyler's "chromatic democracy" (64), the utopian state that the American civilization has reached after the races are technologically homogenized by Black-No-More, Inc., demonstrates the absurdity of racially oriented thought. This is an important point, for Schuyler departed radically from the assimilationism of the New Negro theorists (Du Bois and Locke), who advocated the whitening of the black man, and the (black) racial chauvinism of Langston Hughes and Marcus Garvey. Like Toomer, Schuyler altogether rejected racial categorization. His satire is an attempt to destroy contemporary attitudes and is equally aimed at both races. The solution to social problems that Schuyler offers is the same portrayed in Hurston's novel *Moses*—that each individual must free himself from the external manipulation of social and political institutions. (At this point, Gurdjieff's philosophy resembles existentialism, and the advocacy of the freedom of the individual that emerges in *Black No More* may anticipate the existentialism of Ralph Ellison's *Invisible Man*.) The result of this project would be the impossibility of racialist thought. The difference between the approaches of Schuyler and Hurston is that Schuyler resolves the extinction of racialism at the collective level, whereas Hurston develops this activity at the individual level: Schuyler is able to depict a utopia at the conclusion of his novel; Hurston's *Moses* cannot achieve "chromatic democracy" and must settle for the possibility of utopia once each individual's consciousness has been raised to the requisite degree.

Schuyler makes his points through two-edged lampoons that strip away pretenses through satiric reduction. On one hand he attacks the civil rights activists (Du Bois and the NAACP), and on the other he mounts even-handed attacks on both white and black supremacist organizations. Schuyler's satire develops the thesis that African-American organizations do not really want civil rights for African-Americans, for that would end a very profitable business. Much of the comedy in *Black No More* is derived from Schuyler's exposure of the supposed behind-the-scenes activities of racially oriented organizations: To destroy Dr. Crookman's conversion of African-Americans into whites, African-American organizations cynically conspire with white hate groups to legislate against Crookman's Black-No-More, Inc. Schuyler also provided caricatures of the most important contemporary race leaders, W. E. B. Du Bois and Marcus Garvey. His unflattering portraits of these figures revealed them to be self-serving, insincere, and pretentious. Schuyler was capable of creating masterfully comic scenes, for instance, where he has the leaders of the Knights of Nordica lynched by their own followers because they have disguised themselves as blacks. The comic acuity of Schuyler's satire, his ability to moderate the direct influence of *Beelzebub's Tales*, and the equally poisonous tendency to write "objectively" by closely imitating Gurdjieff, provided him a large measure of success as a satirist.

Despite Schuyler's stylistic distance from Gurdjieff, *Black No More* was very much influenced by *Beelzebub's Tales* insofar as he followed the "objective" strategy of setting out to devastate ordinary ideas and attitudes about race. For followers of Gurdjieff there was no correct opinion concerning race, because for them race did not exist; only "real" ideas and "exact language" made up the esoteric system, and race did not belong in those categories. Throughout *Beelzebub's Tales*, Gurdjieff shows that conventional institutions are illusions: He uses a vocabulary that emphasizes the anti-institutional approach, for example, calling learned discourse "wiseacring" and art and literature "bon ton," "word prostitution," and "nullities." Similarly, by depicting race as a confidence game or "con" (as in KON, the abbreviation for Knights of Nordica), Schuyler was trying to cause his readers to realize that race was only useful to institutions that profited from it. In both *Black No More* and *Beelzebub's Tales*, the exposure of confidence trickery is fundamental. In *Black No More* this is inescapable: Max Disher is introduced into the narrative as a con man; after he becomes white, he immediately takes over the KON. Santop Licorice, Schuyler's caricature of Marcus Garvey—the would-be black emperor—was named after the black baseball star Louis Santop, who was renowned for calling home runs in the manner of Babe Ruth—in other words, a "ballyhoo" figure (Hill 275). Likewise, Du Bois's tendency toward conspiracy is pointed out by the exaggerated name that Schuyler gave him—Dr. Shakespeare Agamemnon Beard (Agamemnon's duplicity was the cause of the wrath of Achilles).

Unlike *Beelzebub's Tales*, Schuyler's focus is narrowed to the subject of American racism. He reduces race to an absurdity—much in the way that Gurdjieff deals with other human institutions—by showing that race is used by the ruling-class manipulators for their own profit. Schuyler wanted to bring his readers to a state of "non-identification," in this case with race (Nott *Teachings* 144).

Schuyler largely subordinates allegory in *Black No More*, employing instead an adaptation of Gurdjieff's "verbal cabbala" (Waldberg 22) that is visible throughout the entire text. There are eight occurrences of the letter g in the first paragraph, a gesture toward Gurdjieff and the Law of Eight. The second paragraph sounds out Ouspensky's name (*"As . . . paid . . . rent . . . struck . . . disgustedly"*; 17), and the novel ceaselessly continues to sound out the names of prominent Gurdjieffians. The numbers three and eight (or seven) also recur many times in the text (e.g., "three-room apartment" [17], "Three Days" [25], "trio" [34], "eight young women" [210], "seven years" [146], "1789 pages" [152]).

One of the more obvious eruptions of Schuyler's verbal cabbala concerns Max Disher. The protagonist of *Black No More* changes his name from Max Disher, the African-American womanizer and confidence trickster, to Matthew Fisher, the organizer of a white, racist, hate group. In this way Schuyler alludes to the Book of Matthew, wherein Jesus takes Matthew, the publican, as a disciple. Max Disher too is a publican, because he is in the Honky Tonk Bar when he meets Helen Givens, the white woman with whom he falls in love. It is because of Helen Givens that Max wants to become white in the first place. There are other allusions to the Bible in *Black No More*. The initials of Dr. Junius Crookman's name are J. C., and Jesus was a shepherd, warranting the association with the shepherd's crook; Crookman is spoken of by Max as a worker of miracles (47); and Schuyler alludes to Matthew 14:1 ("At the time Herod the tetrarch heard of the fame of Jesus") by describing Max designing a KON poster: "Matthew, in 14-point, one-syllable word editorials painted terrifying pictures of the menace confronting white supremacy" (106).

Another level of *Black No More* can be used to assign meanings to Schuyler's conflation of the devil, Jesus, Matthew, Dr. Crookman, and Fisher. When Max begins to organize his hate group, he finds that Dr. Crookman is described on a KON poster as "a scientific black Beelzebub" (65). On the first page of the novel, the narrator describes Max as having a "satanic" appearance, and he is associated with the devil throughout the text (e.g., 17, 111, 185). The KON propaganda calls Black-No-More, Inc.'s technology "devices of the Devil" (106). This particular usage is at root Gurdjieffian, for according to Gurdjieff men see the world upside-down: In esoteric thought, it is understood that mankind takes angels for devils and devils for angels (Waldberg 20). (Gurdjieff wrote the enormous text in which Beelzebub, the fallen angel, is the protagonist to reverse conventional perceptions.) Thus, by eradicating race, Crookman is behaving "angelically." Schuyler provides "objective" proof that man lives with reversed values because in *Black No More* the process of ending racial discrimination is equally denounced by both white and black racists. Although Matthew Fisher, as the Grand Exalted Giraw, wears a name suggestive of Gurdjieff's initials, it is not he, but Dr. Crookman, who represents Gurdjieff. Dr. Crookman depictions the cosmic Christ of the Gnostics, who comes to issue in a new age—here, an age of raceless harmony or "chromatic democracy" (64). By a parallel analogy, Matthew Fisher is identified with Christ's disciple, Matthew; on another level, the association of Gurdjieff with Dr. Crookman and Christ and the association of Matthew Fisher with Dr. Crookman suggest that Fisher may be a version of Jean Toomer.

If we step back from reading *Black No More* as science fiction, it is apparent that language is the central issue in the text. Science fiction texts explore the convention that it is the latest scientific discovery and its technological applications that effect change and solve problems. Yet, the science behind Dr. Crookman's machine-generated, racial-conversion process is not developed in detail, and Crookman's explanation (borrowed by Schuyler from a Japanese quack) sounds like the language of a scientific mirage. Crookman does not generate science so much as a utopian vision that functions as a critique of the dystopian vision of a racist pseudoscience (Hoyrd 70). However, Schuyler seems to have followed Gurdjieff's example by equally demoting genuine science as well. Science is further degraded and parodied by Max Fisher, who passes himself off as an anthropologist to penetrate the KON. This makes more sense than might initially be apparent: The racial problem does not require a scientific solution, it asks for a social, philosophical, or spiritual resolution or a combination of the three. For Schuyler to overly invest in a realistic treatment of science would undermine the thrust of his argument; thus his novel must refuse the valorization of science beyond the structural needs of his "science fiction" narrative.

Language is given a central role in *Black No More* chiefly through Max Fisher; like Santop Licorice, Max is a speechmaker. The war between the races and Black-No-More, Inc., is waged in the media and uses little scientific evidence and much invective. The need for speeches increases as Dr. Crookman's technological solution to the race problem approaches the end of its task: Black-No-More, Inc., has turned all but a few black Americans into white Americans. The backlash against the ultrawhites also comes through language. Once the population understands that to be extremely white means that you once were black, language begins to collapse into a hopeless confusion of signifier and signified. With the black referent having vanished altogether, the population reaches a stage in which people use skin darkeners to prove that they are white. In this way race is finally deconstructed, decentered, and emptied of difference.

Schuyler's interest in a logocentric solution to the racial problem was made explicit in a 1944 article, "The Caucasian Problem," in which he called for a complete reorganization of our social system. He indicated that the words "'Negro,' 'white,' 'Caucasian,' 'Nordic,' and 'Aryan' would have to be permanently taken out of circulation" (Gates 31). Schuyler was not pursuing an eccentric course in formulating such views of language and society, for his linguistic determinism anticipates George Orwell's insights into totalitarian language (Young 13–18). In Schuyler's approach to conceiving the relationship between language and society, we can also recognize "the liberation of the signifier, the rebellion against idealist repressions, and the unleashing of the forces of difference and desire against the law and order of identity" (B. Johnson 41) that foregrounds revolutionary theories of writing derived from the work of Ferdinand de Saussure.

Schuyler was neither a philosopher nor a linguist, and he did not clearly formulate his ideas about language. There remains an unresolved tension between Schuyler's proposed use of mind-control (techniques derived from behavioristic psychology that he felt were required to perfect civil society) and his contradictory interest in expanding the compass of human freedoms. Schuyler, like Toomer, Hurston, Thurman, Fisher, Larsen, and Tolson, had definite, often controversial, ideas about solutions to the racial problem and did not recoil from publishing them. This is significant because not all writers are capable of pointing to possible solutions for social ills; for instance, Orwell's work offers no antidote to totalitarianism (Young 34).

One feature that sets *Black No More* apart from the texts of Thurman, Fisher, and Larsen is the inclusion of a "legominism" on Gurdjieff and *Beelzebub's Tales.* *Black No More* contains a section that is obviously set off from the rest of the novel. The concluding portion of *Black No More* moves into new material that is altogether different from the theme of the "irrationality of color prejudice" (Bell *Afro-American* 143) as Schuyler takes up the narrative of Happy Hill, Mississippi, and the machinations of Rev. Alex McPhule and his True Faith Christ Lover's Church. Read literally, the outlandish episode seems to exist solely to provide for the comic lynching of Snobbcraft and Dr. Buggerie. The two men arrive disguised as blacks, remove their disguises to avoid being lynched, only to be seized upon and lynched, because in the absurd collapse of their racist universe, their white skins betray them as newly whitened "blacks." Although this episode is entertaining and comic, the ten pages of development that bring the racist scoundrels to their grisly demise is structurally unjustifiable. Also, McPhule's variety of homebrewed religion does not require the creation of an elaborate satire to expose its demented illegitimacy.

The McPhule episode takes on quite another appearance when its subtext is examined, for beneath the surface Schuyler presents the esoteric material that comprises his "legominism." In *Black No More* the theme of organizing a group is specifically developed: We see Max Disher become Matthew Fisher, Grand Exalted Giraw of the KON, a secret operative for Black-No-More, Inc. In this guise, Fisher organizes racists for a hidden purpose, because "so long as the ignorant white masses could be kept thinking of the menace of the Negro to Caucasian race purity and political control, they would give little thought to labor organization" (65). Moreover, Schuyler repeats a phrase found in slightly different forms in Thurman's *Infants* and Hurston's *Moses:* "He had the average Negro's justifiable fear of the poor whites and only planned to use them as a stepladder to the real money" (70–71). Schuyler intimates that there is more here than meets the eye, because when asked what a giraw is (as in Grand Exalted Giraw), Fisher's answer is circular, coded, and multivalent: "I can't tell you; I don't know myself. Ask Givens sometime. He invented it but if he can explain it I'll give you a grand" (114). Considering that Henry Givens is an Imperial Grand Wizard, this answer is all wordplay. Besides the puns on "Give" and "grand," Fisher states that he "does not know himself," which alludes to the foundation of the work: "To be able to keep a secret a man must *know himself* and he must *be.* And a man such as all men are is very far from this" (ISM 15). Fisher's words also echo the ancient formula, "know thyself," which was much used by the Gurdjieffians, as in Kathryn Hulme's "*Know thyself*—short simple-sounding words that hold the most difficult lesson in the world to learn" (2).

We are alerted to the presence of a "legominism" by the introduction of the subject of reading early on in the McPhule episode, for the community of Happy Hills has an "inordinately high illiteracy rate" (203). Also, we are presented with one of their signs, a phonetic rendering of a warning to black people. The narrator states that "The literate denizens of Happy Hill would sometimes stand off and spell out the words with the pride that usually accompanies erudition" (204). Schuyler has lodged his "attack on reading" in his satirical treatment of the self-assured adherents of McPhule's cult: We are not meant to laugh at these ignoramuses and pass on, but to recognize ourselves in Schuyler's satire. If the reader hopes to penetrate Schuyler's veil, it will be necessary to abandon "The pride that usually accompanies erudition" (204) and to assume an attitude of illiteracy. Once this has been done, the "legominism" can be read by sounding out the words hidden in the text of the McPhule episode.

The principle characteristic of a "legominism" is that it signals its presence by the inclusion of what Gurdjieff called "lawful inexactitudes." Strictly speaking, these "lawful inexactitudes" consist of violations on universal laws (such as the Laws of Three and Seven) in ways that would attract attention to the existence of the laws themselves. To bring the reader's attention to the "illiterate" level of this episode, Schuyler misspells three words: We find "rivals" instead of "revels" (206), "groove" instead of "grove" (209), and "amended" instead of "amened" (210). The first two misspellings precede the words "take place" to indicate that they are not accidental; similarly, the first and third misspellings are placed within descriptions of McPhule's congregation.

Rev. Alex McPhule's name is a key to the "attack on reading": "Phule" is a homonym of "fool," and from "lex" in Alex we can make out "looks." We are to read the name as "looks a fool," with the connotation being that McPhule "looks a fool" on the surface level as a means to both reveal and obscure the esoteric level. If we read on the syllabic level of the text, we see that the first message given in the McPhule episode is "all and everything," the original title of Gurdjieff's *Beelzebub's Tales.*[2]

From this point on, we have little trouble recognizing that McPhule is Gurdjieff in another of his many disguises. We are told that McPhule is the author of his own Bible, "a crudely-bound manuscript about three inches thick" (207), which he has placed beneath the painting of "a huge eye." These items are allusions to *Beelzebub's Tales,* the Law of Three, and the Gurdjieffian concept of "real 'I.'" Additionally, the eight young women in the Happy Hill True Faith Choir (210) allude to the Law of Eight. The circles in which McPhule's congregation sits (210) represent "the three esoteric circles of more highly developed humanity" (Walker 189), exoteric, mesoteric, and esoteric, which were also arranged concentrically with the esoteric circle as the innermost. The presence of Orage's and Toomer's names throughout this episode should come as no surprise: We can read A. R. Orage and Jean Toomer in "*Ar*my . . . *courage*ous" (204) and "*gen*eral . . . cus*tom* . . . *or*gies" (204–5).

Schuyler's detailed instructions on reading are couched in his description of the "literate denizens of Happy Hill" as they "stand off and spell out the words" (204). Reading through Schuyler's "attack on reading" requires a considerable suspension of the conventions of reading. His code requires that the reader connect widely separated phonemes. (Generally speaking, Schuyler sounds out one phoneme in each paragraph, but the phonemes are not always presented in the correct order that they are in words.)

As a prominent journalist, George Schuyler was uniquely placed to contribute to the Harlem group's "attack on race." Schuyler wrote lead editorials for the *Pittsburgh Courier;* investigative series for the *New York Evening Post;* a popular satirical column, "Views and Reviews," for the *Courier;* satirical articles in the *American Mercury;* and serialized fiction for newspapers. Schuyler's career equipped him for communication with a popular audience; his energetic, confident, sociable, and adventurous personality and his attitude toward life, which blended romanticism and skepticism, allowed him to take a practical, workmanlike, approach to "objective" writing. *Black No More* was one impressive result of Schuyler's pragmatic approach to writing. He was able to place his argument about the devastating social pathology of racialism in an artful, satirical novel that has been read by millions. However, he was not restricted to corrosive satire and investigative journalism. As a writer of serials Schuyler could put a story across, projecting whatever lurid, violent, and sensational elements were required to capture the imagination of the black mass audience. Schuyler was careful to disguise the serious, antiracialist purpose behind the entertaining pieces that he wrote, referring to his serials *The Black Internationale* and *Black Empire* as "hokum and hack work of the purest vein" (Hill 260); in 1935 he stated that he was "grinding out material by the yard and the pound" (Hill 265).

Schuyler was a complex individual, and critics consider many aspects of his thought and writings to be problematic and enigmatic. The debate over Schuyler's writings emerged again with the publication of *Black Empire* in 1991. John C. Gruesser states in his review of the volume that

Black Empire makes available to scholars and the general public two virtually unknown literary works about a successful African American–led conspiracy to liberate Africa from European colonial powers and establish a black empire that will unify the continent. Moreover, it contains a sixty- five-page afterword on Schuyler and the significance of the novels written by the volume's editors, Robert A. Hill and R. Kent Rasmussen, as well an annotated bibliography of Schuyler's fiction written for the *Courier* between 1933 and 1939 under a variety of pen names. This combination of previously unavailable texts and new information, coupled with a recent *New York Times Book Review* essay about the writer and the *Black Empire* novels by Henry Louis Gates, Jr., almost guarantees an imminent critical rediscovery of the author. (679)

Gruesser's fact-based refutation of Gates's reading of Schuyler as a "literary schizophrenic" (Gruesser 679) arrives at a reading of Schuyler that comports with a Gurdjieffian reading (however, with the Gurdjieffian component remaining out of view). Gates's determination that "Schuyler's fragmented self reached schizophrenic proportions" (Gruesser 681) does not recognize that Schuyler's "double-consciousness" was not real, that he was wearing a mask. Gruesser states that "I view Schuyler as a black writer who responded to white racism and the pressure to toe the line within the black community by creating a variety of personae for himself (Samuel I. Brooks being just one of these). . . . Schuyler told a colleague that he donned and doffed these masks to 'avoid monotony' " (683). Gruesser argues that the key to understanding Schuyler is to compare him with the protagonist of *Black No More*, for "The similarities between the main character, Max Disher, and his creator are numerous and notable" (683). Gruesser states that "This ability to remember who he [Max Disher] really is underneath the mask is the key to Max's survival in race-crazy America, an ability that Schuyler himself possessed during the 1920s and 1930s" (684).

Gruesser's idea strikingly resembles what we know of the Gurdjieffian concept of Experiment—conscious role-playing. We have seen that Toomer's group worked to achieve "mental freedom" as a means to escape dependence of externality: In the case of the black American this was an escape from racism. On the psychological level, the Harlem group sought to escape from racism by practicing the Method, which separated the individual from identification with a false reality. According to Gurdjieff "A man who has 'I' and who knows what is required in every respect can act. A man who has no 'I' cannot act" (Gurdjieff *Views* 178). Thus the "mask" is essential, and is the means to a release from society's constrictions. The "mask" concept is perhaps the most elusive part of the Gurdjieffian system. It does not fall under the scope of the introductory lectures on "self observation without identification" in Toomer's 1926 notebook, "A New Group," nor is it included in Ouspensky's comprehensive record of Gurdjieff's early lectures, *In Search of the Miraculous*.[3] C. S. Nott's chapter "New York and Fontainebleau 1925-6" in *Teachings* does indicate, however, that "self observation without identification" was a fundamental technique in the version being taught when Schuyler encountered Gurdjieff's system. Nott describes the idea of "mask" in vivid detail, although he does not use that specific term: "In ordinary life people play roles unconsciously. Gurdjieff played them consciously, and those who worked closely with him usually knew when he was playing a role. . . . In 'A Letter to a Dervish', he wrote:'I finally reached a state when nothing from the outside could really touch me internally' " (*Teachings* 112). The idea of playing roles also appears in Toomer's 1926 lectures, where he speaks of "non-identification with external reality" being a requirement for the African-American living in a racist society. At this early stage in teaching the work Gurdjieff and Toomer do not yet employ the term "mask," however, they link the idea of role-playing to the idea of reaching a state of "non-identification." Although Toomer's confrontation with American racism greatly expanded the applicability of non-identification, his statement that "one should not be dependent upon externality for what happens to one" ("A New Group, 1926") is identical in meaning to Gurdjieff's "nothing from the outside could really touch me internally," from which Toomer's statement was derived.

In addition to the resemblances between Max Fisher and Schuyler that Gruesser observed, there is a further example that deserves comment. Just as Max Disher's pseudonym, Matthew Fisher, contained a hidden meaning, we also discover a cipher in the name under which Schuyler wrote *Black Empire*, Samuel I. Brooks. In fact, it seems more significant that Schuyler's pen name has remained unprobed than that it can be read as a cipher.

The contents of Schuyler's coded messages are warnings and invitations. The simple method of encryption, the imperative discourse, and the direct address that Schuyler employed suggests that he intended these messages to be solved by some of his readers. Although Schuyler's middle name was Samuel, when we look at "Samuel I. Brooks" as wordplay, we see a cipher that is not excessively difficult to read. Its key is the Bible, and Schuyler probably assumed that anyone in the Bible-reading public would be able to recognize the biblical text alluded to by his nom de plume. The passage is in the first Book of Samuel (Samuel I, 17:38) in which David rejects military weapons and decides to face Goliath with the one weapon that is familiar to him, his shepherd's sling: "Then he took his staff in his hand and chose five smooth stones from the brook, and put them in his shepherd's bag, in the pouch; his sling was in his hand, and he drew near to the Philistine." Schuyler's allusion to Samuel I belies his assertions that his work in pulp journalism was nothing but "moron fodder" and that he finally quit writing for the *Illustrated Feature Section* (for which he began writing under the name Samuel I. Brooks) "in order to save what intelligence I possess" (Hill 264). The connotative meaning of Samuel I. Brooks suggests that Schuyler was sustained in his writing of pulp fiction by a serious purpose—he was battling the Goliath of racialism.

A similar approach may be taken in decoding Schuyler's other pen names: Danton Smith (Daniel 10:6, "and the sound of his words like the roar of a multitude"); John Kitchen ("join in it"); Rachel Call ("call all races"); Edgecombe Wright ("come be right"); William Stockton ("I am one stock"); Verne Caldwell ("call all even"), Rachel Love ("love all races"), and D. Johnson ("join in").[4] The combined effect of these names points to Schuyler's desire to create social harmony through his publications.

During the 1930s Schuyler was forced by reduced economic circumstances to publish pulp serials in newspapers. In 1937 Schuyler wrote *Black Empire*, a story that he claimed was "hack work and hokum," written to pander to the race chauvinism of the black masses. The enthusiastic response to *Black Empire* caused him to write to a friend that "The result vindicates my low opinion of the human race" (BE 260). In contrast to these disparaging statements by Schuyler, Hill and Rasmussen are able to note that Schuyler's pulp serials "possess profound thematic affinities with his contemporary 'serious' essays, affinities that transcend the 'genre gap' and suggest—Schuyler's comments notwithstanding—an overarching commonality of literary purpose and concern" (BE 260). Hill and Rasmussen observe that Schuyler's *Black Empire* "contains a wealth of personal, political, and literary allusions, testifying to Schuyler's evolution as a thinker and writer, and, as a historical document, reflecting the turbulence of the crisis-ridden decade during which it was written. Into this highly imaginary story of the liberation of Africa and the elevation of the African-American Schuyler crowded just about everything that he knew or felt about race, psychology, pedagogy, international politics, history, war, technology, health, and modern science" (Hill 261). Gruesser's reading of *Black Empire* is yet more telling, for he suggests that "Schuyler, instead of creating a utopia in the *Black Empire* serials, wrote an anti-utopia reminiscent of *Black No More* to once again expose the dangers of race chauvinism" (683).

We have seen that Schuyler wrote *Black Empire* to be "objective," although he approached this project from a curious perspective. Critics have placed Schuyler as an assimilationist, but they construe *Black Empire* as advocacy of racial elitism or worse (Gruesser 681–82). Gruesser reads Schuyler as concerned to show "the dangers of race chauvinism" (683) to resolve the question of Schuyler's contradictory handling of race in his texts. Considering that Schuyler's *Black Empire* is pulp fiction, it seems to have produced an unfortunately confusing reaction. Gruesser indicates that the problem is that the text is far more subtle than it appears; he states that "With their often stirring black nationalistic rhetoric, the *Black Empire* serials almost beg to be read straight. . . . To do so, however, one must disregard Schuyler's repeated references to the cold-blooded brutality and regimentation of Dr. Henry Belsidus's Black Internationale and the ambivalence of the serial's narrator Carl Slater, to the organization he finds himself forced to join at gunpoint" (682).

Schuyler did not intend the mimetic level of *Black Empire* to present the meaning of the text. Therefore, we must confront the difficulty in sorting out the various coded levels of Schuyler's text. In particular, we must consider the relationship between the Gurdjieffian material that Schuyler included in *Black Empire* and the various pen names that he used in his *Pittsburgh Courier* fiction between 1933 and 1939. Because the thrust of Harlem's Gurdjieffians was to attack race (which agrees with Gruesser's reading of Schuyler's texts as expressing a rejection of race chauvinism [683–84]), it seems unlikely that Schuyler's pen names ("love all races," "call all races," "call all even," etc.) suggest the philosophical sophistication required for "mental independence" and "self-observation." Although Schuyler probably did not approach the work as a mass movement, it seems that he used his pulp stories to recruit those individuals who could penetrate the ciphers as keys to the Gurd-jieffian subtext. Schuyler provided enough material to reify a "racial chauvinist" reading that, at the same time, contained a subtle counter-argument that satirized and undermined Dr. Belsidus's unreflective racialism. The text also contained an "objective" level that included many elements found in the texts of Schuyler's colleagues: the names of Gurdjieff, Ouspensky, and Orage; lists of ciphered names (e.g., 81, 85); allusions to *Beelzebub's Tales;* the Laws of Three and Eight; and various techniques that belong to the Method.

Schuyler's text expresses a number of Gurdjieffian themes, although we must recall that we are speaking of the Harlem group's version of the work, with its additions of secrecy, Blavatsky's racial ideas, and the plan to influence world history through a knowledge of cosmic laws. The plot of *Black Empire* is constructed around events that transpire after the protagonist, Carl Slater, becomes involved with a secret black organization, the Black Internationale, which is headed by a black genius, Dr. Henry Belsidus. Hill and Rasmussen derive the name from Belisarius, the sixth-century Byzantine general who conquered Africa and Rome, and Sidis, the surname of the great early-twentieth-century child prodigy (Hill 309). They also observe that Carl Slater repeatedly describes Belsidus as "diabolic," "satanic," and "demoniacal," and they indicate that such allusions evoke images of Beelzebub (Hill 287). In another context this might be melodramatic hyperbole; however, here it designates *Beelzebub's Tales* and the Gurdjieff work. We must also note the similarity of the "diabolic" Max Fisher/Matthew Disher of *Black No More* to the "satanic" Dr. Henry Belsidus of *Black Empire.* Moreover, the name Henry is a carryover from the complicated wordplay of *Black No More;* Schuyler gave the name Henry Givens to Matthew Fisher's father-in-law, the Grand Imperial Wizard who conferred on Matthew the title of Grand Exalted Giraw. We can read the name Henry Belsidus as an anagram, "be insiders"—a construction whose meaning parallels Schuyler's ciphered pen names, such as "join in it" (John Kitchen) and "come be right" (Edgecombe Wright).

In *Black Empire* Schuyler has limited his "legominism" to names and abbreviations of Gurdjieffian lore. The "legominism" is mainly located in the provocatively titled third chapter, "Dr. Belsidus Reveals Source of His Secret Wealth to Secretary." When Carl Slater ("last call") first meets Belsidus in the genius's opulent town house, Belsidus tells him not to be taken in by what he sees, because "There is method in what you might call my madness" (12). This statement refers to the concept of the "mask" that the Gurdjieffian presents to the world, a concept that Schuyler also incorporated into *Black No More.* The sentence also contains an important pun on the word "method," which is revealed as the secret source of Belsidus's wealth. The first paragraph in this chapter presents Ouspensky's name through the repetition of its phonetic components: "mysteri*ous*," "Belsid*us*," "w*as*," "inter*es*ting," "*spen*t," "*spun*," "*spoon*," "conspira*cy*," "brea*kf*ast," "*sch*eme," "smirk," "history," "alternately." Schuyler also points to Gurdjieff in the sentence "With a golden spoon he traced geometric designs on the green linen cloth as he outlined the most amazing conspiracy in history" (12). In this case we also see an allusion to Gurdjieff as Mr. G., his most common nickname, suggested by the sound of "geometric." Wordplay taking the form of anagrams is also present in *Black No More;* for example, there is the sounding out of Orage's name in the second paragraph ("sardonic," "corners," "ornate,") and the Law of Eight is alluded to in "There were eight shelves." The theme of racial harmony is suggested by the name of a minor character, Alton Fortune ("all for one"). This practice continues throughout the text in many ways: the continual appearance of the numbers three and eight ("three-pointed crown" [9], "3 o'clock" [129], "at 8:30 P.M." [197]) and other mysterious names, such as Teyoth ("the toy"; 11), Hasha Momodu ("sham human"; 33), Ransom Just ("some are just"; 113), and Henry Pilkington ("one kin"; 32). Also Schuyler gives distorted presentations of Gurdjieffian practices, such as the admonition to "Cast down thy eyes!" (61) and the wild, drug-induced dancing (62), which contrast with the Gurdjieffian struggle against the "false 'I,'" the idea of man's multiplicity of small "I"s (ISM 228, 61), and the series of sacred dance movements that Gurdjieff taught that were based on mathematics and performed in full consciousness. Schuyler truly lifts the veil with Carl Slater's insistence that in Belsidus's dystopian religion, the goal was to return control to "the inner man, the subconscious mind, the primeval urges born in the Mesozoic ooze" (62) and that as a result "my mind went completely blank, and I knew nothing" (63). All of this represents an inversion of Gurdjieffian principles, the goal of which is to unify being with doing and thereby to become conscious. Schuyler's style is subtle, but his intention is to parody and satirize conventional religion by presenting an exaggerated version that achieves the same reduction of humanity to its animal essence without any pretense at uplift or enlightenment.

The Black Internationale is a secret organization similar to Dr. Crookman's Black-No-More, Inc. Through a long and costly struggle, the Black Internationale is ultimately successful in reorganizing the world's political structure. Although Belsidus's organization uses superweapons against its enemies, there is an aspect of the story that reflects political realities extant in Europe and Africa during the period in which it was written—from 1936 until 1938. The world that results from the Black Internationale's efforts is not shown, presumably because Schuyler was not sympathetic to the totalitarian program of his victorious superman; however, the world that Belsidus struggles against is more like the world of the 1930s than a wholly fictional world.

Schuyler's two books in which supermen change the world beyond recognition supports the suggestion that there was a real attempt by Toomer and his Harlem followers to change the course of history through their Gurdjieffian endeavors. Based on the coded materials in his texts, we can infer that Schuyler and his

Harlem colleagues were involved the elimination of racial thought through the application of Gurdjieffian teachings and concepts. The surface text may have also been intended to influence the masses by stirring up the feelings of the less sensitive readers, those who did not recognize the esoteric level, thus inciting them to a crude form of political agitation that could be usefully manipulated by the "supermen."

Belsidus also represents another prominent Gurdjieffian theme, that of the superior man: here he appears in a Nietzschean demeanor, similar to Hurston's Aaron *(Moses)*, Fisher's N'Gana Frimbo *(The Conjure-Man Dies)*, Thurman's Raymond *(Infants)*, and Larsen's Dr. Anderson *(Quicksand)*. Dr. Belsidus is derived from extraliterary conventions—movie villains, mad scientists, and other popular conceptions of the strong man. However, beneath this veneer, there are specific references to Gurdjieffian themes in connection with this character. Through the use of the latest discoveries in science, technology, and engineering, Dr. Belsidus is able to conquer Africa and to defeat the colonialist-imperialist armies without the use of large armies of his own. He has little use for the masses, although he does plan to govern them. Both African-Americans and Africans are equally in need of reconstruction, and Belsidus completely reeducates them and restructures every facet of their culture. He provides black people with a new dispensation based on science: Belsidus hands down a new black religion, new schools, a new diet based on radical ideas of nutrition, new farming techniques, and a new social structure. This is all imposed from above. In a speech that expands on Raymond's credo of the unimportance of the masses in Thurman's *Infants*, Dr. Belsidus tells Slater, "We're not worried about the masses. . . . The masses always do what they are told often and loud enough. We will recondition the Negro masses in accordance with the most approved behavioristic methods. The church will hold them spiritually. Our economic organization will keep control of those who shape their views. Our secret service will take care of dissenters. Our propaganda bureau will tell them what to think and believe" (47).

Belsidus's embrace of behaviorism aligns Schuyler with the Oragean version of Gurdjieffian thought. As with many ideological groups, there was a fragmentation of Gurdjieffianism, with the American schism coming between followers of Gurdjieff and followers of A. R. Orage. C. Daly King was particularly interested in seeing Orage's teachings of the Method as a scientific religion. His book, *Beyond Behaviorism* (1927), explored the similarities between the views of Dr. John B. Watson's behaviorism and the Gurdjieff work. In fact, Gurdjieff was so struck by Watson's view of man as a machine that he arranged a meeting between himself, his New York group, and Watson and other behaviorists. Nothing useful came of this meeting, and Gurdjieff concluded that the intelligentsia of America were "nonentities" (Moore 239). However, the American groups conceived the similarities between behaviorism and the Method as being very close; therefore, Orage exploited the general familiarity that most educated people had with behaviorism as a starting place in his lectures on the Method (Webb 306). Thus Schuyler would have been aware of Watson's psychology and of the "scientific" nature of the Gurdjieffian system; his use of a scientific religion in *Black Empire* further suggests that he was familiar with the writings of C. Daly King.

Several revealing continuities come to light when *Black No More* is compared to *Black Empire*. Although on the surface *Black Empire* appears to be a very different book, much is consistent with the earlier work. In both novels the protagonist disappears, Max Disher into a white hate group and Carl Slater into the Black Internationale, a secret organization that is also a hate group. Both protagonists assume key roles in the groups and work directly with the leaders. In a sense Max Disher also belongs to Black-No-More, Inc., and serves in the capacity of a secret agent— although the organization of Dr. Crookman's group is not developed in the novel. As a technologically sophisticated cosmetics business, Black-No-More, Inc. does not need to be organized to the extent of the militarily and socially comprehensive Black Internationale. While enriching himself, Fisher also engineers the destruction of the KON. Both black organizations are successful in altering the world: Black-No-More, Inc., achieves entirely utopian ends in eliminating race conflict altogether, whereas the Black Internationale creates a black empire. In that outcome we discover the very different intention that led Schuyler to write *Black Empire*. At the end of his serial, race still exists, and what at first seems to be a scientifically ordered utopia is a nightmarish dystopia ruled by a psychopathic mass murderer. Dr. Belsidus's promise of a "higher civilization than Europe has ever seen" (258) is hollow. Schuyler communicates Belsidus's rejection of humane behavior and peaceful reconciliation by ending the novel with the brokenhearted tears of Martha Gaskin, the rejected white woman who loves the relentlessly cruel ruler of the Earth. Martha Gaskin's name is a code that has a number of readings. Like Larsen's Gertrude Martin *(Passing)*, it imparts "Mr. G." The name also suggests "heart," "mask," and "skin"—all of which meaningfully apply to the text. The presentation of Gurdjieff as a woman is parallel to both Gertrude Martin and The Pig Woman *(Infants)*.

Both black organizations are successful because they employ scientific solutions to social problems. However, as we have seen, Dr. Crookman's science is undermined by various biological and sociological factors; social equality is finally attained only through his perspicacious ability to manipulate people to the point where race is exhausted as a meaningful sign. The comic-satiric mode of *Black No More* presents a cartoon world that does not allow for the development of Crookman's character. In *Black Empire* Dr. Belsidus can be placed at the center of the narrative and developed to a further degree. However, it is his convictions, not his personal life, that we see portrayed in the narrative. Like Dr. Crookman, Dr. Belsidus enters the narrative fully formed and without a personal history. Dr. Belsidus's shocking view of mankind can be thoroughly expressed, because the space necessary for this is allowed to his character. Through Dr. Belsidus we are allowed access to a superhuman analysis of the life of mankind, which stands in profound contrast to Carl Slater's pedestrian view of the world. This aspect of Belsidus's character compares very well with Gurdjieff's Beelzebub.

Like Gurdjieff's Beelzebub, Schuyler's Belsidus belongs to a higher magnitude of consciousness. Belsidus, described as "determined, educated, suave, immaculate, cruel, immoral" (Hill 267) is a more highly evolved human who assesses normal man as a small, broken creature sadly in need of rehabilitation. Beelzebub, who has been exiled to Mars, makes five trips to Earth in vain attempts to keep man from destroying himself. On each of these trips he is confronted with a different problem: the use of money, human sacrifice, meat eating, false religion, and war. The problems that Beelzebub attempts to resolve are the same concerns that face Belsidus, who reorganizes society and provides for all of his subjects's needs without money. He saves Carl Slater and Patricia Givens from cannibals and then eradicates the practice. Dr. Belsidus has all food centrally prepared and served to his new society, thus he is able to eliminate the cooking of food, which he believes to be the cause of many diseases. Belsidus's new religion uses advanced drugs and hypnotism to efficiently provide the religious feeling that his masses of underlings require. Belsidus's enlightened approach to war is to use science and terror to entirely destroy his enemies, and in this way spares his own population. Beelzebub defined war as "reciprocal destruction," however, for Belsidus the destruction is not reciprocal; in his perfectly efficient system only the enemy is destroyed.

Schuyler's solutions to human problems are not markedly different from those enacted by Beelzebub; both Gurdjieff and Schuyler agree that man is the problem and that the solution is to reformulate man. Gurdjieff proposes to do this by waking up men with the idea of humanity's unlimited possibilities. According to Gurdjieff "*two hundred conscious people,* if they existed and if they found it necessary and legitimate, could change the whole of life on the earth" (ism 310). Belsidus proposes to do this by imposing on men a new social system that will eventually produce a new type of human being. For Belsidus, ideas are insufficient; there must be active force. Gurdjieff's belief in the limitations determined by cosmic law would prevent him from viewing Belsidus's solution as a realistic one, because the Law of Seven (or the Law of the Octave) determines that human aims, when applied forcefully, deteriorate into their opposite forms. According to the Law of the Octave, Belsidus's fascist, technocratic, and rationalistic order would eventually deteriorate into degeneracy and irrational social chaos. However, we do not need to attach a futuristic proviso in reading *Black Empire;* it is only required that we affirm Gruesser's reading of Carl Slater's "ambivalence" toward Belsidus's "cold-blooded brutality" (682) to realize that the text already contains a sufficient critique of the mad scientist's racial utopia.

Schuyler's remote, vengeful, calculating, driven, and terrifying superman, Dr.

Belsidus, is a far cry from Gurdjieff's kindly, garrulous Beelzebub. Yet there is a fundamental similarity in their views of man's construction and of man's place in the universe. In the creation of Belsidus and in Schuyler's use of black secret organizations, we come closest to penetrating the "mask" drawn over his fiction: What we glimpse beneath the "mask" is the Harlem group.

Zora Neale Hurston:
The Self and the Nation

6

Zora Neale Hurston's first novel, *Jonah's Gourd Vine* (1934), is a fictional treatment of the contentious marriage of her parents. The story of a smooth-talking, wife-beating, philandering, jack-leg preacher who runs away whenever he is confronted by difficulties did not provide Hurston with a vehicle for the comprehensive presentation of Gurdjieff's system. Hurston is primarily a storyteller, and her solutions to the problems posed by the "objective" aesthetic tend to achieve a high degree of literary polish. Hurston allegorizes, mythologizes, and symbolizes Gurdjieff's esoteric concepts, where Toomer and her colleagues in the Harlem group often allowed jargon, didacticism, abstract schemes, and impracticable narrative devices to overwhelm the story at the expense of presenting the system. Hurston includes material from the work only in so far as her narrative structure allows the superimposition of discursive materials to be aesthetically effective.

Consequently, although Gurdjieff's name, along with those of his major prose-lytizers, is present throughout the subtext, the continual but highly refined recurrence of these names does not disrupt the verisimilitude of the text compared with the crude effects used in *Passing* or *The Walls of Jericho*. Gurdjieff's name appears on the first page of *Jonah's Gourd Vine:* The eighth paragraph begins, "Ned ignored Amy and shuffled," which supplies "gnored . . . shuff," in a characteristically nondisruptive manner. Ouspensky's name may be found on many pages: "us . . . pint . . . slavery" (5), "Miss Pinkney" (7), "Ah kin pint" (11), "dusk . . . suspiciously . . . utter" (19), and "pantry . . . house" (20). Orage appears as "parlor organ" (135) and "rampage parsonage" (138); in a noteworthy example Orage's name is emphasized by John Pearson's encounter with a woman named Ora: a dilemma develops around whether or not he will go to the ga*rage* or go off with *Ora* (196).

Jean Toomer's name is coded into " 'Naw, Hattie, 'tain't gonna wait. Don't *keer* if youse so nelly *barefoot* 'til yo' *toes* make prints on de ground. She's goin*ter* git h*er* remembrance-stone first. You done wo*re* out *too* *m*any uh h*er* shoes already. *Here*, take dis *two* bits and do anything you wanta wid it.'

She threw it back viciously. 'Don't come lounchin' me out no *two* bits when Ah ast you fuh shoes' " (146; emphases added).

A few lines later, there is the sentence from which the title of the novel was derived: "Ah'd cut down dat Jonah's gourd vine in uh minute, if Ah had all de say-so" (146). The Bible verse to which the speaker alludes, Jonah 4:6–7, contains no specific mention of a gourd vine, merely "the plant." The gourd vine is Hurston's invention, and it introduces a "lawful inexactitude" that indicates a coded subtext or "legominism." Because the phrase "Jonah's gourd vine" appears between the wordplay with Toomer's name and the declaration that Moses "learnt how to call God by all his secret names" (147), it seems likely that Hurston's "gourd" points to Gurdjieff as a "secret name." Hurston was not alone in establishing a homophonic equivalence of "God," "gourd," and Gurdjieff; there are also parallels throughout Tolson's texts, for example, "gored . . . chaff " (HG 21) and "God . . . chef " (HG 151). Hurston's use of indeterminacy in the construction of characters, narrative sequences, embedded texts, and the controvertible relationship between what is looked at and what is perceived (focalization) compose her highly refined "attack on reading." Hurston continually approaches the destruction of the text's verisimilitude, although her artistry in manipulating this level of her text preserves a sense that the unfolding narrative acceptably represents reality.

Jonah's Gourd Vine is based on an esoteric dualism that, despite its importance to the design of the narrative system, does not obtrude on the effectiveness of her story. Through this esoteric scheme, Hurston has personified the themes of "sleep" and the superman so subtly, using John Pearson and Alph Pearson, respectively, that the contrasts between them are only vaguely suggested by the narrator; the reader is allowed to establish the contrast between them as the action of the novel unfolds. Hurston makes her esoteric point, but she does so by exploring and expanding upon the conventions of the novel, not by deforming and violating the genre.

The protagonist, John Pearson, is on the path of destruction, and there is nothing that can save him. In Hurston's text, Pearson is described not as one who is asleep but as one who is blind. Because Hurston substitutes blindness for the more common Gurdjieffian metaphor of "sleep" used to signify a low level of consciousness, we see that she is not committed to a doctrinaire faithfulness to Gurdjieffian terminology. Hurston used the ideas in Gurdjieff's system as an armature for her creative imagination, supporting her propositions on its ideas but moving freely within it. Blindness is equally effective in indicating Pearson's inability to grasp the truth of his position in life. Thus Hurston characterizes her protagonist by pervading the text with images of sight and blindness.

In Hurston's fiction, names are important indicators of the multivalent nature of the text. John Pearson is first called John Buddy Crittenden, and he has been given the nickname Two-Eye-John because of a preaching that his mother once heard. The latter name refers to John the Baptist, who recognized Jesus as the Messiah, thereby seeing something that was invisible to other men. Moreover, in the first chapter of the Book of John, which describes the baptism of Jesus by John the

Baptist, several of the verses are concerned with sight. However, as events transpire, it becomes evident that the name Two-Eye-John is ironic, even derisory, because John Pearson overlooks the very things that everyone else sees. In the final analysis, this name underscores the defining flaw in his character. In Gurdjeffian terms, this defect is his "chief feature": "Every man has a certain feature in his character which is central. It is like an axle round which all his 'false personality' revolves. Every man's personal work must consist in struggling against this chief fault" (ISM 226). Thus, *Jonah's Gourd Vine* is an allegorized version of the story of her father's life, and John Crittenden's life is played out within the confines of Gurdjieff's psychology. Hurston uses her father's story to express several fundamental concepts that were emphasized in Orage's version of the work, primarily "chief feature" as an attribute of man's mechanized functioning.

The struggle against "chief feature" is the central problem that determines the action in the novel. However, Hurston does not name this concept in the novel, she allegorizes it. John Buddy is informed both by Alph Pearson and by a dream (185)—two "objective" perspectives—that he must change the pattern of his life. The specific meaning of Hurston's allegory can be recovered only by reading the allegory in the Book of Jonah. The gourd vine alludes to a life that has been devoured by a worm (or snake) like Jonah's vine. The worm that eats the shade-giving vine symbolizes the active, fatal flaw in John Pearson's character. Hurston has maintained the integrity of the biblical story: When Jonah loses the shade of the vine, he becomes enraged and asks for death. Thus in the modified Gurdjieffian trope of blindness (sleep) and the scriptural trope of anger-unto-death, Hurston symbolizes a central concept in the Gurdjieffian psychology, the "chief feature," or the negative factor that every human most manifests in his behavior toward others. Instead of gaining vision and repulsing the psychic worm of his "chief feature," John Pearson flees the abundant consequences of his ceaselessly negative actions. By doing so, he carries the worm (blindness, his "chief feature") with him into each new situation, and his life rapidly runs downhill until he is utterly destroyed by his own pathological behavior. The novel becomes an approximation of self-observation in which a human machine (John Crittenden) is observed by the narrator; optimally, the reader also might be engaged by the text in the analytical observation of the protagonist. Of course, this is not what happens in the practice of work on oneself, and what the novel provides is a literary representation of "self-observation." In contrast, in Hurston's later novel *Moses*, the protagonist has access to esoteric knowledge and he is shown in the act of "self-observation" (e.g., 100–101, 105). However, no such scene is possible in the world encompassing John Crittenden's path to destruction.

Another prominent symbol in the novel also evokes Gurdjieffian thought. According to Gurdjieff, man is a broken-down machine. Such terms as "automatism," "mechanization," and "machine" are important concepts in the Gurdjieff work—and were particularly emphasized by Orage. All of the works of man, even art and philosophy, are mechanical actions, for a machine can produce nothing that is not mechanical (ISM 18). The mechanical aspect of life is specifically represented in *Jonah's Gourd Vine* by railroad trains. John Pearson is obsessed by trains; he wants to understand what they say. He is told by a fellow bystander that the trains just make a "racket," but he is convinced that the trains are saying words too (16). In John's final sermon the metaphors for salvation and damnation are two trains and the end of time and man's judgment are depicted as the collision between two trains, when "two trains of Time shall meet on de trestle and wreck de burning axles of de unformed ether" (181). John Pearson's attraction to trains can be read as a symbol of his mechanical functioning: Like a train, he can only go where the tracks lead. Finally, it is a train—the symbol of John Pearson's mechanical level of life—that crushes his car and kills him, carrying out the death sentence on "sleeping," mechanical man.

When John Pearson is confronted with an "objective" view of his place in life, the truth of his situation does not penetrate the defenses of his ego. Gurdjieff repeatedly insisted that "nobody wants to know the truth" (ISM 21). The contrasting views of man seen from a higher level of consciousness is provided by Judge Alph Pearson, who tells John Buddy Pearson, "Of course you do not know. Because God has given to all men the gift of blindness. That is to say that he has cursed but few with vision. Ever hear tell of a happy prophet? This old world wouldn't roll on the way He started it if men could see. Ha! In fact I think God himself was looking off when you went and got yourself born" (99). In this passage, sleep can be substituted for blindness without altering the meaning. The idea that sleep is a predominant characteristic of human life is fundamental to Gurdjieff's analysis of man's psychological functioning: "A modern man lives in sleep, in sleep he is born and in sleep he dies" (ISM 66). Moreover, blindness, rather than sleep, better fits the situation of Hurston's protagonist, who struggles with the conflict between religion and uncontrolled sexuality. Alph Pearson's speech comes after he has said to John Pearson, "I'm not going to ask you why you've done these things, partly because I already know, and partly because I don't believe you do" (99). This inability to see the truth is explained by Gurdjieff through reference to "buffers": " 'Buffers' lull a man to sleep, give him the agreeable and peaceful sensation that all will be well, that no contradictions exist and that he can sleep in peace" (ISM 154).

Although she has found her own way to present Gurdjieff's conception of man's true condition in *Jonah's Gourd Vine*, Hurston has not entirely substituted the trope of blindness for the trope of "sleep." When John Pearson is killed by a train, the engineer says: "He musta been sleep or drunk. God knows I blowed for him when I saw him entering the track. He wasn't drunk. Couldn't smell no likker on him, so he musta been asleep" (200). *Jonah's Gourd Vine* proffers a warning: The novel is an "objective" work of art because it shows that to live in "sleep" is to resign control of one's fate to the laws of nature and accident and to die and be "food for the moon"—Gurdjieff's phrase used to describe living for the Earth's needs (subject to the Law of Reciprocal Maintenance) and not for one's own needs (ISM 57).

Much in the text comes into focus when it is realized that the character Alph Pearson introduces the superman theme. Alph Pearson is allowed an understanding of John Pearson's psychology, because *Jonah's Gourd Vine* is based on Gurdjieff's parable of the carriage, horse, driver, and master, and Alph Pearson is the master. Just as Linda, the master in Fisher's *The Walls of Jericho*, possesses an unaccountable store of wisdom and psychological insight, Alph Pearson has a penetrating understanding of those around him. Hurston has not established a rationale to account for Alph's prodigious psychological insight beyond his sociocultural assignment to the master class. However, she does intimate the motive behind his concern for John Buddy, namely that Alph may be John's father; the implication is made, yet their relationship remains shadowy. When Alph Pearson's first encounters John, his reaction is extreme: "Instead of answering the boy directly he stared at him fixedly for a moment, whistled and exclaimed, 'What a fine stud! Why boy, you would have brought five thousand dollars on the block in slavery time! Your face looks sort of familiar but I can't place you. What's your name?'" (17). Alph's anachronistic appraisal of "John Crittenden" is markedly unpromising in that he evaluates John Buddy in the degrading terms of the southern white planter class. However, it is also true that Alph Pearson—in the terms of the racial hierarchy of the South—pays John Buddy a fine compliment. More to the point, the "objective" assessment delivered by this socially and spiritually superior being was not comprehended by John Buddy. Alph immediately hires John Buddy and gives him several important responsibilities. It is soon conveyed that Alph has decided to make something of John Buddy Crittenden, although what results will be limited by John's inferior social status. Thus, Alph is the agent through which Buddy is offered a way to reach higher—to evolve into a more complete human being.

Hurston has loaded the language with signifiers of developmental possibilities: This is not only manifested in the change of name from Buddy Crittenden, with its puns on "bud" and "critter," but also in the new name John Pearson, with its double denotation of the homophone "peer" (to look intently; nobleman). The southern setting of the novel relegates John Buddy to a low social status. However, his evolution and his ability to make the best of possibilities is what is at issue—not the second-class nature of the possibilities allowed John Buddy. Alph Pearson tells John Buddy to go to school and learn to read and write. Suggestively, he also gives John Buddy some suits that are no longer worn by his son. At the school the teacher, every inch a martinet, learns that his new pupil does not know who his father is; he gives Two-Eye-John the name John Pearson. When John's mother takes him home to help her plant a crop, Alph tells John that he can always have a job if he needs it: "No matter where you are, don't steal and don't get too biggety and you'll get along" (42). Alph Pearson has become a surrogate father to John Pearson, and he tries to impart some notion of conscience in John as they part. Although this action is not emphasized in the text, from the Gurdjieffian standpoint, it is tremendously important. Because man is mechanical and "asleep," he has no conscience: "'Buffers' help a man not to feel his conscience . . . as we have no consciousness we have no conscience" (ISM 155).

We get another look at John from Alph's perspective when John's ability to attract women begins to cause trouble. Alph warns him away from a married woman, but John defends himself by saying the woman was chasing him. Alph's reaction reveals the nature of his character as well as John's: "Alph Pearson laughed heartily and gave John a playful shove. 'Get along you rascal you! You're a walking orgasm. A living exultation'" (50). Naturally enough, John does not understand Alph's vocabulary. In Gurdjieffian terms, Hurston here indicates that John lives on the moving-instinctive level, that is, he uses only the lowest of his faculties to get through life. According to Gurdjieff, to evolve, man must harmonize all three centers, moving-instinctive (physical brain), thinking (intellectual brain), and feeling (emotional brain). *Jonah's Gourd Vine*, then, can be read as an "objective" allegory about the dangers of living on one level.

In the context of a Gurdjieffian reading of *Their Eyes Were Watching God* (1937), the doubling that has been widely discussed by Hurston's critics takes on a new significance.[1] The aim of the Method is the integration of the fragmented self, the defective ego referred to in Gurdjieff's lectures as "false personality" and man's "mechanization." According to Gurdjieff, the most characteristic feature of the normal state of man is duality; he consists entirely of dualities or pairs of opposites; thoughts oppose feelings, and moving impulses oppose instinctive craving for quiet (ISM 281). At the same time, the self that is being integrated must be protected by a consciously contrived "mask." The doubleness of the developing or developed man is a matter of intention. In a discussion of "chief feature," Gurdjieff stated that "If you find a way to struggle with this feature and to destroy it, that is, to destroy its *involuntary manifestation* [his emphasis], you will produce on people not the impression that you do now but any impression you like" (ISM 267). Toomer addresses the same subject somewhat differently in his 1926 notebook, the record of the ideas that he and Orage imparted to the Harlem group.

Janie Starks discovers the idea of "chief feature" for herself in *Their Eyes* when she is forced to separate herself from her externality by her husband's brutality: "She had an inside and an outside now and suddenly she knew how not to mix them" (112–13). In the following chapter, Hurston returns to this theme, delineating the expansion of consciousness that the separation from externality provides for Janie. In the first stage of separation, there is still a residual identification of Janie with her demeanor: "The years took all the fight out of Janie's face. For a while she thought it was gone from her soul" (118). Eventually she comes to make no further identification with her exterior manifestations or to internalize the random and "mechanical" manifestations of her husband's negativity: "Then one day she sat and watched the shadow of herself going about tending store and prostrating itself before Jody, while all the time she herself sat under a shady tree with the wind blowing through her hair and her clothes. Somebody near about making summertime out of lonesomeness" (119).

Eventually, Janie's intermittent periods of separation from externality become permanent and she is no longer troubled by the uncontrolled passage from one emotional state to another. "This was the first time it happened, but after a while it got so common she ceased to be surprised. It was like a drug. In a way it was good because it reconciled her to things. She got so she received all things with the stolidness of the earth which soaks up urine and perfume with the same indifference" (119). Janie's indifference to good and bad phenomena suggests that she has attained a measure of unity, but the nature of the unity is in question: Janie has ceased to react automatically, but she is a long way from being a developed person by esoteric standards. In the allegory presented by the narrative, Janie has awakened to a certain point because of the difficult nature of her life; we may even say that she has had a mechanical awakening. She has progressed to a point of mystical understanding, yet, lest we assume that Janie has progressed very far, the narrator establishes her psychic location. Two paragraphs before we learn of her "stolidness," we are told about her place on the scale of evolution: "She didn't read books so she didn't know that she was the world and the heavens boiled down to a drop. Man attempting to climb to painless heights from his dung hill" (119). This is a remarkably telegraphic passage: It compresses an entire philosophy into a few lines, while also stimulating further questions by offering profound information in a matter-of-fact discourse. What books does Janie not read? Surely they are unusual books despite the narrator's generalized demarcation of them as "books." They are the books in which a particular philosophy is presented, yet which books and which philosophy? Also, if Janie does not read them, who does? Apparently the narrator knows of them. If nothing else, Hurston has revealed her narrator's vast intellectual distance from Janie. (Hurston's narrator alludes to the narrator of *Beelzebub's Tales*, whose view is from a very great distance above man and his Earth.)

The narrator's choice in books identifies her as a Kabbalist, familiar with the body of Jewish mystical knowledge. Gurdjieff spoke of the Kabbalah as a more ancient version of his system, and it is mentioned twice in *In Search of the Miraculous*. Hurston states that Janie "didn't know that she was the world and the heavens boiled down to a drop." The source of this phrase is a Kabbalistic concept formulated in the *Zohar* (the Book of Splendor—the "bible of the Kabbalah" and its most influential text) and rendered by Halevi: "Man contains all that is above in heaven and below upon earth, the celestial as well as the terrestrial creatures; it is for this reason that the Ancient of Ancients chose Man as his divine manifestation. No world could exist before Adam came into being, for the human figure contains all things, and all that exists by virtue of it" (*Tradition* 13). The second phrase, "Man attempting to climb to painless heights from his dung hill," is also a condensation of a very complex Kabbalistic doctrine. In Kabbalah "All that has come into being from the Crown of Existence to the emptiness beyond the waves and particles that compose the atom, is sustained by the Will of the Absolute, that it might complete its purpose so that God should see God" (KU 155). Hurston's phrase summarizes man's role in the process of God's attainment of self-consciousness: "The work of creation for mankind is conscious participation in the realization of the Divine intention. . . . The Work of Creation is slowly refining the mirror of existence into a higher and more subtle state in order to reflect in the evolving consciousness of Adam a clearer and more lucid image of God" (Halevi *Tradition* 29–30).

In Kabbalah, to name is to create. Hurston broaches the subject of creative naming early in *Their Eyes Were Watching God*. In the second chapter Janie is recounting her early days, and cannot pick herself out in a photograph. She then reveals that she did not know that she was "colored" and that "Dey all useter call me Alphabet 'cause so many people had done named me different names" (21). The subject of writing and naming returns when Janie describes her attempts to work in Joe Starks's store and the difficulties that ambiguous "literacy" causes her: "Then too she couldn't read everybody's writing. Some folks wrote so funny and spelt things different from what she knew about" (86). In the first proposition, Hurston has thrust directly into the Kabbalah. In Kabbalistic lore the letters are the prime cause of matter; by their union with the forms, letters originated the world of corporeal beings (I. Epstein 227). A Kabbalistic reading of the opening words of the Bible is "In the beginning, God created the alphabet of the heaven and the alphabet of the earth" (Sheinkin 57). Beneath the many appearances of Janie is her essence, which is codified as unification through the revelatory name, Alphabet, the inescapable identity. Janie's multiplicity of names is indicative of her divinity. Hurston's texts are manifold: *Their Eyes* includes Egyptian myth, Kabbalah, and Gurdjieffian secret names. In the cases of Kabbalah and Egyptian myth, Hurston's treatment was comprehensive, consistent, and systematic. It must also be emphasized that these inclusions were superimposed and must be considered simultaneously. For instance, Frazer identifies the Egyptian goddess Isis as the holder of many titles: "Her attributes and epithets were so numerous that in the hieroglyphics she is called 'the many-named,' 'the thousand-named,' and in the Greek inscriptions 'the myriad-named'" (443). In calling Janie "Alphabet" because of her abundant names, Hurston has merged the Kabbalistic conception of alphabetic creation with the numinous and fertile multiplicity of Isis. Hurston sounds the names of Gurdjieff, Ouspensky, Toomer, and C. Day King throughout *Their Eyes* in the same manner as Thurman, Fisher, Larsen, and Schuyler.

Janie's discovery that her essence is literal is identical to the practices of the Kabbalists who "on the one hand, contemplated the sacred Name through the medium of the tree of spheres (The Zoharic school) and, on the other (like [Abulafia]), permuted the twenty-two Hebrew letters to gain prophetic wisdom" (P. Epstein 83). Chapter 2 of *Their Eyes* begins with the contemplation of the Great Tree, which represents the unification of the letters and the "divine manifestations" that the tree (or ladder) of the Sephirot symbolizes (Idel 54): "Janie saw her life like a great tree in leaf with the things suffered, things done, things enjoyed, things done and undone. Dawn and doom were in the branches" (20). Janie's fourfold division of the tree is equivalent to the Kabbalistic Tree of Life, which contains within it the Four Worlds: "The Four Worlds interpenetrate the whole of existence. Schematically they may be seen as a 'Jacob's Ladder,' with the Tree of one World growing out of the structure of the last, so that the will of God, and the flow which connects all that exists, is present in everything that is manifest" (KU 11). The Four Worlds, which have many evocations in Kabbalah, may also be thought of as the worlds of archetypes, creation, formation, and action—a concept comparable to Hurston's description of the tree as four states of "doing." The "Jacob's ladder" is synonymous with the "ray of creation" and is referred to throughout the writings of the Harlem group as a ladder (e.g., Hurston *Moses* 329, DTR 345; Schuyler BNM 70–71; Thurman *Infants* 142; Tolson *Libretto* 13, HG 19). It was also given a graphic representation on an advertising card that Aaron Douglas designed for Carl Van Vechten's *Nigger Heaven*.

A close study of *Their Eyes* unveils two distinct levels, Kabbalistic and Egyptian; both equate to certain aspects of Gurdjieff's system. However, each is consistent within its own system. Gurdjieff's system recognized a kinship with Kabbalah in that both systems encompassed "the unity of everything existing" (ISM 283). Janie's third husband, Tea Cake Woods, has been understood to resemble Osiris (Lowe 195); while the story of Janie's marriage occupies the surface text, an Egyptian subtext recapitulates a detailed rendition of the myth of Osiris and Isis. Tea Cake dies after he is bitten by a rabid dog and Janie shoots him when he grows delirious and tries to kill her. According to the myth of Osiris, although not in the commonly known version of the myth as told in Frazer's *The Golden Bough*, Osiris is bitten by an insect and dies of the resulting infection. (As an anthropologist, Hurston had access to variant versions of the Egyptian myths, and we should not be surprised that she chose elements that suited her plotting better than the most commonly available versions of the myths.) Mythically speaking, as Osiris, Tea Cakes is already dead when Janie shoots him.

Looking beyond Egyptian myth into Egyptian culture, we can identify Janie's speech at her trial for killing Tea Cake as the "Negative Confession" that was de-livered at the trial of the dead soul during which the heart was weighed in the Hall of Maat. Janie's judgment is the rite by which Tea Cake is installed as Osiris, the judge of the dead: "Osiris gained possession of the 'order' of nature in his capac-ity of spirit of growth in vegetation. The transcendent god was removed from the world in order to make room for the immanent deity who assumed all his attributes except that of Creator" (R. T. R. Clark 178).

Also, we learn that "Osiris is now the barley in all its vicissitudes" (R. T. R. Clark 143). The bag of seed that Janie brings back from the muck is Osiris himself: Janie is then sought out by her old friend Pheoby to whom she tells her story throughout the night. This action parallels the myth, in which Isis and Nephthys keep "night watches" over the body of Osiris "until the coming of Horus" (R. T. R. Clark 109). In the myth, Isis used her magical powers to become pregnant by temporarily reviving Osiris; it is consistent with the Egyptian reading of *Their Eyes* to deduce that Janie is pregnant by Tea Cake at the denouement of the novel. Admittedly, this assertion is a radical shift away from contemporary readings of Hurston's text. Nevertheless, this view is in keeping with Hurston's demonstrated understanding of the social uses and meaning of myth and her consistent adaptation of the tradi-tional form of the myth. Consequently, her use of the Osirian cycle is only mean-ingfully completed if "Osiris is 'he who establishes justice over the two lands; he leaves the son [Horus] in his father's place'" (Neumann 64). The narrative cycle can only be fulfilled if Janie is pregnant with "Horus" at the conclusion of the novel.

Turning to Hurston's use of the Kabbalah in *Their Eyes*, we see that a similarly detailed and exacting scheme comes to light. The starting place of the literal Kab-balah is the equivalence of the Hebrew numbers and letters, although only the He-brew alphabet applies to Kabbalah. Isidore Epstein states that "Language and number, conjoined together, are thus declared to be the instruments whereby the cosmos in all its infinite variety of combinations and manifestations was called into existence by God" (228). From there, the letters of the alphabet are assigned a complex series of correspondences. This system originates from the sounds of the letters, the soft-breathing *alef*, the mute *mem*, and the hissing *shem*, respectively air, water, and fire (I. Epstein 227). Using this system, the Kabbalists manipulated an elaborate system of numerical rules that allowed them to explore the hidden meaning of texts (Regardie 106). Hurston was limited in what she was able to ac-complish along these lines; although what she produced is breathtaking in its scope, what we can see of her Kabbalistic usages is fairly simple.

One of Janie's names was Alphabet. There are 22 letters in the Hebrew alpha-bet: *aleph, beth, gimel, daleth, he, vau, ʒayin, het, teth, yod, kaf, lamed, mem, nun, samekh, ayin, pe, [ts]sadhe, koph, resh, sin [shin], tau.* One of the traditions of Kabbalah is that each of the 42 letters of the divine name is a divine name in itself

(Idel 99), and we have already seen that some the characters in *Their Eyes* are Egyptian divinities. If we assign divine Hebrew letters to the characters in the novel, we see that Jody is *yod;* Janie's mother, Leafy, is *alef;* Pheoby is *pe;* and Nunkie is *nun.* Janie is *ayin;* in Kabbalah *ayin* is "God the transcendent, beyond existence, separate from any-thing [sic], absolute nothing" (KU 7).

Although a more extensive Kabbalistic reading of *Their Eyes* would be highly rewarding, this is not the place for such a reading. However, to give a better idea of how Kabbalah is integrated into *Their Eyes*, it will be best to sketch some of Hurston's most significant usages. For example, the phrase "God is everywhere" (72) is the name of God as *Ayin Sof,* the "Absolute All" found at the zenith of the Great Tree (the Sephirot). The proposition "He [God] made nature and Nature made everything else" (101) relays the Kabbalistic idea of the absolute discontinuity of God with creation (Waite 99). The latter phrase occurs in a debate between Sam Watson and Lige Moss: Sam Watson ("Samson") is *Zimẓum,* the contraction within the Godhead that allows existence to come into being, and Lige Moss is *Masseh Bereshit,* the work of creation. Thus the subject of the disagreement—the question of the primacy of God or Nature—expresses their respective cosmic roles.

The equivalence of Joe Starks (Jody) to both the letter *yod* and the number ten (which is represented by the letter *yod*) casts him as a personification of the tension between the *monad* and the *decad*—"the need to unify the ten powers" (Idel 120). This in turn identifies him as Aaron, the false priest of the Golden Apis calf and a parody of Moses (a theme that Hurston returns to in *Moses*). Hurston's intended conjunction of *yod* (and Jody) with Aaron is evident from the episode in which Joe Starks purchases Matt Bonner's yellow mule (itself a parody of the golden calf) and gives the mule a mock funeral, which is in turn parodied by the truth-revealing buzzards.

Hurston has also encoded the Kabbalah into *Their Eyes* by disguising Hebrew phrases as English. Hurston interrupts the realistic form of the novel to introduce a story about a flock of buzzards (Davie 453). The buzzards perform a ritual before consuming a dead mule. The buzzard-parson's query, "What killed this man?" is given answer by the chorus, "Bare, bare fat." This response is a phoneticized contraction of the Hebrew sentence that opens the Bible—*Berashit bara Elohim et hashamayin Vaet ha-aretẓ*. Translated, this means "In the beginning He the God Names created the Heaven and the Earth" (KU 41). Hurston's contraction of the original refers only to the creation of *Vaet,* the Earth, which is rendered by Hurston as "fat."

I have discussed Hurston's inclusion of Egyptian mythology and use of the Hebrew alphabet to make the point that Hurston's treatment of hidden levels is methodical and systematic. On the "literal" level of the novel, Hurston applied the Kabbalistic idea of *Temurah,* or permutation. Although because her aim was to produce permutations that could be read as English, Hurston departed somewhat from the exact method of *Temurah*. However, the alphabetic level of the novel also encompasses the level at which names open beyond the narrative. When Hurston's language is probed at the "literal" and syllabic level, it divulges yet another inclusion, the names of figures who were important to Zora Neale Hurston because of their association with Jean Toomer and his teachers of human development.

In *Their Eyes* Hurston's rendering of the most important name, Gurdjieff, is Jeff Bruce (78). By reversing the order of the two names and reversing Bruce, we discover the phonetically approximate "cur jeff." Ouspensky's name is given as "dust-bearing bee sink" (24) or "us-sink-bee." Orage's name appears throughout the novel because the story takes place in Orange County. Jean Toomer's name appears as "tuhmorrer" (120). Hurston also continually plays word games; throughout the text she points to these names by reiterating the sounds that are their key components. For instance, she plays with Toomer's name as "toes uh Time" (85) and "tomatoes" (86). Similarly she rehearses Orage's name syllabically on many pages (e.g., 90, where the phonemes "ar" and "or" predominate).

Their Eyes is both a novel and an "objective" allegory. In writing an "objective" novel, Hurston needed to incorporate a theory and practice into a form that both inhibits and distorts a reliable version of Gurdjieff's system. The form of the novel reflects the threefold composition of man (body, intellect, and emotions) and Janie's three marriages represent the integration of the three centers. However, the novel is an esoteric romance: Gurdjieff insisted that "One man can do nothing" (ISM 221), that to awaken one must participate in a group effort, a school, and realistically Janie cannot join an esoteric school. Therefore, her third and last marriage signifies her final stage of integration into a school. Tea Cake takes Janie through a number of stages, which are indicated by her changes in dress. First she lets down her hair as she begins to sensually explore the physical realm through his caresses. Janie's next stage moves from Gurdjieffian theory to myth as she is invested in her role as Isis when Tea Cake is cut in a gambling game: The cutting by Double-Ugly parallels the dismemberment of Osiris by Set. The meaning of the name Vergible "Tea Cake" has a simple solution, because we know that he is Osiris. Frazer's account of Osiris details the slimy, seed-bearing, cakelike effigies that worshipers made in his honor, his association with trees as a tree spirit, and that he "represented the yearly decay and revival of life, especially of vegetable life" (378). Thus, in Vergible "Tea Cake," we read "vegetable tree cake." After Janie tends his wounds, Tea Cake tells her that they are going to the muck; the result is that "her soul crawled out of its hiding place" (192). Under the tutelage of the agricultural god surrounded by the members of his school—who are disguised as agricultural workers—Janie learns to do a number of necessary things: to play, to work joyfully, to live in the moment, even to exercise violence. On yet another level, this episode depicts Gurdjieff's Institute for the Harmonious Development of Man.

When she begins to wear overalls, Janie attains a state of unity in which her three centers are united. The name of the garment is a wordplay that makes a pun on what has happened to Janie developmentally. In Janie's psyche there now resides a single "I" that has conquered the multitudinous lesser egos of her "false personality." We first see the overalls when Janie experiences recurrent moments of reverie or self-regard: "Sometimes Janie would think of the old days in the big white house and the store and laugh to herself. What if Eatonville could see her now in her blue denim overalls and heavy shoes?" (200). The difference between her former and present circumstances is that although people do the same things in both places, on the muck she is a participant: "Only here, she could listen and laugh and even talk some herself if she wanted to" (200). The theme of laughter is underscored in this passage, for we are told that "No matter how rough it was, people seldom got mad, because everything was done for a laugh" (200). What Hurston seems to be indicating is the esoteric idea that "people must sacrifice . . . their suffering" (ISM 274).

Hurston's method for writing "objectively" was to craft a successful novel that embodied esoteric principles only so far as they did not interfere with the narrative, structural, and aesthetic unity of her texts. For example, in *Their Eyes* the narrator's omniscience must be understood to be more than a narrative convention. The narrator speaks directly to the reader at the beginning of the novel; subsequently, the characters speak in indirect discourse because the story is told through the narrator's consciousness. The narrator is a higher being reminiscent of the Being at the end of Toomer's play "The Sacred Factory," who signifies the possibility of possessing cosmic consciousness. In Gurdjieff's writings, this figure is Beelzebub. Like the narrator of Jens Peter Jacobsen's *Marie Grubbe*, which Hurston used as a template for the form of *Their Eyes* (Woodson 620), the narrator intrudes at various points and comments on the action. Therefore, Hurston's narrator is a combination of Jacobsen's intrusive ironist and Gurdjieff's Beelzebub, who assesses human life from an "objective" point of view. However, this "objective" use of the narrator is not pedantic or dogmatic; like Alph Pearson, the narrator of *Their Eyes* evokes the nurturing and compassionate superman. Through the device of the superman-narrator, Hurston suggests the existence of a higher form of consciousness that sees life from a cosmic perspective without undercutting the significance of Janie's developing consciousness.

In her novel, *Moses, Man of the Mountain* (1939) Hurston retells the biblical story of "Exodus" by substituting African-Americans for the Hebrew tribes. This is made explicit because the speech used by the "Hebrews" in *Moses* is an African-American vernacular. In a Gurdjieffian context, the superimposition of African-Americans over Hebrews in the story of "Exodus" suggests Toomer's program for transforming African-Americans into a new race through the use of Gurdjieff's system. Toward the end of the text, Moses reviews the events of his life:

His dreams had in no way been completely fulfilled. He had meant to make a perfect people, free and just, noble and strong, that should be a light for all the world and for time and eternity. And he wasn't sure he had succeeded. He had found out that no man may make another free. Freedom was something internal. The outside signs were just signs and symbols of the man inside. All you could do was to give the opportunity for freedom and the man himself must make his own emancipation. He remembered how often he had to fight Israel to halt a return to Egypt and slavery. Responsibility had seemed too awful to them time and time again. They had wanted to kill him several times for forcing them to be men. (344–45)

Moses's assessment of the condition of the Hebrews upon their removal from slavery in Egypt coheres with the views Toomer expressed in his unpublished study of race, "The Crock of Problems" (1927). The view of race that Hurston advocates is that racial identity, national identity, and ethnic identity are debilitating and delusional mental concepts that lead men into destructive behaviors; this aligns with the Gurdjieffian approach of living a completely conscious life.

Hurston's portrait of Moses, the would-be builder of a nation from an unruly horde of slaves, is her attempt to imagine a superman intervening in history. We can only suppose that in this Hurston intentionally took a superficial approach to the concepts on which she drew. It is clear from Tolson's "Libretto" that to a Gurdjieffian the idea of intervening in history required applying the Law of the Octave. We see this as well in Fisher's *The Conjure-Man Dies* in Frimbo's discussion of the means to control the order of events (228). In Hurston's novel, the theory that Moses applies is psychological, yet it does not advance beyond the rudimentary psychological exercises of the Method; it is limited to the materials with which a beginning student would be familiar.

In *Moses* Hurston casts the superman—a peripheral figure in her other texts—as the central figure in the narrative. This represents an advance over *Jonah's Gourd Vine* and *Their Eyes*, where the theme was implicit in both texts. In both *Jonah's Gourd Vine* and *Their Eyes* history is absent from the texts, which precludes a sufficient field for the superman's agency. Although the superman theme is the focus of *Moses*, and the themes of evolution and mental freedom are also important, other esoteric themes appear. Hurston endows Moses with many of the psychological factors that Gurdjieff discussed in explaining the possibilities of man's evolution. Moses's character is largely constructed from a pastiche of Gurdjieffian-Oragean ideas and exercises couched in an oracular, narrational voice suited to the discourse of conscious humanity and the presentation of a man—Moses—becoming a superman. One such exercise appears in chapter 11. Moses is trying to plan his future, and he sits and retraces his life from the past to the present: "He walked backwards over his road from the palace to the seat on the rock in a strange nation. He looked back and the glance changed him like Lot's wife" (105). In Toomer's

1926 notebook, he lists forty-eight exercises that were included in the Gurdjieff syllabus; number forty-three was "Unroll the film." The exercise was an important part of self-observation, and was to be practiced each night while falling asleep. Thus, we see the way Hurston drew directly on the syllabus of the Oragean version of the work for episodes in her fiction.

In chapter 10, Moses sets out to answer certain questions about the gods and divine knowledge; this is what Gurdjieff called "wish." In one sentence Hurston combines two important Gurdjieffian concepts, "sleep" and "magnetic center" (the factor that holds the desire for a spiritual life): "He realized now how Mentu had aroused his thought, and that once you wake up thought in a man, you can never put it to sleep again" (101). This sentence makes a further allusion, because the first chapter of *Beelzebub's Tales* is "The Arousing of Thought." Hurston also appropriates Gurdjieff's concept of man's division into three brains or centers (mental, moving, emotional) to portray Moses's psychic development: "Thinking and walking and feeling, he was at home before he knew it" (96).

There is a noticeable continuity between *Moses* and *Jonah's Gourd Vine*. Both novels develop stories from the Bible and employ a similar method for handling Gurdjieffian material. *Moses* follows the pattern in *Jonah's Gourd Vine* of using blindness to indicate the inability of humans to function above an operational level of consciousness, the state that Gurdjieff called "sleep." As we have seen, the question of blindness and sleep is one of consciousness. Both metaphors are equivalent: Human beings have eyes, but, as Jesus said, they do not see, and they are awake, but from the point of view of "conscious humanity," they behave as though they are asleep. According to Gurdjieff, the real world is hidden from them by the wall of imagination (ISM 143). Moses, who is evolving a higher level of consciousness, represents man at the level of "waking consciousness." He is constantly made aware of the debilitating nature of the consciousness of his associates who still operate with one dominant center (instinctive, emotional, or mental). Frustrated with his struggles to reform the Hebrew people, Moses says at one point "These people were blind" (254) and later he tells Aaron directly "You are blind" (334), just as Alph Pearson tells John Buddy that he is blind.

In Hurston's texts, the evolutionary distance between the superman and men at lower levels of consciousness does not absolve the superman from a responsibility for the lower men. In this vein Moses states that "You do not mock a man for being blind. You lead him" (347). It is leadership that is the real subject of *Moses*, for according to Gurdjieff's system, leadership is entirely problematic. The system dooms Moses's efforts to advance his people, because "The evolution of large masses of humanity is opposed to nature's purposes" (ISM 57). In comparison with the supermen created by Schuyler (Drs. Belsidus and Crookman) and Fisher (N'Gana Frimbo) and the superman theorized by Thurman in *Infants*, Hurston's

Moses is conceived along more compassionate lines. Her salvationist conception of the superman is similar to those of Gurdjieff's Beelzebub and the mysterious figures in Toomer's long poem "The Blue Meridian."

Moses represents a unique approach to "objective" writing—it is at the same time allegorical, historical, and mythic. The narrative concentrates on the superman, but unlike *The Conjure-Man Dies* and *Black Empire*, it proceeds in the direction of evolution. Moses does attain spiritual awakening and he tries to awaken his people, but in doing so he learns that a general awakening violates the laws of nature. *Moses* is no less imbued with an esoteric level than other texts by the Harlem group, however, the text contains very little that can be seen as an "attack on reading." Reading does hold an important place in the story, because Moses travels in search of the Book of Thot, finds it hidden in a river, and copies it (154). However, despite this episode, which serves as instructions on hermeneutic reading, and the intimations of "real knowledge" (81) contained elsewhere in the text (e.g., "secret words" 151, 281), the antinaturalism of the surface text (with its African-American Jews) provides few clues to guide the reader to the esoteric subtext. Even the location of the "legominism" in chapters 6 and 7 is but dimly announced in her introduction, where she states that "*The Sixth and Seventh Books of Moses* [are] being read and consulted in secret" (xxii).

In his introduction to the 1984 edition of *Dust Tracks on a Road*, Robert E. Hemenway states that the text is "one of the most peculiar autobiographies in Afro-American literary history," because it "presents an image of its author that fails to conform with either her public career or her private experience" (ix). Hemenway details the many paradoxes presented by the text, including inconsistent political views, a lack of analysis of segregation, an insignificant treatment of her career as a novelist, a negligible discussion of the Harlem Renaissance, a confusing treatment of her marriage, an obscuring of her personal chronology, and a general disinterest in history. Hemenway's conclusion is that through these devices, Hurston "asks for a considerable suspension of scrutiny" (xiii), which he is willing to allow, because "it provides a fascinating self-portrait" (xiv).

The inconsistencies noted by Hemenway constitute some of the most aggressive and ostentatious manifestations of Hurston's "attack on reading" in *Dust Tracks on a Road*. By denying the reader the very aspects of her life that are expected, Hurston throws into question the verisimilitude of the text and raises the question of how the text is to be read. There are many signs that are intended to guide the reader, the most prominent being those connected to reading and writing, a theme that is of considerable importance in the text.

One episode that puts nearly everything else into perspective takes place during Hurston's account of her schooling (159–60). This episode is remarkable for the conciseness of its "attack on reading." She recounts that while working her way through Howard University, she earned money as a manicurist. Rather than doing her own translations from Xenophon's *Cyropaedeia* for her Greek course, Hurston allowed a client to do it for her. The translator was a man from whom she had been assigned by another client to pry secrets. However, in appreciation of the honorable character of her translator, Hurston states that she intends to keep his secrets. The Greek text in question is a pseudohistorical account of the life of Cyrus the Great, which has an emphasis on the king's early life and education. The story line of the *Cyropaedeia* flagrantly contradicts other source material about Cyrus the Great. Hurston's episode is not only a comment on the unreliable nature of *Dust Tracks on a Road*, it explains why the text takes such a strange approach to Hurston's life: It is to keep secrets. The episode also anticipates that the reader will be able to negotiate the text, despite its inherent difficulties.

Another episode provides a solution to the "attack on reading" announced through the *Cyropaedeia*. Hurston attributes her love for literature to a book that she found:

So I went off to another town to find work. It was the same as at home so far as dreariness and lack of hope were concerned. But one thing did happen that lifted me up. In a pile of rubbish I found a copy of Milton's complete works. The back was gone and the book was yellowed. But it was all there. So I read Paradise Lost [sic] and luxuriated in Milton's syllables and rhythms without ever having heard that Milton was one of the greatest poets of the world. I read it because I liked it.

I worked through the whole volume and then I put it among my things. When I was supposed to be looking for work, I would be stretched out somewhere in the woods reading slowly so that I could understand the words. Some of them I did not. But I had read so many books that my reading vocabulary at least was not too meager. (127)

From what we are told in connection with Hurston's study of Greek, we realize that nothing in the episode is true. Hurston uses the word "work" four times in a short space to mean employment, reading, and oeuvre. This is certainly a case of overuse designed to call attention to the word. Like Gurdjieff's *Beelzebub's Tales*, *Paradise Lost*, the "yellowed" volume that she is supposed to have found, has Beelzebub as its protagonist. "Yellowed" is a reference to Gurdjieff's complexion. Also, the volume of Milton is both "all there" and "complete," which suggests the main title of *Beelzebub's Tales*, "All and Everything." The second paragraph is a lesson in reading the coded subtext of *Dust Tracks on a Road:* It is necessary to read slowly and to look for the "stretched out" words.

As in many of the texts by the Harlem group, episodes set in the theater were used to include the "mask" concept and to indicate the superficiality of the surface text. Hurston recounts an episode in which she obtains her first real job working for an actress as a dresser. To entertain themselves while on the road, the actress invents a game: "She would take rouge and paint her face all over a most startling red. Then I must take eye-shadow and paint myself blue. Blue Jake and Red Jake would then chase each other into closets, across beds, into bathrooms, with our sheet-robes trailing around us and tripping us up at odd moments. We crouched and growled and ambushed each other and laughed and yelled until we were exhausted" (140). In this episode Hurston played a role to get her job as a dresser (as she did in her previous position as a nanny). Not content to merely work as an actress, the actress also spends her leisure time romping around in additional dramas. Hurston means to indicate something more substantial with the Red Jake–Blue Jake episode, namely that the political positions adopted by members of the Harlem group (and Tolson) were exercises in playing roles, but here it further underscores the polysemic nature of *Dust Tracks on a Road*. The eighth chapter is also heavy with references to a subtext, including "code" (130), "secret" (139), "lying" (122), "gags" (138), "sly digs" (138), "double-talk which went over my head" (137), and "sly trick" (137).

It is no exaggeration to state that *Dust Tracks on a Road* is the most densely coded text produced by a member of the Harlem group. Not only do the names Jean Toomer, C. Daly King, Gurdjieff, and Ouspensky resound continually through the text, but names of the Harlem group do as well. There is also an intricate relationship between what is encoded and what is offered on the surface. Nearly everything in the text contains at least one hidden level. For instance, the anagram "trust code" contained in the title *Dust Tracks on a Road* may be used to read the title of the eighth chapter, "Backstage and Railroad" as "code, staged, liar." The eighth chapter is a "legominism" replete with esoteric significance. Hurston states "They know how to call names" (135). Then, using a list of invectives purportedly known to every southern child, Hurston names the Harlem group in a coded list, adding to it the thrice-repeated name of C. Daly King ("eyes loo*king* like s*king*-ginny nuts, and mouth loo*king* like a dish-pan full of broke-up crockery" [emphases added]).

In her foreword to the 1991 edition of *Seraph on the Suwanee*, Hazel Carby noted the resemblances between the marriage of Arvay Henson and Jim Meserve in *Seraph* and Janie Killicks and Jody Starks in *Their Eyes Were Watching God*. Arvay's subservient role parallels Janie's dominance by Jody (*Seraph* xv). The marriage in *Seraph* eventually resembles Janie's marriage to Tea Cake in a number of important respects. *Seraph* repeats much of the material in *Their Eyes* not only on the narrative level but also on the levels of symbols, myths, allegories, and "objective" material. Both texts also explore the same archetypes and "hieroglyphic" signs—such as the net, tree, moon, and horizon. From the esoteric point of view, *Seraph* is a significant advance on *Their Eyes*, for it contains significantly more Gurdjieffian material, and the material is more accessible. The text of *Seraph* is heavily coded throughout, although not intrusively. To accomplish the coding of the esoteric subtext, Hurston developed a new approach to the Gurdjieffian technique of "lawful inexactitudes" (BT Book 2 51–52), the keys to the hidden knowledge in "legominisms." Hurston's revised method involves the inconsistent portrayal of characters.

The text's characterological coding has been observed by critics but not systematically assessed. Lowe states that "In fact, Arvay appears more racist toward the new arrivals; she calls Mr. Corregio 'the Gee' and his wife 'The Georgia Cracker,' obviously forgetting her own origins" (308). Arvay's overreaction to such a degree that she forgets her own origin identifies the passage as a "lawful inexactitude." Read as a "legominism," the passage hides Orage's name in Corregio and "the Gee" and "Georgia Cracker" refer to George Ivanovich Gurdjieff. Throughout the narrative, we are alerted to similar subtextual elements by repeated admonitions that "common sense" must be used when a joke is encountered. Jim tells Arvay that she has misread the Bible because she has not realized that it contains jokes: "Now take this same man, Cain, that you have been reading about. He never would have got into all that trouble if he could have seen a joke. . . . Common sense ought to have told him God wouldn't stand for him stinking up Heaven and all like that" (66). Jim says nearly the same thing about his insistence that Arvay not have a girl baby: "But Arvay, I thought that anybody at all would see through a joke like that. Anybody with even a teaspoon of sense knows that you can't tell what a child'll turn out to be until it gets born" (103). John Lowe has noticed the "common sense" lapse put forth as a joke; however, he has turned it back onto Arvay as a further demonstration of her "lack of humor, Puritanism, and apparent racism" (307). Although Hurston expends a great deal of energy in attacking the reader's assumptions about how the novel is to be read and how her fictional world is to be interpreted, the devices that she used to signal the other levels of the text are visible but remain enigmatic for most readers.[2]

It is possible that the biblical and Freudian inclusions in *Seraph* were themselves meant as jokes or even blind alleys. Because Hurston has barely hidden the "objective," Gurdjieffian subtext, it seems likely that she used her surface text to give an ironic treatment to "subjective" concepts with which she did not sympathize. Furthermore, by presenting the argument between Arvay and Jim over the interpretation of the Bible, Hurston attacks her readers's certainty that they should read her novel in the accustomed way. Behind *Seraph* lies *Beelzebub's Tales*, which according to Orage "is a sort of Bible . . . a kind of bible for the future" (Nott *Teachings* 194). It is also a bible that is full of jokes. In *Seraph* Hurston repeatedly links her jokes to common sense. Arvay and Jim's argument over whether there are jokes in the Bible revolves around "the dumbness of those who couldn't see a joke," and as a consequence, "Arvay found out that Jim thought her a trifle dumb" (66). Hurston makes it plain that the text of *Seraph* is, among other things, an attack on the literal reading of the text. She may do this in the hope that her readers will apply not the Bible, Freud, or black traditions to her novel but their own common sense.

Speaking about the hidden level of *Beelzebub's Tales*, Orage states that

"According to Gurdjieff, the key to the Legominism [coded text] and the key of the inexactitudes are both in our hands, the latter to be discovered by intuition. The key to the Legominism is the Method. Our understanding of this book can be said to be a test of our understanding and realization of the Method" (Nott *Teachings* 194). In the light of Orage's comment, Hurston's performance seems paradoxical: Because her readers have no awareness of the Method, they have no ability to read the esoteric level of her novel, with or without common sense. The advice that common sense is the solution to the problem of reading the text is given by Jim, the emblem of advanced consciousness. However, Hurston does not depict the biblical text being read with common sense. Likewise the clues that have been provided by the surface text are insufficient to alert most readers to their presence.

As in Hurston's other texts, in *Seraph* myth constitutes an important subtextual level. However, Hurston conducts the esoteric narration of the Osiris cycle with different emphases in *Their Eyes* and *Seraph*. The god Osiris lends himself to a Gurdjieffian interpretation; his dismemberment and dispersal can be read as an allegory of the theme that man contains not one self but multiple "subpersonalities," because of the disharmonies introduced by his three unequally apportioned centers, body, emotions, and intellect.

Seraph is an allegory of spiritual progress that relates the cosmically defined roles of women and men. In their violent courtship, Jim and Arvay reenact the primordial creation of the heavens and the fertilization of the Earth. The distinctly gendered roles in this creation have been transmitted down through the ages of man. Thus, the mystery that surrounds Jim Meserve arises because he seems to be conscious of simultaneously inhabiting and expressing a number of divine roles as he interacts with Arvay. Jim is successively Geb, the father of the gods; Osiris, the god of growth; and Ra, the god of the sun. The domestic struggle that characterizes the marriage is designed to show Arvay that in her "real self" (334) she inhabits divine "woman-mother" (BT Book 3 174–75) roles—Nut, Isis, and Hathor—that complement the divine male personae that Jim projects. Arvay is in a state of spiritual wakefulness at the conclusion of *Seraph;* she is not merged into anything beyond herself. Hurston's point is that at last Arvay has located and unified her self in accordance with her "objective" role in the universe, service to her fellow beings.

In the role of Osiris, Jim shoots their son, Earl (who is the evil god Set on the Egyptian mythical level of the subtext), after he has attacked a young girl. Hurston then has Arvay and Jim double back on their roles as Geb and Nut and give birth to children who are also forms of Osiris and Isis. The son, a form of Osiris, is a blues musician who becomes wildly popular, and the daughter exhibits the beautiful and fertile qualities of Isis. The turning point of the novel is Jim's struggle with a snake. Frozen in fear, Arvay does nothing to free Jim from the snake's coils; he would have been crushed had not one of the hired hands walked around Jim and uncoiled the snake. This scene is a reenactment of the Egyptian myth of "Straightening out Apopis," the revival and resurrection of Osiris from the cosmic mound and the destruction of the monstrous snake that symbolizes death. At the conclusion of the novel, Arvay and Jim sail into the sunrise in a fishing boat, which represents the Egyptian Boat of the Sun. Hurston subliminally roots her novel in cosmic creation and fertility myths, which were intended to endow the text with a numinous aura. We are led to conclude that Hurston used the myths enacted in her subtext to unconsciously affect the majority of her readers and not to divulge the cosmic or esoteric level of the novel.

In *Seraph*, Arvay portrays a role similar to Janie in *Their Eyes*, but she does so by boarding the fishing boat given her name. We have seen that some of the Harlem group texts were based on Gurdjieff's parable of the orderly house: At the conclusion of *Infants*, for example, Niggerati Manor is converted to a home for wayward girls under the direction of the Pig Woman. To clarify one meaning of Hurston's use of seacraft, we only have to realize that the difference between a house and a boat is that a boat has a captain. As captain, Jim assumes the role of the "real 'I'" that Arvay must develop. That is, allegorically, Jim is her "real 'I.'" In this arrangement, there is no opportunity for Hurston to develop the theme of the dismemberment of Osiris. Hurston may have been influenced by variant materials from the Egyptian corpus of sacred texts, such as the "Legend of Ra and Isis," which Budge included in *The Book of the Dead*. In that text, Ra is saved by Isis after he has been bitten by a serpent. Isis saves him by using his secret name, which Ra tells to her by abrogating himself from time and space: "Then the divine one hid himself from the gods, and the throne in the Boat of Millions of Years was empty. . . . Thus was the great god made to yield up his name" (Budge 124). This Egyptian text helps to clarify the murky conclusion of *Seraph*. First we see that Jim will not come to Arvay's cabin until she calls out to him, and then they flirt verbally. Arvay must invoke Jim's name in a somewhat ritualistic manner, much as in an Egyptian litany: "Who's been pomping you up so? Who's been telling you that you're pretty?" asks Jim. Arvay's answer is "Jim Meserve, that's who" (347). Arvay goes on to aver that she has come to understand what Jim's essence contains: She insists that now "I can read your writing" (347). Although the dismemberment of Osiris communicated an esoteric truth in a dramatically and graphically powerful way, in *Seraph* Hurston substituted esoteric naming for the original scheme.

In Hurston's writing none of the three threads—narrative, myth, or esoteric system—will suffice on their own. Her novels are not purely literary exercises. Hurston is not merely telling a story, as we see in novels by Hemingway or Fitzgerald; nor is she relating a myth, as James Joyce does in *Ulysses;* nor is she illustrating esoteric concepts, as Toomer does in "Eight Day World." In *Seraph*, Hurston's fiction reaches its culmination in a form in which she applies the Law of Three, the esoteric idea that all phenomena can be understood as the meeting of three different and opposing forces or principles (Waldberg 97). These forces may be thought of as positive, passive, and negative or impulsion, mediation, and resistance. A review of Hurston's fiction demonstrates that she consistently explored the Law of Three, such as in Janie's three marriages in *Their Eyes* and the three components of *Seraph* that contribute to its structural unity, namely, myth, narrative, and the Gurdjieff work. Without the inclusion of the work, readings of her novel that interpret the mythic level against the narrative level are likely to remain enigmatic. We also see this Law of Three operating within the narrative of *Seraph:* Arvay (passive force) comes between the crewman (negative force) and Jim (positive force), thereby allowing Jim to continue sailing the boat to safety. Without Arvay's intervention, all of them would have died. Similarly, the mythic component and the narrative line cancel out one another, which produces an allegory with an indefinite meaning. When the themes of the work are factored in with the other two levels, the novel takes on its complete form as a unified work of "objective" art.

The threefold synthesis of myth, esoterism, and narrative is given its clearest expression through the two episodes that describe Arvay's crisis and its subsequent resolution. When a huge snake attacks Jim, Arvay is powerless to aid him; at the end of the novel, the scene is repeated when one of the crew fastens onto Jim and threatens his life. The second attack on Jim is based on another section of *The Book of the Dead* that describes a struggle between Osiris and Apopsis, although now they are called Ra and Aapep. These attacks on Jim portray an identical cosmic event, the mythic rising of the sun. In *The Book of the Dead*, Budge describes the rising of the sun as Ra's battle with the great serpent, Aapep, who attempted to bar his progress. All Aapep's attacks failed, because Ra cast immobilizing spells on him. The supporters of the Sun-god bound Aapep in chains, hacked him to pieces, and burned him in Ra's flames (Budge 166).

The first episode acts out the mythic attack of Osiris by the evil god Apopsis, who takes the form of a giant snake. Arvay does not protect Jim (Osiris), and another person must unwind the monstrous Apopsis. When the scene repeats on board the *Arvay Henson*, it does so with remarkable faithfulness to the Egyptian original. Jim imitates Ra's "spells" as he roundly curses the mate because he is praying: "Don't you be praying on my damn boat, you bastard you! Get up off your damn rusty knees!" (329). The issue here is exactly that addressed in the title of *Their Eyes Were Watching God*, the idea that men are dependent on illusory faith in outside forces instead of depending on their own energized wills. Esoterically, the attack of Aapep on Ra represents Arvay's inability to align herself with a "real 'I.' " At the conclusion of *Seraph*, having destroyed her old "house," her system of multiple selves, Arvay protects her unified "I" against the hysterical crewman, who represents a component of her fragmented self, one of her "subpersonalities."

In the esoteric account, we understand that the allegory takes place within

Arvay's psyche. She burns her parental home to exorcise her dysfunctional past; her psychic setting is then shifted from the outworn house that she has shed like a psychic chrysalis to the boat, the *Arvay Henson*, that symbolizes her new, unified self. Hurston probably drew the ship metaphor from Orage's habit of speaking of the Method as a vessel on which his disciples were to sail (Webb 306). *Seraph* concludes with Arvay having come to terms with her provisional, manifold, and "false" self; she has not dissolved into oceanic formlessness but has contracted into psychic unity.[3] This is given mythic form by depicting the boat of Ra, the Boat of Millions of Years, as it sails into the sunset. We see a vigilant Arvay watching the sun rising as she embraces her sleeping husband: "The few hours left of the darkness passed away with Jim held in her arms" (351). This scene reconfigures the vignette for plate XX of the "Papyrus of Ani" that Budge describes in connection with the "Hymn to Ra": "Isis embraces the body of the god with her right arm" (296). In discussing Ra's insistence that he believes in the power of Osiris, Budge notes that "Ra and Osiris are only two forms of one god" (296). Accordingly, Hurston has justifiably conflated in Jim the two gods Ra and Osiris, "the king of eternity" (Budge 350).

In her versions of "objective" texts, Hurston largely concerned herself with a human- centered universe and human psychology. She worked best with the theme of three centers and found ways to work feeling, thinking and doing into the fabric of the language and the form of her novels in efficacious, graceful, and accomplished ways. She also successfully concentrated on evoking the important themes of "mental independence" and "sleep." Although an important feature of her novels, Hurston's attack on racialism is understated. She handles attitudes about race not as an empirical social condition but as a determinant of individual psychology, such as Tea Cake's fear of white people that emerges with tragic consequences in the dementia of his rabies infection. It is primarily in *Dust Tracks on a Road* that Hurston reveals herself as an uncompromising antiracialist: The concept underlying her text is that "Negroes are just like anybody else" (329), a conviction that she shared with the other members of the Harlem group. Throughout *Dust Tracks on a Road*, Hurston illustrates and expounds upon the idea that "What the world is crying and dying for at this moment is less race consciousness" (326).

Hurston also successfully gave her novels a religious atmosphere without concerning herself with religious values. In doing so, she followed Gurdjieff's method of modernizing mysticism by attacking science through the irreligious devices of parody, satire, and irony. In addition, such unmodern devices as parable, allegory, fable, fantasy, and magic spells have been used to restore emotional flexibility to the impoverished modern self. Here Hurston's approach resembles the "mythical method" outlined by T. S. Eliot in "*Ulysses*, Order and Myth." In that essay, Eliot speaks of the application of myth to literature as a "step toward making the modern world possible for art . . . order . . . and form" (178).

Hurston gave the superman a major role in her fiction. Her conception of this important but unfashionable figure is essentially that of a religious leader inspired with a deep and direct spirituality. In doing this, Hurston contrasts with Toomer's existential position, of "I, single and alone in this vast universe,—all points of which are equally 'remote'" ("The Meaning of 'Individual'" "A New Group, 1926"). Hurston's supermen embody the preeminence of compassion, psychological insight, and a visionary perception of human possibilities. As we have seen, Hurston's achievements should not be taken for granted, for other Harlem writers made the superman a central theme and yet passed over the constructive themes that Hurston explored. When Hurston's texts are compared to other texts by the Harlem group, we see that she is more concerned with guiding man to a higher consciousness and a utopian future than with looking down on the world from an ethereal distance. As a body of work, Hurston's fiction repudiates the view that "those who know" are justified in laughing sardonically at the masses who suffer in ignorance at the foot of the cosmic ladder.

Conclusion

Wallace Thurman's *Infants of the Spring* concludes with a description of the title sheet, which is all that remains of Paul Arbian's illegible novel: "Beneath this inscription, he had drawn a distorted, inky black skyscraper, modeled after Niggerati Manor, and on which were focused an array of blindingly white beams of light. The foundation of the building was composed of crumbling stone. At first glance it could be ascertained that the skyscraper would crumple and fall, leaving the dominating white lights in full possession of the sky" (184). Ekphrasis (the verbal representation of visual art) is not common in the texts of the Harlem group, and its use at the finale of *Infants* is trenchant. The image that closes Thurman's novel is a dramatic chiaroscuro of the latent destruction that propelled the Harlem group into fervent creativity. Destructions, plunges, and downfalls permeate their texts, from the title of *The Walls of Jericho* to a play about the fall of Jerusalem to Titus in A.D. 70 that Hurston was writing in 1947 (Hemenway 343). Although the Harlem group texts do depict ascensions, my point here is that the writers believed that drastic means were required to save the human race from imminent and inevitable destruction. The Harlem group saw themselves poised decisively "between the ass and womb of two eras" (HG 125). Strangely enough, the group believed that they were the determinants of whether the future would be doomsday or paradise.

The theme of destruction has not been dealt with directly in this study. Certainly, Gurdjieff and Orage held the attention of their followers by a constant reiteration of this theme. In their system, because man is situated at the foot of the "ray of creation" (octave, ladder, or cosmos) everything reaching man from above is mechanical-involution; evolution requires conscious labor, voluntary suffering, and the struggle against the descending ray (Nott *Teachings* 135). Niggerati Manor, the three-storied house in which Thurman set *Infants* and the prototype of Paul Arbian's toppling skyscraper, was itself a key symbol in the process of evolution. The central doctrine that spurred the Harlem group was that man produced "a substance needed by some entity [the moon (ISM 304)] . . . thus serving the evolution or involution of that entity" (Gurdjieff *Views* 210). Although formerly warfare could produce a form of the "food" required in the reciprocal exchange of the cosmos, it would not do so forever: Either man produced a finer food than war or man would be useless to the cosmos, for man's failure to evolve was retarding the evolution of higher worlds (ISM 305). Gurdjieff believed that this "finer food" could be produced by two hundred conscious men, the "inner circle of humanity." John G. Bennett comments that *Beelzebub's Tales* is concerned with two themes:

awakening man to the significance and purpose of his existence and war (27). The centrality of "periodic reciprocal destruction" (BT Book 3 247) in Gurdjieff's "objective" view of man partly accounts for his conviction that man only rises to fall again. The reason for this belief is that Gurdjieff traced the origin of wars to planetary influences ("Solioonensius") that propagate mass hysteria (Bennett 28). Not only was future destruction a topic of perennial pondering by the Gurdjieffians, past destructions were also examined as beacons from which great lessons could be learned. Orage was fond of such austere ruminations as "Why is it that we fail . . . to preserve the treasures of each succeeding civilization . . . Egypt . . . India . . . Chaldea . . . China? . . . Why do we believe and hope in 'progress,' when all around us there are proofs that we are deteriorating and are working day and night to produce forces that will destroy even such as *we* have built up?" (Nott *Teachings* 132–33). However, these destructions did not only affect civilizations, man's devolution was also given graphic depiction: "It may be that if the degeneration of man continues, if his energy continues to be diverted to trivialities, if scientists continue to invent more fantastic means of destruction, if men continue to pollute and poison the rivers and the earth with chemicals and sprays—then Nature may do to them what she did to the ants and bees" (Nott *Teachings* 140). Writing in his highly refined version of Orage's teachings, C. Daly King notes that "the programme of our Western civilization, entered upon unwittingly so far as concerns its deepest motive and carried forward to-day [sic] with ever-mounting fury, is bankrupt and impossible. It is obvious that consciousness cannot be gained unconsciously" (King *Psychology* 144).

Beelzebub's Tales is a direct confrontation of the eventuality of destructions. Exiled to Mars, Beelzebub makes six descents to Earth from his observatory to try to preserve human civilization—the first in the time of Atlantis to warn against sentimental reformers and the last to find out why the span of man's life is shortening. Gurdjieff's book tells of man's origin and describes him from a higher realm. The book recovers lost information, it does not present new information (Nott *Teachings* 134).

This establishes a background for the place of literature in a scheme grounded in the primacy of destruction, a threatened future, loss, and unconsciousness. Such a literature is, first of all, concerned with texts that have survived from other destructions. In this vein, Orage made constant reference to esoteric schools: "Gurdjieff says that there has existed from Atlantean times a chain of esoteric schools, custodians of secret knowledge, which, from time to time, is interpreted and taught by teachers who are sent out from these schools" (Nott *Teachings* 186). Orage stated that the troubadours were emissaries of an esoteric school (Nott *Teachings* 142). Thus, secret knowledge can be recovered from any number of similar sources. However, it is difficult to recognize a book that contains esoteric information because the nature of the text has been disguised.

Speaking of the difficulty of reading *Beelzebub's Tales*, Orage noted that "there are three 'versions' of the book—an outer, an inner, and inmost: also, every complete statement in the book has seven aspects" (Nott *Teachings* 136). A further hint is offered in the statement that "*Beelzebub's Tales* are [sic] not wholly allegorical; some parts are historical, some contemporary. We must be able to read parabolically the thought between and over the lines" (Nott *Teachings* 214). Therefore, Gurdjieff's book is on the surface a fantastic story about a voyage through space, on the inner level a description of man, and inmost an account of the cosmos. It was necessary to write in such a fashion because of the limited utility of language from the "objective" view: Nott states that "Gurdjieff spoke and wrote in a picture-form of speech, symbolical language, which is necessary for understanding, because words, being counters or characters of account, result in definitions, and definitions eventually freeze language, for when all is defined and determined it is lost, or leaves only a shallow impression on him who hears or uses the definitions" (*Teachings* 228). Orage's theoretical analysis of Gurdjieff's writings implies an important relationship between the use of "symbolical language" and the historical treatment of texts. If destruction is in every case the rule, then for texts to preserve the attainments of knowledge, they must take a form that will communicate to those in the future. To do this, the text must be endowed with qualities that are more substantial than most language: These texts are what Gurdjieff called "legominisms," and they are characterized by inexactitudes, which can be discovered by intuition (Nott *Teachings* 194).

Each text written by the members of the Harlem group is, essentially, a reduced version of *Beelzebub's Tales*. The reaction of Toomer and his group was conditioned by a number of factors: their preliminary grasp of the esoteric system (in contrast with Gurdjieff's deeper understanding), their exoteric status as students, their need to respond to the racial problem, and their own roles in the salvation of civilization (on one level) and of humanity (on another level). Finally, history played a role: Shortly after the Harlem group began its literary efforts, America entered the Great Depression. The collapse of the world's economy must have seemed to them like the beginning of the end of civilization. Actual depictions of the Depression are absent from the Harlem group's texts written after 1929, although it certainly contributed to the central role of destruction and involution in their writings.

In writing the "objective" text, Jean Toomer made few advances beyond reproducing the vocabulary of the system in "Eight Day World" and "The Gallonwerps." Toomer's major contribution to the Harlem group was to join Gurdjieff's system of self-development with a comprehensively intellectual and spiritual response to the racialization of American culture. Thus, the racial component in the writings of the Harlem group is their special contribution to addressing the problem of the world's condition. This study began by citing W. E. B. Du Bois's famous words about the status of race in determining the future course of history. Although the Harlem group's texts struggle against the concept of racialization, this theme occupies only the outermost level of their texts. Had the Harlem group believed that this struggle would be brought to a successful conclusion, there would be no need for the inner and the inmost levels in their texts. As with *Beelzebub's Tales*, the inner text is partly historical and imparts information about the Harlem group itself and the inmost level is concerned with cosmic laws.

It is a matter of speculation as to whether the inmost level of these texts is more obscure than the inner level, because neither seems to have been detected by most readers. However, it seems that the original intention was to make the inner, racial level less opaque than the inmost level. On the texts' inner level, pen names, themes, and plot elements revolve around conspiracies, disguises, codes, and secrets; these are more apparent than the inmost level, which contains encoded names of obscure mystics (Gurdjieff, Ouspensky, Toomer, and King) and abstruse concepts. Through these texts, the Gurdjieffians hedged their bets: Should the world prove to be beyond salvation, as "legominisms" their texts would help to reconstruct the esoteric system that they believed to be the crowning achievement of civilization. By writing in this way they were simply imitating Gurdjieff.

As with esoteric literature in general, intertextuality is a major and consistent feature of the Harlem group's texts. Although Toomer's unpublished works and Van Vechten's *Nigger Heaven* influenced the Harlem group to some degree, it is not difficult to make out the outline of Gurdjieff's *Beelzebub's Tales* in many of the Harlem texts. Gurdjieff's text also played a generative role in shaping Toomer's writing. Therefore, we can acknowledge *Beelzebub's Tales* as the urtext of the "objective" tendency in Harlem.

The Harlem group wrote allegories of spiritual advancement. In addition to Gurdjieff's influence, however, the Harlem group also made innovations of their own. Thus, the surface of the texts by Larsen, Thurman, Fisher, Schuyler, Hurston, and Tolson express several Gurdjieffian themes in disparate ways. However, this diversity is deceptive: The inner texts have many commonalities and the inmost level is identical and equivalent to the "objective" level of *Beelzebub's Tales* and to texts by other schools of Gurdjieffians.

Evolution and involution (or creation and destruction) are found in all of the texts discussed in this study. Races evolve in texts such as *Black No More; Moses, Man of the Mountain;* and *Harlem Gallery.* However, the Gurdjieff system places the individual at the center of the cosmos, and thus most of the "objective" texts treat the theme of individual evolution (e.g, *Their Eyes Were Watching God, Seraph on the Suwanee,* and *The Blacker the Berry*). "Objectively" speaking, involution is the same theme with the octaves of vibrations working in the opposite direction. However, this is seldom recognized by people exclusively aware of the "subjective" level—such as the characters in the texts. Involution was worked out in such texts as *Passing, Quicksand, Jonah's Gourd Vine, The Walls of Jericho*, and *Harlem Gallery*.

The Harlem group's literary production began in 1928 with the publication of an evolutionary novel, *The Walls of Jericho*, by Rudolph Fisher and an involutionary novel, *Quicksand*, by Nella Larsen. Fisher's text was based on Gurdjieff's parable of the horse, carriage, driver, and master and featured the theme of sleep. Larsen's text was based on another of Gurdjieff's parables, the well-ordered house; sleep was an important theme in Larsen's novel also. Next followed the evolutionary *The Blacker the Berry* (1929) and the involutionary *Passing* (1929). Thurman's text featured the theme of mental independence and Larsen's relied heavily on the three-centers theme both in form and content. After 1929, Larsen did not publish and Thurman was silent until 1932. Schuyler then produced the evolutionary *Black No More* (1931) and the involutionary *Slaves Today* (1931). In the figure of his first superman, Dr. Crookman, Schuyler presents Beelzebub, whereas *Slaves* is based on Gurdjieff's parable of the escape from prison.

Rudolph Fisher, Wallace Thurman, and A. R. Orage died in 1934. Larsen continued to write, although she destroyed her manuscripts. Fisher's *The Conjure-Man Dies* (1932), Thurman's *Infants of the Spring* (1932), and Hurston's *Jonah's Gourd Vine* (1934) are all involutionary texts. Fisher and Thurman largely concerned themselves with the "ray of creation," and Hurston's first novel explores the theme of sleep. Fisher follows Schuyler in featuring Beelzebub, whereas Thurman imitates Larsen's use of the parable of the house.

Hurston's *Their Eyes Were Watching God* (1937) is almost exaggeratedly evolutionary, whereas Schuyler's *Black Empire* (1936–1938) plunges to new depths of violence, hatred, and spiritual death. Although *Their Eyes* follows Larsen's second novel in featuring the three-centers theme, the text is diverse and the parables of the house and of the horse, carriage, driver, and master may be found in it. Hurston's use of myth was not one dimensional; T. S. Eliot's ideas on myth were likely a contributing factor, as may have been Carl Jung's. But another important component came from the Gurdjieff system: Orage stated that "We are like the dismembered Osiris. With the help of the Method we can re-member [sic] ourselves; re-collect ourselves, become whole" (Nott *Teachings* 130). Although not in the story, in *Their Eyes* Hurston reproduces the myth of Isis and Osiris in "symbolical language." In *Seraph* she relates other episodes in the cycle of the Egyptian gods; although she represents Osiris throughout the text, she does not reproduce the familiar myth of Isis and Osiris that she relates in *Their Eyes*. Schuyler's superman, Belsidus, is reminiscent of Fisher's N'Gana Frimbo, particularly in that both explore Beelzebub as an involutionary figure.

Moses, Man of the Mountain (1939), Hurston's evolutionary treatment of the superman, is an ambiguous text—it is difficult to assign it a direction, although from the Gurdjieffian approach it is clearly an evolutionary text. The novel argues for the impossibility of the evolution of groups, instead it follows the path of Moses's individual evolution. Hurston's next two texts are also evolutionary. *Dust Tracks on a Road* (1942) is one of the only texts that extensively deals with advanced material, namely, Experimentation or role-playing. *Seraph on the Suwanee* (1948) returns to the parable of the horse, carriage, driver, and master.

Melvin B. Tolson's "Libretto for the Republic of Liberia" (1953) is the first text to take up one of Gurdjieff's favorite themes, the idea that political and religious movements of the purest intentions become their opposites. This theme is given an elaborate exposition in *Beelzebub's Tales,* particularly in "Beelzebub's Opinion of War" in Book 3. On its surface, "Libretto" expresses an evolutionary and prophetic account of Africa's ascendancy, and it may be thought of as having a complex relationship to Schuyler's *Black Empire. Harlem Gallery* (1965) is Tolson's last book-length poem and concludes the Gurdjieffian tradition of African-American writing. The poem recapitulates all of the texts discussed in this study. Tolson was fond of stating that the poem's theme was that movements become their opposites, although he did not identify the Gurdjieffian source of this proposition (see ISM 129). Specifically, Tolson intended the poem to be the first book of a five-volume treatment (Flasch 149) of the metamorphosis of Christianity into slavery: "There was no racial prejudice as such in the history of the world until . . . the Christian ethic had to find a way to justify . . . slavery" (Bickman 6). Tolson's protagonist is an albino Negro who keeps company with an African scholar, Dr. Obi Nkomo. Nkomo is an evolutionary version of Fisher's involutionary superman, N'Gana Frimbo. Nkomo is also Gurdjieff in disguise, but his name plays a familiar joke. We have seen that Thurman and Hurston left clues that Langston Hughes was not a Gurdjieffian and was not aware of the Harlem group's activities. Dr. Obi Nkomo's name is an anagram for "do be common," which in turn is a parody of Hughes's mouthpiece, Jesse B. Semple. Through this elaborate play on words, Tolson indicates that he has hidden Gurdjieff in a character who seems to express a Hughesian brand of racial chauvinism.

Previously, the literature of the Harlem Renaissance has been understood by critics to consist of a volatile sociological mixture of the fad of the exotic and primitive black, the "bourgeois-uplift of the Du Bois–Brawley school" (Singh *Novels* 26), and the failure of Alain Locke and Charles Johnson to organize a cohesive literary movement (Singh *Novels* 31). Critics have overlooked Toomer's Gurdjieffian school of "objective" literature because they tend to assign Harlem literary works to one of the three categories above or to emphasize certain exceptions. For instance, Singh states that

Harlem Renaissance writing is marked by racialism, but the writers reflect the spirit of the times in their refusal to join causes or movements. 'Individuality is what we should strive for. Let each seek his own salvation,' says Raymond Taylor, the alter ego of Wallace

Thurman in *Infants of the Spring*. (20) As a creative writer, Zora Neale Hurston was interested not in social problems, but in the problems of individuals, black or white. . . . Wallace Thurman, lost in the world of contemporary bohemia, would not compromise with the high artistic standards he set for himself and others. There were, however, many black writers of the period who—independently or under Locke's influence—resolved their dilemmas of conflicting racial and artistic loyalties in ways resembling Locke's approach. Among these writers are Langston Hughes, Jean Toomer, Rudolph Fisher, Eric Walrond, Sterling Brown, Arna Bontemps, and Zora Neale Hurston. (*Novels* 20–21)

Most of the writers that Singh assigns to the coterie of "individuality," were members of Toomer's Gurdjieff group, namely, Thurman, Toomer, Fisher, Walrond, and Hurston. Moreover, we can recognize in Thurman's call for "individuality"—the source of Singh's terminology—the Gurdjieffian principle of "mental independence," a central a part of the doctrines that Toomer presented to his Harlem followers. The writers that remain—Hughes, Bontemps, Brown, and Locke—were advocates of some form of racialism. These "racialists" stand in stark contrast to those others identified by Singh as "independents"; rather than embracing the concept of "race consciousness," the "independents" wholeheartedly rejected racial categorization. In fact, Toomer, Hurston, Thurman, and Tolson stated categorically that the "Negro" did not exist. The uniformity of the rejection of racialism on the part of the "independents" points more to their common embrace of an ideology of antiracialism than to their adherence to a formless, subjectless "independence."

To communicate the illusory and socially deleterious nature of racial thought and behavior, the members of the Harlem group took up the novel in its most popular forms—romance, suspense, adventure, detective story—as the means to reach a wide audience with their views. In some cases, critics read these antirace novels as works celebrating color. In this way, Hurston becomes the author of "the most famous lines in African American women's literature" (Kafka 174). Where a reading that celebrates race has been difficult or impossible, the texts have been declared to be lamentable expressions of Hurston's racial confusion and ambiguity. The result is that particularly in the cases of Schuyler's *Black No More* and Hurston's *Seraph on the Suwanee*, the ironic and complexly inapplicable handling of race (compounded with the unfashionable handling of gender in *Seraph*) has accorded the texts little sensitive attention from critics.

There are perhaps as many questions to answer at the conclusion of this study as at its inception. Whatever else remains to be investigated, it seems that no longer can we look at the career of Jean Toomer in the same way. The revised conception places Toomer as a bridge between the unique and controversial George Ivanovich Gurdjieff and his mystical teachings, dances, and writings and an important school of American writers. In turn, the revised Toomer relocates an important body of African-American literature, which now may be seen to contain far more cohesion, depth, and artistry than was suspected before the key to their inner and inmost levels had been disclosed. Along this line, we have Gurdjieff's observation—a warning and an invitation—that "Pure knowledge cannot be transmitted, but by being expressed in symbols it is covered by them as a veil, although at the same time for those who desire and who know how to look this veil becomes transparent" (ISM 284).

Notes

Introduction

1. The designation of these writers as the "Harlem group" is my own and was not used by the individuals to whom it refers. Although it was suggested by the title of Melvin B. Tolson's master's thesis "The Harlem Group of Negro Writers" (1940), my intention is merely to use a convenient label for the writers under discussion—Thurman, Fisher, Larsen, Schuyler, Hurston, (and Tolson). The Harlem group encompassed more than the five writers directly treated in this study, and also included Bruce Nugent, Dorothy Peterson, Aaron Douglas, Harold Jackman, and Eric Walrond.

2. A typical statement along these lines is John Bennett's comment that "Ideas are powerful, not organisations [sic]" (42).

3. See James Webb's detailed discussion of C. Daly King's *The Oragean Version* (304–10).

4. Melvin B. Tolson's *Harlem Gallery* is included in the comparative study because he came at the end of the "objective" tradition in Harlem and distilled and clarified its practice.

Chapter 2

1. Michael Riffaterre's definition of this term is as follows: "Sociolect: language both as grammar and repository of the myths, traditions, ideological and esthetic stereotypes, commonplaces, and themes harbored by a society, a class, or a social group. Literary texts exploit the sociolect as does any other utterance, shaping their own original usage *(ideolect)* in conformity or in contradistinction to the sociolect. Aside from syntactic structures, the sociolect contains ready-made narrative and descriptive models that reflect a group's ideas or consensus about reality. Verisimilitude depends on references to such models" ("Glossary" 130).

Chapter 3

1. This is not to say that Fisher had access to Gurdjieff's words through Ouspensky's text. *In Search of the Miraculous* was circulated through the various groups in a mimeographed form for many years before it was published in 1949. It is not known whether Fisher had direct access to Gurdjieff's words during the composition of *The Walls of Jericho*, and he may or may not have derived the metaphor of the wall from Gurdjieff. Nevertheless, the meaning of the figure of speech is identical, and if the usage is coincidental, it is an instructive concurrence.

2. "[T]he Negro is a sort of seventh son, born with a veil, and gifted with second-sight in this American world. It is a peculiar sensation, this double-consciousness, this sense of always looking at one's self through the eyes of others, of measuring one's soul by the tape of a world that looks on in amused contempt and pity. One ever feels this twoness—an American, a Negro; two souls, two thoughts, two unreconciled strivings; two warring ideas in one dark body, whose dogged strength alone keeps it from being torn asunder" (Du Bois 45).

3. It is instructive to compare Fisher's description of N'Gana Frimbo to James Webb's biographical description of Gurdjieff with "a glint of stratagem in his eye" (19), Schuyler's fictional description of Dr. Belsidus with "deep-set eyes [that] smoldered like twin volcanos" (*Black Internationale* 11), and Larsen's fictional description of Gurdjieff as Mrs. Hayes-Rore with a "direct penetrating gaze" (*Quicksand* 68).

Chapter 4

1. Kenneth Walker notes that Freud's psychology leaves out much that Gurdjieff discourses on at length. Freud ignored mysticism and the soul and located the ego as a function of body image. Freudian psychology does not recognize the states of consciousness (waking "sleep," "clear consciousness," "self-remembering," and the "objective state of consciousness" or cosmic-consciousness; see ISM 141) that are basic to Gurdjieffian psychology; nor does Freudian psychology recognize the fundamental fragmentation of man's being into three centers: emotional, physical, and mental.

2. See, for example, Butler (167–85), McDowell, Blackmore, Hostetler, Dearborn (59–60), Tate, Thornton, and Du Cille.

3. James Webb gives a good account of the differences in the system that developed between 1924 and 1929. Orage ran the American groups with no supervision, and he gradually developed his own vocabulary and methods. When Gurdjieff visited America in 1930 he disbanded Orage's groups and repudiated his disciple's innovations. At this point, it is not clear whether Toomer's Harlem group followed the so-called Oragean Version after 1930 or returned to an "orthodox" version of the Method. See Webb (305–11).

4. This paragraph (39), besides commenting negatively on the Harlem "school" sounds out the name of Langston Hughes ("*long*," "*st*udents," "*op*en," "Ent*hus*iasm"). Both the enciphering device and the condemnatory opinion are reminiscent of Hurston's treatment of Hughes in *Seraph*.

5. See xxiii of Deborah E. McDowell's introduction to *Quicksand and Passing* and David L. Blackmore.

6. Gurdjieff's esoteric psychology emphasizes that men and women have functional differences: "Gurdjieff and his teachings developed the masculine in men and the feminine in women" (Nott *Teachings* 118). The conception of these differences has nothing to do with conventional gender stereotypes, which are cultural and shift with the times. In the "objective" view, women and men are equally "asleep." See *Beelzebub's Tales* (Book 3 171–86).

7. The use of these names raises an interesting question about the origin of this practice. Schuyler's pen name, John Kitchen, is also comparable to Wallace Thurman's character Campbell Kitchen in *The Blacker the Berry*. Were these names created as a group effort?

Chapter 5

1. "Impressions" can mean both external sensory stimuli (ISM 181) and life experiences (Wilson *War* 68–69).

2. The word "all" is emphasized for the first two pages by its frequency and its prominent placement at the beginning and end of some sentences. On page 205 "ever" occurs twice in a paragraph that also contains "the Evil One" (Beelzebub) and two "all"s. On page 206 the "y" sound is emphasized with four occurrences in a short paragraph. The next paragraph takes up the "ing" sound. We find "thing" in "nothing" on page 207. There are more in-

stances of these inclusions, as Schuyler has saturated the text with elements that compose the words "all" and "everything."

3. Although the term "mask" does not occur in *In Search of the Miraculous*, it is implied. For example, Gurdjieff observes that "In order to see types one must know one's own type and be able to 'depart' from it" (247).

4. John Kitchen, the pen name that George Schuyler used to publish "The Philanderer" (1934), is comparable to Campbell Kitchen, the Carl Van Vechten analog and tutor to the protagonist of Wallace Thurman's novel *The Blacker the Berry* (1929). We can read John Kitchen as "join in it" and Campbell Kitchen as "come be in it."

Chapter 6

1. In "Poetics of Embalmment" (147–48) Kathleen Davies provides a useful summary of the critical response to Hurston's ambiguity. Davies's comments include the views of Mary Helen Washington, Robert E. Hemenway, and Henry Louis Gates.

2. I am indebted to Craig Werner (1991) for noticing that there are more than two dozen times in *Seraph* that characters fail to understand jokes (Lowe 260–61). Lowe himself calls for "a special reading" (260–61) of the text due to its allegorical (293) and psychological (271) nature.

3. John Lowe adjusts Freud's "mistaken dismissal of the oceanic as 'regressive.'" Lowe gives the oceanic a positive valence and then "aligns the oceanic with the Afrocentric" to conclude that "The African view of the cosmos assumes the interrelatedness of all things and argues for community and union rather than for difference, hierarchy, and individual dominance" (333). This reading not only runs afoul of the entire Gurdjieffian project (and Hurston's involvement in it), but also the goal of the individual worshiper in the Egyptian religion to persist eternally as an individual and to "be content with nothing less than living in the absolute presence of the god [Ra] himself" (Budge "Hymn to Ra" 296).

Bibliography

Barrett, Francis. *The Magus.* New York, N.Y.: Citadel, 1967.

Bell, Bernard W. "Jean Toomer's *Blue Meridian:* The Poet as Prophet of a New Order of Man." *Black American Literature Forum* 14 (Summer 1980): 77–80.

————. *The Afro-American Novel and Its Traditional.* Amherst: University of Massachusetts Press, 1987.

Bennett, John. *Talks on Beelzebub's Tales.* York Beach, Maine: Samuel Weiser, 1988.

Bickman, Jack. "Flowers of Hope." *Orbit. Sunday Oklahoman* August 29 (1965): 6–9.

Blackmore, David L. " 'That Unreasonable Restless Feeling': The Homosexual Subtexts of Nella Larsen's *Passing.*" *African American Review* 26 (1992): 475–84.

Blavatsky, H. P. *Abridgement of the Secret Doctrine.* Wheaton, Ill.: Theosophical Press, 1968.

Bone, Robert. *The Negro Novel in America.* New Haven, Conn.: Yale University Press, 1958.

Bresky, Dushan. *The Art of Anatole France.* The Hague: Moton, 1969.

Budge, E. A. Wallis, ed. *The Book of the Dead.* Secaucus, N.J.: University Books, 1960.

Butler, Judith. *Bodies That Matter: On the Discursive Limits of Sex.* New York, N.Y.: Routledge, 1993.

Byrd, Rudolph P. "Jean Toomer and Writers of the Harlem Renaissance: Was He There with Them?" In *The Harlem Renaissance: Re-evaluations.* Ed. Amritjit Singh, William S. Shriver, and Stanley Brodwin. New York, N.Y.: Garland Press, 1989. 209–18.

————. *Jean Toomer's Years with Gurdjieff: Portrait of an Artist 1923–1936.* Athens: University of Georgia Press, 1990.

Calverton, V. F. *An Anthology of American Negro Literature.* New York, N.Y.: Modern Library, 1929.

Campbell, James L., Sr. *Edward Bulwer-Lytton.* Santa Barbara: University of California Press, 1986.

Carby, Hazel. "Foreword." In *Seraph on the Suwanee.* Zora Neale Hurston. New York, N.Y.: Harper, 1991. vii–xviii.

Clark, Gordon H. "Epicureanism." In *Selections from Hellenistic Philosophy.* Ed. Gordon H. Clark. New York, N.Y., Appleton-Century-Cofts, 1940. 1–8.

Clark, R. T. Rundle. *Myth and Symbol in Ancient Egypt.* London: Thames and Hudson, 1978.

Coleman, Leon Duncan. *The Contribution of Carl Van Vechten to the Negro Renaissance: 1920–1930.* Ann Arbor, Mich.: University Microfilms, 1969.

Crane, Hart. *The Complete Poems and Selected Prose of Hart Crane.* Ed. Brom Weber. New York, N.Y.: Anchor Books, 1966.

Daumal, Rene. *Mount Analogue: A Novel of Symbolically Authentic Non-Euclidean Adventures in Mountain Climbing.* Trans. Roger Shattuck. Baltimore, Md.: Penguin, 1974.

Davie, Sharon. "Free Mules, Talking Buzzards, and Cracked Plates: The Politics of Dislocation in *Their Eyes Were Watching God.*" *PMLA* 108 (May 1993): 446–59.

Davies, Kathleen. "Zora Neale Hurston's Poetics of Embalmment: Articulating the Rage of Black Women and Narrative Self-Defense." *African American Review* 26.1 (1992): 147–59.

Davis, Thadious. *Nella Larsen, Novelist of the Harlem Renaissance: A Woman's Life Unveiled.* Baton Rouge: Louisiana State University Press, 1994.

Dearborn, Mary V. *Pocahontas's Daughters: Gender and Ethnicity in American Culture.* New York, N.Y.: Oxford University Press, 1986.

De Jongh, James. *Vicious Modernism: Black Harlem and the Literary Imagination.* New York, N.Y.: Cambridge University Press, 1990.

Draper, Muriel. Papers. Beinecke Rare Book and Manuscript Library, Yale University, New Haven, Conn.

Du Bois, W. E. B. *The Souls of Black Folk.* 1903. *Essays and Sketches.* New York, N.Y.: New American Library, 1969. 45–53.

Du Cille, Ann. *The Coupling Convention: Sex, Text, and Tradition in Black Women's Fiction.* New York, N.Y.: Oxford University Press, 1993.

Eliot, T. S. "*Ulysses,* Order, and Myth." In *Selected Prose of T. S. Eliot* Ed. Frank Kermode. New York, N.Y.: Harcourt, 1966.

Epstein, Isidore. *Judaism.* London: Pelican, 1960.

Epstein, Perle. *Kabbalah: The Way of the Jewish Mystic.* Boston, Mass.: Shambhala, 1988.

Fisher, Alice Pointdexter. "The Influence of Ouspensky's *Tertium Organum* upon Jean Toomer's *Cane.*" *CLA Journal* 17.4 (1974): 504–15.

Fisher, Rudolph. *The Walls of Jericho.* New York, N.Y.: Arno Press, 1969.

———. *The Conjure-Man Dies.* New York, N.Y.: Arno Press, 1971.

Flasch, Joy. *Melvin B. Tolson.* New York, N.Y.: Twayne, 1972.

Flint, R. W. "Introduction." In *Marinetti—Selected Writings.* F. T. Marinetti. Ed. R. W. Flint. New York, N.Y.: Farrar, Strauss, and Giroux, 1971. 3–36.

France, Anatole. "The Procurator of Judea." In *Tales from a Mother-of-Pearl Casket.* Trans. Henri Pene Du Bois. New York, N.Y.: Books for Libraries Press, 1972. 1–26.

Frazer, J. *The Golden Bough: A Study in Magic and Religion.* Abridged ed. New York, N.Y.: The Macmillan Company, 1922, 1972.

Fritzsche, Peter. "Nazi Modern." *Modernism/Modernity* 3.1 (1996): 1–22.

Fulcanelli, pseud. *Le Mystere des Cathedrales: Esoteric Interpretation of the Hermetic Symbols of the Great Work.* Suffolk, U.K.: Neville Spearman, 1977.

Fuller, Hoyt. "Introduction." In *Passing.* Nella Larsen. New York, N.Y.: Collier, 1971. 11–24.

Gates, Henry Louis, Jr. "A Fragmented Man: George Schuyler and the Claims of Race." *The New York Times Book Review* 7 (1992): 31.

Gossett, Thomas F. *Race: The History of an Idea in America.* New York, N.Y.: Oxford University Press, 1997.

Gruesser, John C. "George S. Schuyler, Samuel I. Brooks, and Max Disher." *African American Review* 27.4 (1993): 679–86.

Gurdjieff, G. I. *All and Everything: An Objectively Impartial Criticism of the Life of Man, or Beelzebub's Tales to His Grandson*. New York, N.Y.: E. P. Dutton, 1973.

————. *Views from the Real World: Early Talks in Moscow, Essentuki, Tiflis, Berlin, London, Paris, New York, N.Y. and Chicago as Recollected by His Pupils*. New York, N.Y.: E. P. Dutton, 1973.

————. *Life Is Real Only Then, When "I Am": All and Everything. Third Series*. New York, N.Y.: E. P. Dutton, 1978.

Halevi, Z'ev ben Shimon. *Kabbalah: Tradition of Hidden Knowledge*. London: Thames and Hudson, 1979.

————. *A Kabbalistic Universe*. York Beach, Maine: Weiser, 1988.

Hayles, N. Katherine. *The Cosmic Web: Scientific Field Models and Literary Strategies in the Twentieth Century*. Ithaca, N.Y.: Cornell University Press, 1984.

Hemenway, Robert E. *Zora Neale Hurston: A Literary Biography*. Champaign: University of Illinois Press, 1980.

Hill, Robert A. and Kent Rasmussen. "Afterword." In *Black Empire*. George Schuyler. Boston, Mass.: Northeastern University Press, 1991. 259–323.

Hostetler, Ann E. "The Aesthetics of Race and Gender in Nella Larsen's *Quicksand*." *PMLA* 105.1 (1990): 35–46.

Hoyrd, Andre. "George S. Schuyler's Shafts and Darts: *Black No More* and the Menippean Tradition." M.A. thesis. Howard University, Washington D.C., 1995.

Hughes, Langston. *The Big Sea*. New York, N.Y.: Thunder's Mouth, 1968.

Hulme, Kathryn. *Undiscovered Country: In Search of Gurdjieff*. Boston, Mass.: Little, Brown and Co., 1966.

Hurston, Zora Neale. Papers. Zora Neale Hurston Collection. Yale Collection of American Literature. Beinecke Rare Book and Manuscript Library, Yale University, New Haven, Conn.

————. *Jonah's Gourd Vine*. New York, N.Y.: Harper and Row, 1934, 1990.

————. *Moses, Man of the Mountain*. Urbana: University of Illinois Press, 1939, 1984.

————. *Their Eyes Were Watching God*. Urbana: University of Illinois Press, 1978.

————. *Dust Tracks on a Road*. Ed. Robert Hemenway. Urbana: University of Illinois Press, 1984.

————. *Seraph on the Suwanee*. New York, N.Y.: Harper, 1991.

Hutchinson, George. "Nella Larsen and the Veil of Race." *American Literary History* 9 (1997): 329–49.

Idel, Moshe. *Kabbalah: New Perspectives*. New Haven, Conn.: Yale University Press, 1988.

Johnson, Barbara. "Writing." In *Critical Terms for Literary Study*. Ed. Frank Lentricchia and Thomas McLaughlin. Chicago, Ill.: University of Chicago Press, 1990. 39–49.

Jung, C. G. "The Spiritual Problem of Modern Man." In *The Portable Jung*. Ed. Joseph Campbell. New York, N.Y.: Viking, 1971. 456–79.

Kafka, Phillipa. *The Great White Way: African American Women Write*. New York, N.Y.: Garland, 1993.

Kellner, Bruce. *Carl Van Vechten and the Irreverent Decades*. Norman: University of Oklahoma Press, 1968.

Kerman, Cynthia Earl and Richard Eldridge. *The Lives of Jean Toomer: A Hunger for Wholeness.* Baton Rouge: Louisiana State University Press, 1987.

King, Charles Daly. *The Psychology of Consciousness.* London: Kegan Paul, Trench, Trubner & Co. Ltd., 1932.

———. *The Oragean Version.* Long Valley, N.J.: privately published, 1951.

Kirschke, A. H. *Aaron Douglas: Art, Race, and the Harlem Renaissance.* Jackson: University Press of Mississippi, 1995.

Kronegger, M. E. "Impressionist Tendencies in Lyrical Prose: 19th and 20th Centuries." *Revue de Litterature Comparee* 43 (1969): 528–44.

Larsen, Nella. Papers. Dorothy Peterson Collection. James Weldon Johnson Manuscript Collection. Yale Collection of American Literature. Beinecke Rare Book and Manuscript Library, Yale University, New Haven, Conn.

———. *Quicksand.* In *Quicksand and Passing.* Ed. Deborah E. McDowell. New Brunswick, N.J.: Rutgers University Press, 1986.

———. *Passing.* In *An Intimation of Things Distant: The Collected Fiction of Nella Larsen.* Ed. Charles R. Larson. New York, N.Y.: Doubleday, 1992.

Larson, Charles R. "Introduction." In *Black No More.* George S. Schuyler. New York, N.Y.: Collier, 1971. 9–15.

———. "Introduction." In *An Intimation of Things Distant: The Collected Fiction of Nella Larsen.* New York, N.Y.: Anchor, 1992. xi–xxi.

———. *Invisible Darkness: Jean Toomer and Nella Larsen.* Iowa City: University of Iowa Press, 1993.

Lewis, David Levering. *When Harlem Was in Vogue.* New York, N.Y.: Oxford University Press, 1981.

Little, Jonathan. "Nella Larsen's *Passing:* Irony and the Critics." *African American Review* 26.1 (1992): 173–82.

Locke, Alain. "The Legacy of the Ancestral Arts." In *The New Negro.* Ed. Alain Locke. New York, N.Y.: Atheneum, 1969. 254–67.

Lowe, John. *Jump at the Sun: Zora Neale Hurston's Cosmic Comedy.* Urbana: University of Illinois Press, 1994.

Marinetti, F. T. "Multiplied Man in the Reign of the Machine." In *Marinetti—Selected Writings.* Ed. R. W. Flint. New York, N.Y.: Farrar, Strauss, and Giroux, 1971. 90–94.

McDowell, Deborah E. "Introduction." In *Quicksand and Passing.* Nella Larsen. Ed. Deborah E. McDowell. New Brunswick, N.J.: Rutgers University Press, 1986. ix–xxx.

McKay, Nellie Y. *Jean Toomer: Artist—A Study of His Literary Life and Work.* Chapel Hill: University of North Carolina Press, 1984.

———. "Jean Toomer in Wisconsin." In *Jean Toomer: A Critical Evaluation.* Ed. Therman B. O'Daniel. Washington, D.C.: Howard University Press, 1988. 47–56.

McKluskey, John, Jr. "Introduction." In *The City of Refuge: The Collected Stories of Rudolph Fisher.* Columbia: University of Missouri Press, 1987.

Moore, James. *Gurdjieff: The Anatomy of a Myth.* Rockport, Mass.: Element, 1991.

Neilson, W. A., ed. *Webster's New International Dictionary of the English Language.* Springfield, Mass.: C. G. Merriam, 1936.

Neumann, Erich. *The Origins and History of Consciousness*. Princeton, N.J.: Princeton/ Bollingen, 1993

Nott, C. S. *Further Teachings of Gurdjieff: Journey through This World*. York Beach, Maine: Samuel Weiser, Inc., 1969.

————. *Teachings of Gurdjieff: A Pupil's Journal—An Account of Some Years with G. I. Gurdjieff and A. R. Orage in New York, N.Y. and Fountainebleau-Avon*. York Beach, Maine: Samuel Weiser, Inc., 1982.

O'Daniel, Therman B. "Introduction." In *The Blacker the Berry . . . : A Novel of Negro Life*. Wallace Thurman. New York, N.Y.: Macaulay, 1970. ix–xix.

Ouspensky, P. D. *In Search of the Miraculous: Fragments of an Unknown Teaching*. New York, N.Y.: Harcourt, Brace & World, 1949.

————. *Tertium Organum*. New York, N.Y.: Vintage, 1950.

Palmeri, Frank. *Satire in Narrative: Petronius, Swift, Gibbon, Melville, and Pynchon*. Austin: University of Texas Press, 1990.

Patterson, William Patrick. *Struggle of the Magicians*. Fairfax, Calif.: Arete, 1996.

Perry, Margaret, ed. *The Short Fiction of Rudolph Fisher*. New York, N.Y.: Greenwood Press, 1987.

Peterson, Dorothy. Papers. Dorothy Peterson Collection. James Weldon Johnson Collection. Yale Collection of American Literature. Beinecke Rare Book and Manuscript Library, Yale University, New Haven, Conn.

Pickthall, Maurice. *Said the Fisherman*. New York, N.Y.: Knopf, 1925.

Plagens, Peter. "The Return of the Limp Watch." *Civilization* 3.5 (1996): 30–32.

Rampersad, Arnold. *The Life of Langston Hughes*. Vol. I, *1920–1941: I Too Sing America*. New York, N.Y.: Oxford University Press, 1986.

Regardie, Israel. *A Garden of Pomegranates: An Outline of the Qabalah*. St. Paul, Minn.: Llewellyn, 1986.

Riffaterre, Michael. *Fictional Truth*. Baltimore, Md.: Johns Hopkins University Press, 1990.

Rosenberg, Samuel. *Naked Is the Best Disguise: The Death and Resurrection of Sherlock Holmes*. New York, N.Y.: Bobbs-Merrill, 1974.

Rusch, Frederik L., ed. *A Jean Toomer Reader*. New York, N.Y.: Oxford University Press, 1993.

Sadoul, Jacques. *Alchemists and Gold*. Trans. Olga Sieveking. New York, N.Y.: G. P. Putnam's Sons, 1972.

Schuyler, George. *Slaves Today: A Story of Liberia*. New York, N.Y.: Brewer, Warren, and Putnam, 1931.

————. "The Van Vechten Revolution." *Phylon* 11 (1950): 362–68.

————. "The Negro-Art Hokum." In *Voices from the Harlem Renaissance*. Ed. Nathan I. Huggins. New York, N.Y.: Oxford University Press, 1976. 309–11.

————. *Black No More*. New York, N.Y.: Collier Books, 1979.

————. *Black Empire*. Ed. Robert A. Hill and R. Kent Rasmussen. Boston, Mass.: Northeastern University Press, 1991.

Shah, Idries. *The Sufis*. New York, N.Y.: Anchor, 1964.

————. *Oriental Magic*. New York, N.Y.: Dutton, 1973.

Sheinkin, David. *Path of the Kabbalah*. New York, N.Y.: Paragon, 1986.

Singh, Amritjit. *The Novels of the Harlem Renaissance*. University Park: Pennsylvania State University Press, 1976.

————. "Foreword." In *Infants of the Spring*. Wallace Thurman. Boston, Mass.: Northeastern University Press, 1992. vii–xxix.

Sollors, Werner. *Beyond Ethnicity: Consent and Descent in American Culture*. New York, N.Y.: Oxford University Press, 1986.

Speeth, Katherine Riordan. *The Gurdjieff Work*. New York, N.Y.: Pocket, 1976.

Talalay, Kathryn. *Composition in Black and White: The Life of Philippa Schuyler*. New York, N.Y.: Oxford University Press, 1995.

Tate, Claudia. "Nella Larsen's *Passing:* A Problem of Interpretation." *Black American Literature Forum* 14 (1980): 142–46.

Taylor, Paul Beekman. "Gurdjieff's Deconstruction of Historical Time in the *Third Series.*" The Proceedings of the International Humanities Conference: All and Everything, 1997. 179–205.

————. Letter to the author. 8 December 1997.

Thornton, Hortense E. "Sexism as Quagmire: Nella Larsen's *Quicksand*." *CLA Journal* 16 (1973): 285–301.

Thurman, Wallace, ed. *Fire!!* 1926. Nendeln/Liechtenstein: Kraus Reprint, 1968.

————. *The Blacker the Berry . . . :A Novel of Negro Life*. New York, N.Y.: Arno Press, 1969.

————. *Infants of the Spring*. Carbondale: Southern Illinois University Press, 1979.

Tolson, Melvin B. "The Harlem Group of Negro Writers." M.A. thesis. Columbia University, New York, 1940.

————. *Libretto for the Republic of Liberia*. New York, N.Y.: Collier Books, 1953.

————. *Harlem Gallery: Book I, The Curator*. New York, N.Y.: Twayne, 1965.

Toomer, Jean. "The Crock of Problems." Box 32, Folder 7. Jean Toomer Collection. James Weldon Johnson Manuscript Collection. Yale Collection of American Literature. Beinecke Rare Book and Manuscript Library, Yale University, New Haven, Conn.

————. "A New Group, 1926." Box 66, Folder 2. Jean Toomer Collection. James Weldon Johnson Manuscript Collection. Yale Collection of American Literature. Beinecke Rare Book and Manuscript Library, Yale University, New Haven, Conn.

————. Notebook entry, 1931. Box 2. Jean Toomer Collection. James Weldon Johnson Manuscript Collection. Yale Collection of American Literature. Beinecke Rare Book and Manuscript Library, Yale University, New Haven, Conn.

————. Papers. Jean Toomer Collection. James Weldon Johnson Manuscript Collection. Yale Collection of American Literature. Beinecke Rare Book and Manuscript Library, Yale University, New Haven, Conn.

————. "The Blue Meridian." In *The Wayward and the Seeking: A Collection of Writings by Jean Toomer*. Ed. Darwin T. Turner. Washington, D.C.: Howard University Press, 1982. 214–34.

————. "The Gurdjieff Experience." In *The Wayward and the Seeking: A Collection of*

Writings by Jean Toomer. Ed. Darwin T. Turner. Washington, D.C.: Howard University Press, 1982. 128–36.

———. "The Experience." In *A Jean Toomer Reader.* Ed. Frederik L. Rusch. New York, N.Y.: Oxford University Press, 1993. 33–76.

———. "A New Race in America." In *A Jean Toomer Reader.* Ed. Frederik L. Rusch. New York, N.Y.: Oxford University Press, 1993. 105.

Turner, Darwin T. *In a Minor Chord: Three Afro-American Writers and Their Search for Identity.* Carbondale: Southern Illinois University Press, 1971.

———. "Introduction." In *Cane.* Jean Toomer. New York, N.Y.: Liveright, 1975.

———, ed. *The Wayward and the Seeking: A Collection of Writings by Jean Toomer.* Washington, D.C.: Howard University Press, 1982.

Ulmer, Gregor L. *Applied Grammatology.* Baltimore, Md.: Johns Hopkins University Press, 1985.

Van Dusen, Wanda. "Portrait of a National Fetish: Gertrude Stein's 'Introduction to the Speeches of Marechal Petain' (1942)." *Modernism/Modernity* 3.3 (1996): 69–92.

Van Notten, Eleonore. *Wallace Thurman's Harlem Renaissance.* Atlanta, Ga.: Costerus New Series 93, 1994.

Van Vechten, Carl. Postcard to Dorothy Peterson, 1939. JWJ MSS 10, Box 2, Folder 50. Dorothy Peterson Collection. James Weldon Johnson Manuscript Collection. Yale Collection of American Literature. Beinecke Rare Book Library, Yale University, New Haven, Conn.

Waite, A. E. *The Holy Kabbalah.* Secaucus, N.J.: University Press, 1975.

Waldberg, Michel. *Gurdjieff: An Approach to His Ideas.* Trans. Steve Cox. London: Routledge and Kegan Paul, 1973.

Walden, Daniel. "The Canker Galls . . , or, The Short Promising Life of Wallace Thurman." In *The Harlem Renaissance Re-examined.* Ed. Victor A. Kramer. Georgia State Literary Studies, no. 2. New York, N.Y.: AMS Press.

Walker, Kenneth. *A Study of Gurdjieff's Teaching.* New York, N.Y.: Award, 1969.

Walrond, Eric. "The Epic of a Mood." *The Saturday Review* October 2 (1926): 153.

Watson, Steve. *The Harlem Renaissance.* New York, N.Y.: Pantheon, 1995.

Webb, James. *The Harmonious Circle: The Lives and Work of G. I. Gurdjieff, P. D. Ouspensky, and Their Followers.* Boston, Mass.: Shambhala, 1987.

Welch, Louise. *Orage with Gurdjieff in America.* Boston, Mass.: Routledge and Kegan Paul, 1982.

Werner, Craig. "Zora Neale Hurston." In *Modern American Women Writers.* Ed. Elaine Showalter, Lea Baechler, and A. Walton Litz. New York, N.Y.: Charles Scribner's Sons, 1991. 221–33.

Wilson, Colin. *The Occult.* New York, N.Y.: Random, 1973.

———. *The War against Sleep: The Philosophy of Gurdjieff.* Wellingborough, U.K.: Aquarian, 1980.

———. *Beyond the Occult.* New York, N.Y.: Carroll & Graf, 1988.

Wintz, Cary D. *Black Culture and the Harlem Renaissance.* Houston, Tex.: Rice University Press, 1988.

Woodson, Jon. "Zora Neale Hurston's *Their Eyes Were Watching God* and the Influence of Jens Peter Jacobsen's *Marie Grubbe*." *African American Review* 26 (1992): 619–35.

Young, John Wesley. *Totalitarian Language: Orwell's Newspeak and Its Nazi and Communist Antecedents*. Charlottesville: University Press of Virginia, 1991.

Index

Accidental events, 2

African-American language, objective writing and, 12

Alchemy, Thurman references to, 57–58

All and Everything: An Objectively Impartial Criticism of the Life of Man, or Beelzebub's Tales to His Grandson. See *Beelzebub's Tales* (Gurdjieff)

Anagrams, 18–19; in *Black Empire*, 19, 140; in *Black No More*, 141; in *Blacker the Berry*, 54–55; in *Dust Tracks*, 20–21, 164; in *Infants*, 19; in *Passing*, 100; in *Quicksand*, 100, 105, 106

Anderson, Margaret, 36

Antiracialism: fiction writing and, 11; Harlem group, 177; Toomer's, 15, 16–17; Van Vechten's social engineering and, 9. *See also* Attack on race

Art, "objective." *See* "Objective," Gurdjieffian

Art as Vision group: forming a new race, 44; studies Ouspensky's writings, 30–31; visionary aesthetic of, 31–32

Artificiality: *Blacker the Berry* text, 51–52; *Infants* text, 63

Attack on race, 27; in *Black Empire*, 139; in *Black No More*, 45, 126, 128; in *Blacker the Berry*, 47, 48, 60–61; in *Infants*, on Harlem writers failure to address, 72–73; in *Passing*, 120–21; Schuyler's, 136, 139–40; in *Slaves Today*, 124; Thurman and, 48; Toomer amplification of, 32–33; in *Walls of Jericho*, 79–80, 85–86. *See also* Chromatic democracy

Attack on reading, 20, 26–27; absence of, in *Slaves Today*, 125; in *Black No More*, 135; in *Blacker the Berry*, 49–50, 61; in

Conjure-Man Dies, 87–89; in *Dust Tracks on a Road*, 162–64; in *Infants*, 63; in *Moses*, 162

Barthe, Richmond, 9

Beelzebub's Tales (Gurdjieff), 10; allusions to in Harlem group writings, 26; attack on modern science, 91; destruction theme in, 45, 172; Harlem group writing and, 23, 173; influence on *Black No More*, 131; lawful inexactitudes of, 11; as successful objective modern text, 11; themes of, 171–72; Toomer's imitations of, 33; as urtext for Harlem group writers, 174; writing/publication of, 21–22. *See also* "Book, the"

Behaviorism, Orage and, 142–43

Bell, Bernard, 111, 124–25

Bennett, Gwendolyn, 47

Bennett, John G., 171–72

Beyond Behaviorism (King), 142

Beyond Ethnicity (Sollors), 29

Biblical allusions: in *Black No More*, 132; Gnostic doctrine and, 60; in *Quicksand*, 104–05; in *Seraph*, 165; in *Their Eyes*, 154, 155; in *Walls of Jericho*, 76, 81, 84–85. *See also Jonah's Gourd Vine; Moses*

Big Sea, The (Hughes): on Toomer's activities in Harlem, 34–35, 36

"Biologist Asserts He Can Remold Man" (article, *New York Times*), 126

Black and Conservative (Schuyler), 123

Black Empire (Schuyler), 17, 136–41; anagrams in, 19, 140; cipher of Schuyler's name in, 138; coded levels in, 139–40; disaster premonitions in, 44, 175; Gruesser review of, 136–37; Gurdjieff

Black Empire (Schuyler) (*cont.*)
character in, 26; legominisms in, 140–41; octaves in, 25; Tolson's "Libretto" and, 176; world change theme of, 143–45

Black Internationale (Schuyler), 136; octaves in, 25

Black No More: Being an Account of the Strange and Wonderful Workings of Science in the Land of the Free, A.D. 1933–1940 (Schuyler), 8, 126–36; anagrams in, 141; attack on reading in, 27, 135; Biblical allusions in, 132; on chromatic democracy, 45, 130; critical reviews of, 177; Du Bois/Garvey caricatures in, 130–31; embedded text in, 28; esoteric science *vs.* pseudoscience in, 127–28; evolution in, 174, 175; Gurdjieffian themes/representation in, 132, 134–36; language as central issue of, 132–33; legominism in, 134–36, 140–41; as Menippean satire, 128, 129–30; new race concept in, 127, 128–29; "objective" strategy of, 131; octaves in, 25, 127–28; sounds of text, 131–32; world change theme of, 17, 143–45

Blacker the Berry, The (Thurman), 47–62; alchemy/magic references, 57–58; artificial narrative of, 51–52; attack on reading and, 49–50, 61; coded text on Toomer's activities in Harlem, 35–36; color-consciousness in, 47, 48, 60–61; Gnostic doctrine in, 57, 59–60; as Gurdjieffian initiatory text, 54–56; Gurdjieffian themes in subtext, 50–51; Harlem Gurdjieffians in, 60–61; individual evolution in, 174, 175; lawful inexactitudes in, 55–56; mental independence symbolism, 54, 62; names as coded messages in, 52–54; octaves in, 25; opinions about, 47–48; organization of, 54; "plot" of, 48–49; secrecy theme/textual nature of, 51–52, 58–59; sleep symbolism in, 50, 56–57, 61; sounds of text, 56, 58–59;

subtext/intratextuality in, 28, 49–50, 53–54

Blavatsky, H. P., 31, 42, 127, 128. *See also Secret Doctrine*

"Blue Meridian, The" (Toomer), 44–45, 162

Boas, Franz, 15–16

Boccioni, Umberto, 38

Bontemps, Arna, 13, 39, 177

"Book, the," 83, 119–20. *See also Beelzebub's Tales*

Book of the Dead, The (Budge), 167, 168–69

Brawley, Benjamin, 47, 176

Breton, Andre, 38

Brook, Peter, 91

Brooks, Samuel I. *See* Schuyler, George S.

Brown, Sterling, 177

Budge, E. A. Wallis, 167, 168, 169

Buffers, Gurdjieffian concept of, 77, 78, 108, 152

Bulwer-Lytton, Edward, 129

Burke, Kenneth, 30

Buwongo ritual, Gurdjieffian concepts and, 93–94

Bynner, Witter, 9

Byrd, Rudolph P., 45, 66

Cabala, Thurman use of, 58

Cabbala, verbal, in *Beelzebub's Tales*, 11

Calverton, V. F., 126

Cane, Melville, 9

Cane (Toomer), 23, 31–32

Carby, Hazel, 164

"Caromb" (Toomer), 33

"Caucasian Problem, The" (Schuyler), 133

"Chief feature" concept, 149, 152–53

Chromatic democracy: in *Black No More*, 45, 129, 130

City of Refuge: The Collected Stories of Rudolph Fisher, The, 73

"City of Refuge, The" (Fisher), 75

Coded text, 17–21; anagrams, 18–19; *Beelzebub's Tales*, 33; Thurman's, 51–52;

transparent wordplay, 18, 27–28. *See also* specific works

Coleman, Leon, 9–10

Color-consciousness: African-American intraracial, 47, 48, 60–61; Harlem group concerns of, 45; Van Vechten's salons and, 8

Conjure-Man Dies, The (Fisher), 75, 86–95; attack on modern science, 91; attack on reading in, 27, 87–89, 125; coded text in, 18–19; detective novel as "objective" form, 86–87; embedded text in, 28; evolving man concept, 93–95; Gurdjieff representation in, 90–91; Gurdjieffian themes in subtext of, 89–90, 91–93, 175; on intervening in history, 160; involution in, 175; lego-minism in, 92–94; "man as a three-storied factory" concept in, 93; names as Gurdjieffian devices in, 90; octaves in, 25, 89; sight theme, subtext and, 87; sounds of text in, 88; superior man theme in, 142

Conscious discrepancies, 26

Consciousness, Animal, Human, and Super-human (Orage), 65

Cosmic physics, Gurdjieff's, 79

Cosmic Web, The (Hayles), 37

Crane, Hart, 30

"Crock of Problems, The" (Toomer), 23, 43, 160

Cryopaedeia (Xenophon), 163

Dance, sacred, 6, 36, 38, 41

Daumal, Rene, 34

Davis, Thadious: on France's story in *Quicksand*, 104; Gurdjieffian reading of *Quicksand*, 105; Larsen biography, 97–98; on Larsen's ironic methodology, 109; on Larsen's use of silence, concealment, secrecy, 119; on *Passing* structure, 114; on *Said the Fisherman* in *Quicksand*, 100

Depression, Great, 173

Destruction: planetary, 43; Schuyler's race-less society after, 45; as theme of Harlem group, 171–72; in *Walls of Jericho*, 81. *See also* Involution

Detective stories. *See Conjure-Man Dies, The*

Devolutionary development, 99, 121. *See also* Involution

Douglas, Aaron, 98; Jacob's ladder and, 155; at party for Larsen publication, 9; Thurman and, 47; at Toomer's lectures, 39; Van Vechten and, 7

Draper, Muriel, 6–7, 9

Du Bois, W. E. B., 1, 173–74, 176; double consciousness theory, Toomer's attack on race and, 33; Fisher satire of, 78; New Negro theories of, 130; reviewing *Black No More*, 129; Schuyler caricature of, 130–31; on Thurman addressing African-American intraracial color prejudice, 47; Van Vechten admiration and, 7

Duality, man's, 152

"Dust" (Fisher), 75

Dust Tracks on a Road (Hurston): attack on reading in, 27, 125, 162–64; coded subtext in, 20–21, 28, 164; Hemenway introduction to, 162; Hemenway on textual construction of, 125; on lawful inexactitudes, 11–12; mask concept in, 163–64; on Negroes like anybody else, 16; octaves in, 25; role-playing in, 176; on secrecy in Harlem group, 13; Van Vechten tribute in, 7

Egypt: culture of, in *Their Eyes*, 155–56; myths of, in *Seraph*, 166–67; myths of, in *Their Eyes*, 154–55, 156; myths of, Law of Three and, 167–69

"Eight Day World" (Toomer), 173

Eldridge, Richard, 39

Eliot, T. S., 169, 175

Epstein, Isidore, 156

Esoteric groups, 12–13. *See also* Secrecy

Esoteric schools: Gurdjieff's New York, 85; reciprocal periodic destruction and, 172
Evolution: Blavatsky's sixth-root race and, 42; Gurdjieffian idea of normal man and, 14; Gurdjieffian Method theme, 26, 99; Harlem group "objective" writing and, 174; racial emphasis of, 17, 143–45; Thurman on, 66; Toomer, Harlem group "objective" writing and, 21. *See also* Involution
"Exile into Being" (Toomer), 40–41
Experiment technique, Oragean version, 13

False personality, 5–6; Gurdjieffian Method theme, 26; in *Jonah's Gourd Vine*, 152; in *Quicksand*, 100, 108; Toomer, Harlem group "objective" writing and, 21. *See also* Masks
Fauset, Jessie, 7
Ferris, Hugh, 9
Fire!! (magazine), 7
Fisher, Rudolph, 75–95, 123, 175; antiracial writing approach of, 11, 15, 24; coding in novels of, 20; McKluskey on, 75; productivity of, 14; Singh's assessment of, 176–77; Tolson and, 15; Van Vechten admiration and, 7; Van Vechten and, 7. *See also Conjure-Man Dies, The; Walls of Jericho, The;* other specific works by
Flasch, Joy, 19–20
France, Anatole, 103
Frank, Waldo, 29, 30
Freudian psychology, 97, 165
Fritzsche, Peter, 1–2
Fulcanelli (alchemist), 58

Gale, Zona, 34; Tolson and, 15
"Gallonwerps, The" (Toomer), 22, 23–24, 33, 173
Galton, Francis, 4–5
Garvey, Marcus: racial chauvinism of, 130; Schuyler caricature of, 130–31; Schuyler deconstructs theories of, 124

Gates, Henry Louis, Jr., 13, 136, 137
Glenn, Isa: at Van Vechten dinner parties, 9
Gnostic doctrine, 59–60; Gurdjieff and, 57; Thurman use of, 58–59
Golden Bough, The (Frazier), 155
Grant, Madison, 5
Gruesser, John C., 136–37, 139
Gurdjieff, George Ivanovich: assessment of modernist historical period, 1–2; biological conception of race and, 16; on change, 17; as disguised character in Harlem group writings, 25–26; Harlem group housecleaning, 12; initiation lecture for Orage students, 12–13; "inner circle of humanity" concept, 171; on Kabbalism, 153; literary works, conceptual power of, 33–34; on man's threefold construction, 11; metaphysics of, 3; philosophy of, as existentialism, 130; psychology of, Larsen and, 97; "reciprocal maintenance" concept, 127, 151; role-playing of, 14; sacred dances of, 36, 38; teaching Orage, 33; on Toomer, 38; on war and planetary influences of, 172; Watson's behaviorism theories and, 142–43. *See also Beelzebub's Tales;* other specific works by
Gurdjieff's Deconstruction (Taylor), 12

Harlem Gallery (Tolson), 15, 176; complex coding in, 19; disaster premonitions in, 44, 174–75; embedded text in, 28; evolution in, 174; Gurdjieff character in, 25; octaves in, 25
Harlem group, 4; antiracial/racial art of, 24; codes in texts of, 17–21; color line concerns of, 45; destruction as theme in, 171; esoteric ideology of, 73, 85; Gurdjieffian literary elements in writings of, 21–22; Gurdjieffian/Oragean themes in writings of, 21; imitating Gurdjieff's writing style, 23; legominisms, effective-

ness of, 174; mystical teachings, 43; "objective" satire of, 23–24; productivity of, 14; secrecy concerns of, 13, 16–17; Toomer influence on, 34–36; Toomer's centrality to, 41; Van Vechten salons and, 7–8

Harlem Renaissance: celebration of, racialism dangers and, 70–71; critical understanding of, 176–77; failure to generate "objective" literature, 72–73; Gurdjieffian activities/ideas and, 9; Toomer and, 16; transformative power of totalizing ideology and, 37

Harris, Dorothy Hunt, 39

Hayles, N. Katherine, 37

Heap, Jean: Gurdjieff's sacred dancing and, 36

Hemenway, Robert E., 125, 162

"Herod the Great" (Hurston), 123

Hill, Robert A., 124, 136, 139, 140

Hoffenstein, Samuel, 9

Holiday (Frank), 31

Hostetler, Ann E., 99

Hughes, Langston: Harlem group and, 176; "objectivity" of, 10; racial chauvinism of, 130; Singh's assessment of, 176–77; socialism, race and, 15; Thurman and, 47; on Toomer's influence in Harlem, 34–35, 98; Toomer's public groups and, 13; on Van Vechten's salons, 7–8

Hulme, Kathryn, 14, 134

Hurston, Zora Neale, 123, 147–70; antiracial writing approach of, 11, 15, 24, 169; Boaz, scientific antiracism and, 15–16; coding in novels of, 20; literary aesthetics in "objective" writing of, 147; myth use of, 175; "objective" writing of, 169–70; productivity of, 14; Singh's assessment of, 176–77; Thurman and, 47; Van Vechten admiration by, 7; vs. Schuyler in approach to antiracialism, 130; writing form using Law of Three

of, 167–69. *See also Jonah's Gourd Vine; Seraph on the Suwanee; Their Eyes Were Watching God;* other specific works by

Hutchinson, George, 45, 97, 98

Illusion, manipulative: Fisher's use of, 78; Gurdjieff's view on modern life as, 22

Imes, Nella. *See* Larsen, Nella

In a Minor Chord (Turner), 35

In Search of the Miraculous (Ouspensky), 6; allegory on "objective" view of human condition, 75; Kabbalism discussion in, 153; "man as a three-storied factory" discussion in, 93; "mask" concept omitted from, 137

Individuality: evolution of, in Hurston's works, 174, 176; Gurdjieffian Method theme, 26; in *Infants*, 70–71; mental independence concept and, 72

Industrial society degeneration, 3

Infants of the Spring (Thurman), 62–73, 171; anagrams of Gurdjieff's system in, 19; artificiality of text in, 63; attack on reading, 63, 69, 125; evolution symbols in, 171; Gurdjieff representations in, 25–26, 66–67; Gurdjieffian vocabulary and, 64–65; involution in, 175; light theme in, 63–64; mechanized man in, 65; names as Gurdjieffian devices in, 69–70; "Negroes like anybody else" formula in, 11, 16; octaves in, 25; as parables, 64–65; racial emphasis of change in, 17; self-development in, 64, 66; sleep symbolism in, 65; sounds of text, 63, 67–68; superior man theme in, 142; Toomer representation in, 68, 69; on Toomer's Gurdjieffian work in Harlem, 41–42, 69–70, 73; wordplay in, 18, 27–28, 65, 68

"Inner circle of humanity" concept, 171

Institute for the Harmonious Development of Man, 5; in subtext of *Their Eyes*, 158; Toomer attends, 32; Van Vechten and, 7

Invisible Darkness: Jean Toomer and Nella Larsen (Larson), 35
Involution: definition of, 174; examples of, 174–75; Gurdjieffian Method theme, 26; Toomer, Harlem group "objective" writing and, 21. *See also* Evolution

Jackman, Harold, 9, 39, 98
Jacob's ladder, 66, 155. *See also* Evolution; Ray of creation
Jacobsen, Jens Peter, 159
Jean Toomer's Years with Gurdjieff (Byrd), 35
Johnson, Charles S., 10, 36, 44, 176
Johnson, James Weldon, 7, 10
Johnston, Mary, 9
Jonah's Gourd Vine (Hurston), 147–52; blindness in, 150; "chief feature" concept in, 149; continuity with *Moses*, 161; Gurdjieffian buffers concept in, 151–52; as Gurdjieffian teaching story, 151; involution in, 174–75; mechanized man in, 149–50, 152; names as codes in, 147, 148–49; "objective" textual verisimilitude in, 147–48; octaves in, 25; self-development in, 151–52; sleep symbolism in, 148, 150–51, 152, 161, 175; superman theme in, 148
Joyce, James, 33–34
Jung, Carl, 37, 175

Kabbalism in Hurston's books, 153–55, 156–57
Kerman, Cynthia Earl, 39
King, C. Daly, 3, 34; at Gurdjieff's initiation lecture, 12–13; Orage and, 37, 142–43; on periodic reciprocal destruction, 172

Language: African-American, "objective" writing and, 12; as central issue of *Black No More*, 132–33; Orwell's totalitarian, 133; Schuyler's ideas about, 133
Larsen, Nella, 97–122, 123, 175; antiracial writing approach of, 11, 15, 24; attack on reading and, 27; coding in novels of, 20; concern with color line, 45; esoteric concepts of, 98; Gurdjieffian psychology in novels of, 97–98; literal text, coded subtext integration, 107; "objective" writing, 98–99; productivity of, 14; psychological symbolism of, 99; response to *Nigger Heaven*, 10; at Toomer's lectures, 39; Van Vechten and, 7, 8; on Van Vechten dinner parties, 9. *See also Passing; Quicksand;* other specific works by
Larson, Charles R., 129
Law of Three: Gurdjieffian Method theme, 26; Hurston application of, 167–69
Lawful inexactitudes, 11–12; in *Black No More*, 135; in *Blacker the Berry*, 55–56; for coding subtext in *Seraph*, 164–65; Harlem group writings incorporating, 26; Orage on Gurdjieff usage of, 173; in Thurman's work, 35–36
Legominism(s), 26; in *Beelzebub's Tales*, 165–66, 173; in *Black Empire*, 140–41; in *Black No More*, 134–35; in *Conjure-Man Dies*, 92–94; in *Dust Tracks*, 164; in *Moses*, 162; in *Passing*, 119
"Letter to a Dervish, A" (Gurdjieff), 137
Liberia, slavery in, 124–25. *See also Slaves Today*
"Libretto for the Republic of Liberia" (Tolson), 15; on intervening in history, 160, 176; octaves exposed in, 25
Life Is Real Only Then, When "I Am" (Gurdjieff), 36; on Harlem group housecleaning, 12
Life of Langston Hughes, The (Rampersad), 35
Light theme: in *Conjure-Man Dies*, 89; in *Infants*, 63–64
Little, Jonathan, 97, 109, 110, 121
Lives of Jean Toomer, The (Kerman and Eldridge), 35
Locke, Alain, 36, 176; New Negro theories

of, 130; "objectivity" of, 10; Singh's assessment of, 176–77; Van Vechten admiration and, 7
Luhan, Mabel Dodge, 29, 34, 36, 97–98

"Magnetic center" concept, 161
Marie Grubbe (Jacobsen), 159
Marinetti, Filippo Tammaso, 37–38, 43
Marinoff, Fania, 8, 109
Marxism, race and, 15
Masks: Fisher's use of, 78, 79–80; Gurdjief-
fian Method theme, 26; Harlem group
and, 128, 177–78; in *Passing*, 109; in
Quicksand, 108; Schuyler's adoption of,
128, 137–38, 145; Toomer, Harlem
group "objective" writing and, 21. *See
also* False personality; Secrecy
McDowell, Deborah E.: on duplicity of
narrator in *Passing*, 116; on Larsen's
ironic methodology, 109; on *Said the
Fisherman* in *Quicksand*, 100; on satire
of *Passing*, 111
McKay, Nellie Y., 34–35
McKluskey, John, 75, 76
Mechanized man: in *Blacker the Berry*, 56;
in *Infants*, 65; in *Jonah's Gourd Vine*,
149–50, 152; Orage on, 12; in *Quicksand*, 108; sex and, 99–100; Toomer,
Harlem group "objective" writing and,
21; in *Walls of Jericho*, 78–79. *See also*
Sleep
Mental independence concept: Harlem
group writings and, 177; individuality
symbolism and, 72; in *Passing*, 121–22;
role-playing and, 14; symbolism, 62;
Toomer, Harlem group "objective"
writing and, 21; in *Walls of Jericho*, 77
Method, the (Toomer/Orage teachings):
themes in, 26
"Miss Cynthie" (Fisher), 75
Modern art, totalism in, 37–38
Moore, James, 59, 90–91
Moses, Man of the Mountain (Hurston),
159–62; attack on reading in, 27, 162;

blindness/sleep symbolism in, 161; continuity with *Jonah's Gourd Vine*, 161;
embedded text in, 28; evolution in, 174,
175–76; legominism in, 162; organizing
principle of, 25; superior man theme in,
142, 160, 161–62
Munson, Gorham, 30, 36

NAACP, 15, 78
Names as coded messages, 28; *Blacker the
Berry*, 52–56; *Conjure-Man Dies*, 90;
Hurston's use of Kabbalism and,
156–57; *Infants of the Spring*, 69–70;
Jonah's Gourd Vine, 148–49; *Passing*,
113–14, 116–17, 118–19; *Their Eyes*,
154–55
Naumburg, Margaret, 26, 29, 30, 97
"Negro-Art Hokum, The" (Schuyler),
70–71
Negro in America, The (Schuyler), 123
"Negroes like anybody else" formula: in
Black No More, 134; in Hurston writ-
ings, 16, 169; Thurman writings, 11
*Nella Larsen, Novelist of the Harlem Re-
naissance: A Woman's Life Unveiled*
(Davis), 35, 97–98
New Age (journal), 65
"New Group, 1926, A" (Toomer): Gurdji-
effian exercises list, 160–61; Harlem lec-
tures/notes, 39–40; "mask" concept
omitted from, 137; synthesizing Gurdji-
eff's system, 40–41
New Negro, The: as gift to Van Vechten, 7
New Negro movement, 24, 130
New race concept: Art as Vision and, 44; in
Black No More, 127, 128–29;
Blavatsky/Ouspensky on, 44–45; in
Moses, 159; spiritual nature of, 45;
Toomer on, 42, 44, 45
"New totality," search for, 2–3
Nigger Heaven (Van Vechten), 7; Gurdjief-
fian objectivity, Harlem group response
to, 10; Jacob's ladder design for, 155; as
"objective" writing, 9–10

Noguchi, Yusaburo, 126
Non-identification doctrine, 33, 71, 137–38.
  See also Masks; Role-playing
Nott, C. S., 57
Nugent, Richard Bruce, 47

"Objective," Gurdjieffian: art, qualities of,
  6; attributes of, 10; Harlem group writing and, 23; lawful inexactitudes of,
  11–12; self-development method, 5;
  view of man, 4
"Objective" writing, Gurdjieffian: attack
  on race in, 27; attack on reading in,
  26–27; coded message in names, 28,
  52–54; embedded text, 28; Gurdjieff as
  disguised character in, 25–26; Gurdjieffian principals' names as text, 28; names
  as ciphers through three-S concept,
  27–28; organizing principles of, 24–25;
  satirical novel of manners *vs.* detective
  novel, 86; text within text, 26; textual
  blueprint of, 24–28
Octave, Law of the, 2–3; evolution and, 72;
  Gurdjieffian Method theme, 26; Harlem
  group textual organization and, 24–25
O'Keefe, Georgia, 34
"On Being an American" (Toomer), 23
Orage, Alfred Richard, 175; *Beelzebub's
  Tales* translation/editing, 22; behaviorism and, 142–43; on discovering lawful
  inexactitudes, 11; early creed of, 65; on
  esoteric schools, 172; Gurdjieff Method
  of, 3, 12, 13; on legominism in *Beelze-
  bub's Tales*, 165–66, 173; on man's
  threefold construction, 11; in New
  York, 6–7; on periodic reciprocal destruction, 172; productivity of, 14; as
  Toomer's tutor, 33, 38
Orage with Gurdjieff in America (Welch),
  38–39
Oragean Version, The (King): on Harlem
  group housecleaning, 12
Oral History (Van Vechten), 9
Osiris, myth of, 155

Ouspensky, P. D.: Art as Vision group
  studies writings of, 30–31; first impression of Gurdjieff, 108; on fragments of
  an unknown teaching, 5; on Gurdjieff
  and Gnostic doctrines, 57; on Gurdjieff
  as dance teacher, 6; Gurdjieff disciple in
  USA, 2; teaching "man as a three-storied factory" concept, 93–94; Tower of
  Babel interpretation, 85. *See also In
  Search of the Miraculous*

Participation technique, Oragean version,
  13
Passing (Larsen), 108–22; anagrams in, 19,
  100; attack of reading in, 119, 125; attack on race in, 110–11, 120–21; consciousness theme in, 114; emotional
  center work in, 114–15, 117–18; esoteric
  nature of, 119; gender character theme
  in, 115; Gurdjieff representation in,
  25–26, 119–20; Gurdjieffian psychology
  in, 118; Gurdjieffian subtext in, 111, 118,
  119; instinct center in, 117–18; intellectual center work in, 115–16, 117–18; involution in, 174–75; ironic methodology
  of, 109; mask theme in, 109–10, 116;
  mental freedom theme in, 121–22;
  names as coded messages in, 113–14,
  116–17, 118–19; on nature of man, 120;
  octaves in, 25, 100; reading, as process
  in, 112; structure of, 114
Passing of the Great Race, The (Grant), 5
Patterson, William Patrick, 43
Perry, Margaret, 75
Peterson, Dorothy, 8, 9, 39, 97
Pickthall, Marmaduke, 100–01
"Procurator of Judea, The" (France),
  103–04
Progressivism, 4–5
Putnam, George, 124

Quicksand and Passing (McDowell), 100
Quicksand (Larsen), 99–108; anagrams in,
  19, 100, 105, 106; Gurdjieff character in,

25; Gurdjieff/Orage vocabularies in, 108; Gurdjieff representations in, 107–08; involution in, 174–75; octaves in, 25; "Procurator of Judea" intertext in, 103–05; psychological symbolism in, 99–100; reading theme of, 103, 104, 106; *Said the Fisherman* intertext in, 101–02; sleep theme in, 100, 102–03, 104, 105; sounds of text, 105, 106–07; superior man theme in, 142

Racialism. *See* Antiracialism; Attack on race
Racism, American: Gurdjieffian assault on, 4–5; Harlem group writers attacks on, 27; Schuyler's ridicule of, 126–27; synthesizing Gurdjieff's system to attack, 40–41; Toomer, "non-identification" concept and, 138. *See also* Attack on race
Randomness: Gurdjieff on, 2
Rasmussen, Kent, 124, 136, 139, 140
Ray of creation concept, 24–25, 175; Gurdjieffian Method theme, 26; in *Infants*, 63–64; Jacob's ladder and, 155. *See also* Evolution
Reading, attack on. *See* Attack on reading
"Reciprocal maintenance" concept, 127, 151; Toomer, Harlem group "objective" writing and, 21
Riordan, John, 9
Role-playing: Experiment technique and, 13–14, 137–38; Gurdjieffian Method theme, 26. *See also* Masks
Russian Revolution, Gurdjieff experience with, 2

Said the Fisherman (Pickthall), 100–01; spiritual nature of, 104
Sant'Elia, Antonio, 38
Satan, as allusion to Gurdjieff, 26
Schuyler, George S., 123–45; attack on race, 136, 139–40; chromatic democracy concept, 45, 129, 130; coding in novels of, 20; language ideas of, 133; Liberian

slave labor research trip, 124; masks of, 128, 137; messages encoded in writing of, 17; objective texts by, 8; "objectivity" of, 10; productivity of, 14; pseudonyms of, as cipher, 18, 138; role-playing of, 13, 14, 137–38; science/behaviorism themes of, 142–43; similarity to Gurdjieff, 123–24; superior man theme, 142; superman theme, 141–42; using names with double meanings, 19; *vs.* Hurston in approach to antiracialism, 130; writing approach of, 11, 15, 24, 136. *See also Black Empire; Black No More; Slaves Today*; other specific works by
Science fiction, *Beelzebub's Tales* as, 22
Science of man, comprehensive, 3
Secrecy: around Toomer, 44; in *Blacker the Berry*, 51–52; Harlem groups concerns about, 13, 16–17, 58–59; Larsen's use of, 119. *See also* Esoteric schools
Secret Doctrine, The (Blavatsky), 42, 44, 129
Self-development, "objective," 5; Gurdjieff's system, 36; in *Infants*, 64, 66; in *Jonah's Gourd Vine*, 151–52; sleep as motif of, 14; Toomer teaching, 10; in *Walls of Jericho*, 79
Self-observation and non-identification technique: in Hurston's novels, 149; Oragean version, 13; Toomer's, 10
Seraph on the Suwanee (Hurston), 123, 164–69; attack on reading in, 27; biblical/Freudian themes in, 165; Carby introduction to, 164; critical reviews of, 177; embedded text in, 28, 164–67; esoterism, Law of Three and, 168–69; on Hughes's status as outsider, 36; individual evolution in, 174, 176; Law of Three application in, 167–69; lawful inexactitudes for coding esoteric subtext in, 164–65; legominism in, 165–66; mental independence as theme in, 169; myth as subtext in, 166–67; myth, Law of Three and, 168; sleep as theme in, 169

Seven types of man, Gurdjieffian Method theme, 26
Shah, Idries, 57, 102
Sight, sound, sense cipher concept: in *Blacker the Berry*, 56, 58–59; Harlem group use of, 21, 27–28; in *Infants of the Spring*, 63, 67; in *Quicksand*, 105, 106–07; in *Their Eyes*, 154–55; Tolson's, 19–20; in *Walls of Jericho*, 82–83
Singh, Amritjit: assessment of Harlem writers, 176–77; on *Blacker the Berry*, 47, 48; on *Infants* and the Harlem Renaissance, 69, 70
Slaves Today: A Story of Liberia (Schuyler), 124–26; attack on reading and, 125–26; Gurdjieff character in, 25–26; involution in, 175; octaves in, 25; parallels to other Harlem group first writings, 124
Sleep concept: *Beelzebub's Tales* and, 22; in *Blacker the Berry*, 50, 56–57, 61; devolutionary strategy of "objective" artist and, 99; Gurdjieffian Method theme, 26; Hurston's substitution of blindness for, 148, 161; in *Jonah's Gourd Vine*, 150–51; as motif of self-development, 14; in *Quicksand*, 100, 102–03, 104, 105; Toomer, Harlem group "objective" writing and, 21. *See also* Mechanized man
Socialism, race and, 15
Solano, Solita, 107–08
Sollors, Werner, 29
Sounds of text. *See* Sight, sound, sense cipher concept
Spingarn, Amy, 7
"Struggle of the Musicians, The" (ballet), 6
Study of Gurdjieff's Teachings, A (Walker), 93–94
Suffering: thematic commitment to, 50–51
Superior man theme: Schuyler's use of, 142
Superman theme, 66; in *Cane*, 31; Gurdjieffian Method and, 26; Hurston's use of, 160, 170; in *Infants*, 66; Schuyler's use of, 126, 141–42; Toomer, Harlem group use of, 21, 127–28
Surrealism, totalism in, 38
Syllepsis: Larsen's use of, 118; Thurman's use of, 48

Teaching stories: Gurdjieffian, 93, 151, 167, 175; Hurston's allegories as, 149, 152–53; Schuyler's cartoons as, 128; *Slaves Today* and, 124, 125; Thurman's use of, 64–65. *See also Said the Fisherman*
Teachings (Nott): on Harlem group housecleaning, 12; "mask" or "role-playing" concept description, 137
Tertium Organum (Ouspensky), 30–31; on forming a new race, 44
Their Eyes Were Watching God (Hurston), 152–59; "chief feature" concept in, 152–53; coded text in, 156–57; disaster premonitions in, 43–44; Egyptian culture in, 155–56; Egyptian myth in, 154–55, 156; as esoteric romance, 158–59; evolution theme in, 160, 175; Gurdjieffian secret names in, 154–55, 158; Harlem group names in, 158; individual evolution in, 174; Kabbalistic themes in, 153–55, 156–57; man's duality theme in, 152; mental freedom theme in, 160; names as creation in, 154; "objectiveness" of, 159; octaves in, 25; sounds of text in, 154–55; subtext design of, 28, 114, 155, 157–58; themes of repeated in *Seraph*, 164
Three octaves of radiation: Gurdjieffian Method theme, 26; as Harlem group writing characteristic, 24–25; reading three times and, 50. *See also* Law of Three; Octave, Law of the
Three-S's (sight, sound, sense cipher) concept. *See* Sight, sound, sense cipher concept

Threefold construction, man's, 11
Thurman, Wallace, 47–73, 98, 123, 175; antiracial writing approach of, 11, 15, 24; attack on reading and, 27; coding in novels of, 20; editing *Fire!!*, 7; on Harlem Renaissance literary production, 10–11; "objectivity" of, 10; productivity of, 14; Singh's assessment of, 176–77; Tolson and, 15; at Toomer's lectures, 39. *See also Blacker the Berry, The; Infants of the Spring*
Time, evolution of humanity and, 42
Tolerance, doctrine of, 75–76
Tolson, Melvin B.: attack on reading and, 27; complex coding of, 19–20; as member of Harlem group, 14–15
Toomer, Jean, 1, 29–46, 123; as accursed poet, 29–30; analyzing/reformulating the Method, 32; antiracist component, Gurdjieff doctrine, 3–4, 15, 16–17, 173; assigned to start Gurdjieff group, 38–39; attractiveness of, 97–98; critical understanding of, 176–77; as Gurdjieff/Harlem group bridge, 177–78; Gurdjieff's impact on, 32; Gurdjieff's sacred dancing and, 36; Harlem group response to, 10; imaginary technological devices in writing of, 22–23; imitates Gurdjieff writings, 33; lectures, self-observation without identification, 39–40; on man's threefold construction, 11; on mental independence, 62; mimicking Gurdjieff teaching persona, 123–24; modernist influences of, 37; new race vision of, 42, 44, 45, 159; new spiritualized American humanity vision, 42–43; Orage and, 36–37; on race in human life, 43, 44; revising Gurdjieff, false personality and, 5–6; role-playing concept and, 137–38; as sacred dance teacher, 41; satirical/"objective" writing of, 23; secrecy cloud around, 44; on spiritual nature of race, 45; superman

theme and, 127; synthesizing Gurdjieff's system, 40–41; Van Vechten admiration and, 7; at Van Vechten dinner parties, 9; wealthy women and, 29. *See also* specific works by
"Transatlantic" (Toomer), 24, 33
Turner, Darwin T., 31

"*Ulysses,* Order and Myth" (Eliot), 169
United Negro Improvement Association (UNIA), 36, 78
Urban League, antiracism of, 15

Van Vechten, Carl: antiracialist social engineering program of, 9; bohemian salons of, 7–8; dinner parties, 8–9; Larsen and, 8, 109; satirical/"objective" writing of, 23
"View and Review" column (Schuyler), 136
Vril: The Power of the Coming Race (Bulwer-Lytton), 129

Walden, Daniel, 69
Walker, Kenneth, 93–94
Walls of Jericho, The (Fisher), 75–86; attack on race/color discrimination in, 85–86; attack on reading in, 27; coding in, 20; dual levels of, 76; embedded text for "objectivity" in, 28, 82–86; esoterism in, 79, 84–85; evolution in, 175; Gurdjieffian buffers concept in, 77, 78; Gurdjieffian themes in subtext of, 90; illusion/masks in, 78, 79–80; involution in, 81, 174–75; mechanized man in, 78–79; Moses theme in, 76, 81; obscurity of ciphers, 83–84; octaves in, 25; racialist thought in, 80–81; self-development in, 79; sleep symbolism in, 77, 81; sounds of text, 82–83
Walrond, Eric, 10, 39, 177
War, planetary influences and, 171–72
Wasserman, Eddie, 7

Watson, John B., 142–43
Webb, James, 119–20
Welch, Louise, 12, 38–39
White, Walter, 7
Whitman, Walt, Ouspenskian visionaries admiration of, 29
Williams, John, 49
Wilson, Colin, 34, 59–60

"Work, the," 5; alchemy as symbol for, 58; emergence of term, 59; as legominism, 262

Youman, Mary Mabel, 109

Zohar (Kabbalistic Book of Splendor), 153–54